W9-BWR-194

The Wooden Spoon Dessert Book

ALSO BY MARILYN MOORE

Baking Your Own
The Wooden Spoon Bread Book

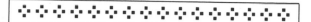

The Wooden Spoon Dessert Book

❖ ❖ ❖

The Best You Ever Ate

Marilyn Moore

1817

HARPER & ROW, PUBLISHERS, New York
Grand Rapids, Philadelphia, St. Louis, San Francisco
London, Singapore, Sydney, Tokyo, Toronto

THE WOODEN SPOON DESSERT BOOK.
Copyright © 1990 by Marilyn Moore.
All rights reserved.
Printed in the United States of America.
No part of this book may be used or reproduced
in any manner whatsoever without
written permission except in the case of brief quotations
embodied in critical articles and reviews.
For information address Harper & Row, Publishers, Inc.,
10 East 53rd Street,
New York, N.Y. 10022.

FIRST EDITION

Library of Congress Cataloging-in-Publication Data
Moore, Marilyn M.
The wooden spoon dessert book:
the best you ever ate/Marilyn Moore.—1st ed.
p. cm.
Bibliography: p.
Includes index.
ISBN 0–06–016250–3
1. Desserts.   I. Title.
TX773.M65   1990
641.8′6—dc20   89–45691

90 91 92 93 94 DT/HC 10 9 8 7 6 5 4 3 2 1

for Viola, Mabell, and Bernice,
who mothered me with their desserts

Contents

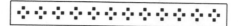

Acknowledgments
xiii

Introduction
xv

Before We Start
the ingredients, equipment, and methods of dessert making
1

High and Handsome Layer Cakes
frosted and filled in a multitude of ways
15

Delicate Cakes
light and luscious for special occasions
35

Tender Cakes
with mouth-watering sour cream and buttermilk flavor
51

Granny's Cakes
recipes from generations past
65

Carrying Cakes
cooled and frosted right in the pan
79

All But Forgotten Icebox Cakes
chilled confections to delight the taste buds
91

Pie Doughs and Crusts
to get you started
99

Fresh Fruit Pies
in celebration of harvest
105

Simple Sugar Pies
for rich indulgence
119

Creamy Custard Pies
with old-fashioned goodness
127

Ordinary Pies
favorites from old-time bakers
143

Deep-Dish Pies and Cobblers
the easiest of all
155

Drop Cookies
to easily fill the cookie jar
163

Straight-Edged Cookies
bars and squares for all occasions
171

Rolled and Molded Cookies
when you want to play
179

Icebox Cookies
to bake for your break while the coffee perks
189

Stovetop Custards
especially for the little ones
195

Baked Custards and Puddings
to take you back to Mother's kitchen
203

Steamed Puddings
a heritage of recipes
213

Fruit Desserts
with down-home goodness
219

Old-fashioned Ice Creams
like Grandpa used to make
231

Smooth Sherbets
such cool, cool pleasure
239

Flavored Ices
for light refreshment
245

Easy Candies
to satisfy a sweet tooth
251

Confections and Sweetmeats
for dainty appetites
257

Sweet Beverages
for mealtime or in between
265

Special Sauces
to top it all off
269

Epilogue
277

Bibliography
279

Index
285

Acknowledgments

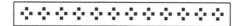

To my mother and mother-in-law, who gave me a heritage of recipes, mostly desserts.

To my husband for tasting anything I put in front of him: good, bad, or indifferent. And for putting up with meals when dessert was the only thing planned.

My hometown of Hoopeston, Illinois, is a rural community where swapping recipes with friends and neighbors is as natural an activity as taking a walk. To those hometown Hoopeston friends for caring and sharing insights and ideas, and for digging out special recipes when needed, especially: Mary Jones, Diane Singleton, and Selma Young.

To those who entrusted me with their family collections of cookbooks, some handwritten on paper brittle with age: Jeanette Groves, Lorraine Hott, and Peter Krimbel.

To my tasters, who ate and analyzed their way through it all, and promised to put off diets until tomorrow. The crew at the library: Louise Griner, Carol Arnold, Scarlet Cropper, Hazel Donaldson, Esther Jarnagin, and Maria Solis. Everyone at Flowers and Gifts by Molly Culbert: Molly and James Culbert, Karen Anderson, Louise Barten, Evelyn Brown, Lois Cade, Judy Custer, Joanne Elliott, Laura Hathaway, Dawn Martin, and Darlene Van Pelt.

To Dole Packaged Foods Company for sending me information about pineapple upside-down cakes.

To Sonoma Antique Apple Nursery and Southmeadow Fruit Gardens for sending me information about apple varieties and their cooking properties.

At Harper & Row, to Bill Shinker and Pat Brown, for being enthusiastic from the beginning, and to Susan Friedland and her editorial staff for giving me the kind of support that all writers need.

To my agent, Elise Goodman, for having the uncanny knack of making things happen just when I'm ready.

The introduction to the recipe Chocolate Angel Food borrows freely from "History of the Mary Hartwell Catherwood Club," dated 1974 and on file at the Hoopeston Public Library, Hoopeston, Illinois. Although based on pieces written earlier by Frances Trego, Elizabeth Bell, and Dorothy Shuler, the author is unknown.

Introduction

When beginning this book, I knew I wanted to impart to others the goodness of the foods that nourished so many of us as we were growing up. I began looking through old family recipes and some early cookbooks for inspiration, and was struck by the fact that the vast majority of recipes were for desserts.

A partial explanation is that early cooks knew all their basic, everyday recipes by heart. It was a special cake or pie, learned from a neighbor, that needed writing down.

But that's not all. Desserts *are* special. They celebrate birthdays, christenings, graduations, weddings, and anniversaries. They broaden the pleasure of sharing with friends. Desserts provide the perfect finish for any family gathering.

I carried some of my old-fashioned desserts out for tasting. The response was immediate and overwhelming. My tasters had tasted for me before and knew what they were in for. When taste-testing chess pies they might have to try ten or twelve before we decided which was best. Unsuccessful efforts had to be tasted as well, in order to analyze what went wrong. Their unbridled enthusiasm for the project cemented my decision to go ahead.

Most of the recipes come from earlier times. Some are more recent variations. They say a serious cook won't leave a recipe alone. Like our foremothers, I didn't hesitate to add my own touches here and there. I have carefully gone through them all, giving the step-by-step instructions as much clarity as possible.

The selections that proved good enough to be included have no regional emphasis. I have been told that I am "so midwestern." That is mostly true. But I am also a little bit southern, a little bit Californian, and a little bit Hawaiian. Temper that with a German Mennonite heritage, and you have a mighty tasty combination.

And how about our diets? Can we have our cake and eat it, too? I think so. In answer to your inevitable question: No, I don't eat desserts every day. But, if I'm going to have company, if I'm going to celebrate, if I'm going to have my grandchildren over, I'm going to have a good homemade dessert. I invite you to do the same.

MARILYN MOORE

The Wooden Spoon Dessert Book

Before We Start

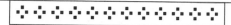

The ingredients, equipment, and
methods of dessert making

If you've been making pies and cakes all your life,
don't bother with this section. If you're unsure of
yourself, read on.

The Ingredients I Use

FLOUR   I use unbleached all-purpose flour most of the time. Cake flour
has less gluten than all-purpose. It produces a lighter texture and finer
crumb, making it the choice for some cakes. To substitute all-purpose
flour for cake flour, remove 2 tablespoons from each cup used. To substitute cake flour for all-purpose, add 2 tablespoons to each cup used.

GRANULATED SUGAR   Pure cane sugar. Being jingoistic, I look for
bags from my birth state of Hawaii.

SUPERFINE SUGAR   Finely ground granulated sugar, sometimes called
"bar sugar." It will dissolve more quickly than regular granulated sugar
and is used when that is an advantage.

BROWN SUGAR   I prefer light brown sugar for most desserts. Choose it
in plastic bags and buy the ones that feel the softest, ignoring labels.
Avoid those that look and feel like grainy sugar moistened with molasses.

CONFECTIONERS' SUGAR Confectioners' sugar is finely pulverized granulated sugar with a small addition (about 3%) of cornstarch to prevent lumping. It should not impart an unpleasant cornstarch flavor to frostings. If yours does, try a different brand.

BUTTER If butter is called for, use unsalted. If you wish to substitute margarine, use firm stick margarine, not soft or whipped. You may wish to reduce salt in the recipe, as most margarine is salted. Margarine is slightly softer than butter, but should not throw a recipe off. If shortening is substituted for butter in a cake recipe, two tablespoons of liquid should be added to the batter for each ½ cup shortening used. Oil cannot be satisfactorily substituted for butter in most recipes.

SHORTENING I use plain (not butter-flavored) shortening. If butter is substituted for shortening in a cake recipe, the liquid should be reduced by two tablespoons for each ½ cup butter used. If butter is substituted for shortening in a pie-crust recipe, the results will not be quite as flaky.

VEGETABLE OIL Any light oil will work. Oil is not interchangeable with butter or shortening. Recipes must be specifically written for its use.

EGGS I use only clean, Grade A eggs, with no cracks, large size. If there is any danger of salmonella bacteria contamination in the eggs in your area, check with your local USDA extension agent and get a recommendation for use. Remember, eating raw cake or cookie batter is the same as eating raw eggs.

Some recipes call for only whites or yolks, leaving you with the leftovers. Whites can be covered and refrigerated for several days. They can also be frozen in airtight packages to be defrosted for later use. You can keep track of how many you have frozen, or measure them after defrosting. One egg white from an egg graded large measures about 2 tablespoons, so 1 cup will hold about 8 whites. Yolks do not store as well as whites. Plan to use them first, saving only the whites.

MILK Use whatever you have on hand to drink. I use skim. It doesn't matter if you use whole.

BUTTERMILK This is skim milk commercially fermented with a lactic-acid bacteria culture, sold as cultured buttermilk in the dairy case.

SOUR MILK A home substitute for buttermilk. Place 1 tablespoon vinegar or lemon juice in a measuring cup. Fill to the 1-cup level with milk. Let the milk stand until it "clabbers," or thickens with tiny white flecks that float. It may not be quite as thick as commercially produced cultured buttermilk, but works pretty well in a pinch. Milk that has soured from being kept too long should not be used. It should be thrown out.

HALF-AND-HALF   Just as it sounds, approximately half milk and half cream, but with a little more milk than cream.

WHIPPING (HEAVY) CREAM   Recipes from early cookbooks often call for country cream, so thick you could mound it in a spoon. I have adapted all recipes for this collection to be successful using ultra-pasteurized whipping cream, because that is what is available in most supermarkets today. If you can, however, buy whipping cream or heavy cream that is not ultra-pasteurized, do so. It will whip more readily and to greater volume.

SOUR CREAM   Cream commercially thickened and soured with a lactic culture. Regular cream that has spoiled or "gone sour" should not be used. It should be thrown out.

BAKING POWDER   To avoid a metallic aftertaste, I prefer one without aluminum.

VANILLA   I use only pure vanilla extract. Artificial vanilla is no substitute.

SPICES   Buy small jars and store in a dark place away from heat. Replace after 3 months. Old spices are tasteless. Small grinders can be used to grind whole spices right before needed. Particularly useful are those made specifically for nutmeg and pepper.

COCOA AND CHOCOLATE   The recipes were all tested with reliable and easy-to-find supermarket cocoas and chocolates. To substitute cocoa for chocolate, use 3 tablespoons cocoa plus 1 tablespoon oil, shortening, or butter, for every square (1-ounce) unsweetened chocolate.

WATER   Use only cold water from the tap. If the water has not been used for a period of time, run it until you can feel a temperature change, signifying that any water that was sitting in the pipes has run out. This procedure helps prevent lead contamination. Be aware that even non-lead pipes are sometimes joined with lead solders.

LEMON JUICE   Squeeze fresh, right before use. Bottled juice tastes old. Frozen lemon juice is a suitable substitute, if used soon after opening.

NUTS   Buy the freshest whole nuts you can find and chop them to size right before use. Taste nuts before adding to a batter. If rancid, they ruin anything you put them in.

APPLES   There are so many apples to choose from. For extensive listings of unique and antique apples you can grow in your own back yard, write to Sonoma Antique Apple Nursery, 4395 Westside Road, Healdsburg, CA 95448, or Southmeadow Fruit Gardens, Box SM, Lakeside, MI 49116. Send $1 to Sonoma to have their catalog sent first class. For $8, Southmeadow will send you their 112-page catalog, which is packed with useful information; the price list is free. The Sonoma nursery holds several apple tastings each year. Check with them for dates. Carolyn Harrison at Sonoma and Theo Grootendorst of Southmeadow sent me their apple recommendations. From their lists, I suggest Red Astrachan, Newton Pippin, Arkansas Black, Duchess of Oldenburg, Tompkin's King, Yellow Bellflower, Northern Spy, Rhode Island Greening, Baldwin, Wolf River, or Willie Sharp for pies; Ribston Pippin, Bramley's Seedling, Gravenstein, Liberty, Stayman Winesap, Almata, Wellington, or Yellow Transparent for sauce. Roadside stands and farmers' markets supply a variety throughout harvest. Don't be afraid to ask about the cooking properties of any apples you see displayed. Supermarkets have a more limited selection. They buy commercial varieties that all ripen at the same time, do not bruise easily, and look pretty on display. Of those more readily available, I like Granny Smith, Golden Delicious, McIntosh, and Jonathan for pies; Jonathan, Golden Delicious, and McIntosh for sauce. Both Cortland and Rome apples are good for baking.

PERSIMMONS   The recipes in this book call for wild American persimmons (*Diospyros virginiana*). They are not interchangeable with commercially grown Oriental varieties. They can be found growing wild in the woods, or domesticated in country farmyards, from central Illinois and Connecticut south to northern Texas and Florida. The fruits vary in size, from one to two inches in diameter, and are yellow or orange in color, with a reddish cheek. Large seeds are embedded in the soft flesh.

Experts disagree on whether the fruits need to be touched by light frost before harvest. Everyone agrees that, if taken too soon, their astringent flavor will pucker your mouth. If unsure, break one open and taste. If it cannot be eaten out of hand, check again later in the season. If the fruit is mature, you can shake the tree's branches to cause a drop. Ripe fruits are best carried in flat boxes to minimize crushing.

ALCOHOLS AND LIQUEURS   A few recipes call for rum, whiskey, or brandy as flavoring. Don't try to save money by buying cheap brands. You will only ruin your good dessert. If you want to avoid alcohol, substitute other liquids in sauces or puddings, such as fruit juice or coffee. Cake batters are more precise, and may not stand up to substitution. If you must eliminate all alcohol from your diet, remember that common extracts, such as vanilla, orange, lemon, and almond, have an alcohol base.

Recommended Equipment

You won't need a lot of fancy equipment to make my recipes. Most things can be mixed in a stoneware bowl with a sturdy wooden spoon. A minimum number of pans will take care of most of the baking. Shop at a restaurant-supply store to find heavy-duty goods at reasonable prices. Check the cookware department of a large department store, or seek assistance in a gourmet cookshop, for the hard-to-find.

BAKING PANS There's no reason to buy the most expensive pans available, but cheap ones may warp or dent. Some inexpensive pans are undersized and won't hold enough batter. Look for straight-sided cake-layer pans. Some have slightly slanted sides, making it difficult to stack an attractive layer cake. Insulated or double-walled pans are a good choice because they are great for turning out evenly baked, straight-sided cakes.

Gather these pans first:

Two or three 9-inch round layer pans, two or three 8-inch round layer pans. These should be 1½ to 1¾ inches deep.
One or two 9-inch pie pans. Metal is best; glass is satisfactory.
One 9-inch tube pan and one 10-inch tube pan. One of the tube pans could be fluted; one could have a removable bottom.
One 8 x 8 x 2-inch baking pan or ovenproof dish and one 9 x 13 x 2-inch baking pan or ovenproof dish.
One 15½ x 10½ x 1-inch jelly-roll pan.
Two baking sheets for cookies. The size should allow a minimum 1-inch clearance from oven walls on all sides for air circulation. The insulated pans, mentioned above, minimize the danger of burning cookie bottoms.
One 9- or 10-inch springform pan, or both. These should be 3 inches deep.

ROLLING PIN A good ball-bearing wooden rolling pin will last a lifetime and is easier to handle than a solid pin. A marble rolling pin is heavy enough to do most of the rolling for you. Fun to use.

PASTRY BLENDER A pastry blender has several arched blades held by a wooden handle. Makes cutting in shortening and flour much easier than using knives.

RUBBER SPATULAS   Get several sizes.

METAL MIXING SPOON   Should be stainless steel, with a handle that will not conduct heat. When a custard recipe says a mixture "coats a spoon," this is the spoon to use.

WOODEN SPOON   I like a medium-size spoon about 12 inches long with a bowl that is 3 inches long and 2 inches wide.

CANDY THERMOMETER   Choose one that will keep the bulb end off the bottom of the pan. If you are comfortable with gauging the stages of candymaking, you can dispense with a thermometer.

MEASURING SPOONS   ⅛ teaspoon, ¼ teaspoon, ½ teaspoon, 1 teaspoon, ½ tablespoon, 1 tablespoon. ½ tablespoon is the same as 1½ teaspoons. Metal is better than plastic. Stainless steel is best. If you do a lot of baking, buy more than one set.

MEASURING CUPS   For dry ingredients: separate measures for ⅛ cup, ¼ cup, ⅓ cup, ½ cup, and 1 cup, with the measure extending to the top for leveling. A coffee measure is the same as ⅛ cup, as is 2 tablespoons. Metal is better than plastic. Stainless steel is best. For liquids: 1 cup, 2 cups, and 4 cups, with measurements marked on the sides. Glass is better than plastic. Again, extra sets come in handy.

SAUCEPANS   You will need 1 quart-, 2 quart-, and 3-quart saucepans, and you should choose heavy-bottomed pans to minimize scorching. They should be nonreactive, that is, they should not react with the foods you cook in them. Stainless steel is best. It is not only nonreactive, even with acid foods, but it can be used with both wooden and metal spoons.

ELECTRIC MIXER   Most recipes can be made with or without a mixer. When I think it is much easier with, I mention the machine.

FOOD PROCESSOR   There is no recipe in this book that requires a food processor. I use one to chop, slice, shred, and purée. I do not use it to mix most dessert doughs and batters. If you want to mix doughs with a food processor, remember to use a light touch to avoid overmixing. On/off pulses will give you better control than continuous processing.

MICROWAVE   My recipes yield better results if cooked on or in a conventional range. I use a microwave to shortcut melting butter, scalding milk, and boiling water.

ICE-CREAM CHURN   If you haven't shopped for an ice-cream churn lately, give it a try. There are electric models that use ice cubes rather than crushed ice, and models that use no ice at all because the canister is frozen before use. There are expensive models, requiring neither ice nor pre-freezing, that need only be filled and turned on to make successive batches of frozen cream. And you can still get the old-fashioned crank-style churn that turns out the best ice cream of all. Why the best? Because you control the speed with which the paddle turns: slowly before the cream freezes, so as not to make butter, and faster as it stiffens, to incorporate air into the beaten mix. All you need is a pair of strong shoulders to go with it. With the variety available, you should be able to find a churn that fits your needs and pocketbook.

Methods

MEASURING INGREDIENTS   Dry ingredients, with the exception of brown sugar, are spooned lightly into the measure, and then leveled off with a straight edge. Brown sugar is packed into the measure and then leveled off.

Liquids are measured by sighting at eye level. If your eyes are not level with the line of measurement, you may measure more or less than you want.

SIFTING DRY INGREDIENTS   Dry ingredients should be blended and fluffy before they are added to a batter. It doesn't matter if they are sifted, stirred, or whisked, as long as the ingredients are well distributed and there are no lumps. Cake flour gets lumpy in storage and is sometimes better sifted before measuring. Be sure to follow the recipe. One cup of flour measured before sifting will weigh more than one cup measured after sifting. You don't need an old-fashioned sifter. Stir through a large sieve held over a bowl or wax paper. Dry ingredients can be buzzed in a food processor, if you don't mind a fine cloud of flour dust settling on everything.

SCALDING LIQUIDS   Heat to just below the boiling point. The liquid should steam and form small bubbles around the edge of the pan.

MELTING CHOCOLATE   Chocolate is best melted in the top of a double boiler over hot, not boiling, water. Take care not to get any water or steam in the melting chocolate, or it will "seize up," turning thick and grainy. Leave the melted chocolate over the warm water, off the heat, until ready to use. Stir and use slightly warm, but not hot, when adding to batters.

Chocolate packages recommend microwave melting of unwrapped chocolate in a nonmetal dish. Barbara Kafka, in her book *Microwave Gourmet*, tells us to wrap the chocolate tightly before microwave melting. Use a high power setting, starting with 45 to 60 seconds for 1 ounce of chocolate, and adding 10 to 30 seconds for each additional ounce. If you use a microwave, remember that chocolate can become overcooked or scorched just as easily as on the stovetop. Take it easy.

BEATING EGG WHITES   Become familiar with the stages of beaten egg whites. Beat 3 or 4 to learn. Use clean and dry beaters and bowl. Start with the slow speed of an electric mixer, gradually turning to medium or high. They will first be foamy with large surface bubbles. Gradually the bubbles will get smaller and closer together as the whites begin to firm. Stop the beaters and raise them often to check progress. Soft peaks will rise and then fold. Firm peaks will hold. Stiff peaks will hold and have pointy tops. Overbeaten whites are dry and come apart in chunks. Beaten egg whites should be used immediately. Do not let them sit while preparing other parts of a recipe. Better to have everything else ready before the whites are begun.

Egg whites can also be beaten with a hand-held rotary beater, or can be whipped into shape with a wire whisk. The process is the same.

MAKING PERFECT BUTTER CAKES: The term butter cakes includes both those made with butter and those made with shortening. Soften the butter or shortening by beating before adding the sugar. Do not soften in a microwave. The batter could become undesirably oily. You can partially soften butter by leaving it out on a countertop. Gradually add the sugar to the softened butter or shortening, beating the mixture to form a creamy texture. The sugar crystals actually cut into the fat layers, forming large numbers of small air cells, and begin the process of lightening the batter. Beat the eggs in one at a time, unless the recipe specifies otherwise, adding more air and lightness. Be sure the eggs are at room temperature. Cold eggs can curdle smoothly creamed butter and sugar, leaving you with lumps that are almost impossible to make smooth again.

For a conventional butter cake, divide the dry ingredients into approximately 3 or 4 parts and add to the batter alternately with the liquid, which is divided into 2 or 3 parts. For example:

1 part dry ingredients
1 part liquid
1 part dry ingredients
1 part liquid
1 part dry ingredients

Each part is well blended, but not overmixed, before the next is added. It doesn't matter if the mixing is done in an electric mixer or by hand.

For a quick-mix butter cake, the dry ingredients, the liquids, the eggs, and the butter or shortening are all mixed together more or less at one time. Then the batter is beaten just until smooth and creamy.

Grease cake pans and lightly flour them to enable the cake to be easily released. Cakes that have a tendency to stick require a lining of wax paper, which is also greased. A dark chocolate cake can fill a pan dusted with a mixture of cocoa and flour. Spread about 1 tablespoon of shortening evenly in a layer pan. Sprinkle in about 1 tablespoon of flour and shake until all surfaces are coated. Remove the excess flour by tapping the pan, upside down, on the side of the sink.

Spread the batter evenly in the pan to avoid a rounded top. If the batter is thick, spread it carefully with a rubber spatula.

MAKING DELICATE FOAM CAKES   These are made without, or with very little, butter. Their lightness comes from the air beaten into eggs, egg yolks, and/or egg whites. The dry ingredients can be folded into the beaten eggs, or the beaten eggs can be folded into the batter. In either case, the best tool to use is a rubber spatula. Stir part of the beaten eggs into the batter to lighten the texture before you fold in the remainder. To fold, cut straight down through the mixture in the bowl, scrape along the bottom toward you, and come back up with a gentle, rolling motion. Rotate the bowl a quarter turn, and repeat the folding. Gentle folding will blend the ingredients without deflating the eggs.

Foam cakes will bake and rise higher in ungreased pans. Two-piece pans with removable bottoms make release possible. The sides and removable bottom require careful cutting with a slender knife or spatula to help free the baked cake.

BAKING CAKES   For baking cakes, place the oven rack in the middle position, unless the recipe tells you to do otherwise. Allow space for air circulation between pans and oven walls and between the pans themselves. Do not open the oven door before the minimum baking time is reached, or your cake may fall. There are three ways to determine if a cake is done: a wooden pick inserted in the center of the cake will come out clean, with no batter clinging to it; the cake will begin to pull away from the sides of the pan; the cake will spring back when lightly touched in the center.

COOLING CAKES   Cool butter-cake layers in their pans for about 10 minutes before turning out. This allows the fragile cake to set, preventing its collapse. Then lay a wire rack over one layer. Holding the pan and the wire rack at the same time, invert the layer and allow it to drop onto the wire rack. Carefully remove the pan. Reinvert the layer, using a second wire rack, so that it stands right side up to cool. Continue with the other layers.

Cool foam cakes completely in inverted pans. Some pans have an extended neck, or feet, to hold the cake away from the counter for cooling. If your does not, you will have to prop it up on something, such as the neck of an empty bottle. After cooling, release the cake carefully, using a thin, sharp knife or spatula.

FROSTING CAKES Unless otherwise noted in the recipe, cool a cake or cake layer completely before frosting. Brush the layers lightly with your hands to remove any loose crumbs. Place the first layer, upside down, on a cake plate. Frost the top of the layer with ½ to 1 cup of frosting. Place the second layer on top, right side up. Frost the top with ½ to 1 cup of frosting. Then frost the sides with ¾ to 1½ cups of frosting. If your frosting is a little bit soft when you begin, it will be just right to do the sides when you get to them.

MAKING FLAKY PIE CRUSTS The tenderest, flakiest pie crusts are made gently with hand tools only. A food processor can be used, however, if you use on/off pulses sparingly, so as to not overwork the dough. In either case, use ony enough water to hold the dough together. Avoid overworking the dough with warm hands, which melt the shortening used. Roll the dough immediately after mixing, or cover and chill for 15 to 20 minutes, to make handling easier. Dust the rolling surface lightly with flour and flatten the ball of dough in that flour by patting gently with your hands. Turn the dough over and pat again. Roll out from the center of the dough toward the edges. Turn the dough over several times during the beginning of the rolling process, to keep the surface lightly dusted and prevent sticking. Just remember to be gentle and unafraid, and a tender, flaky crust will be your reward.

MAKING SMOOTH STOVETOP CUSTARDS AND PIE FILLINGS Stovetop custards can be made in a saucepan or double boiler. In a saucepan over direct heat, the custard will cook faster and require more diligent stirring. In a double boiler, the slower cooking demands only an occasional stir. Since the double-boiler method takes longer, my lack of patience makes me opt for the direct method. You can adapt my recipes to a double boiler, but you will have to allot more time.

Cooked in a saucepan, the custard needs to be stirred continuously and watched closely. Stirring should alternate between a circular stir and one that draws a series of figure 8s across the bottom of the pan. The stir need not be frantic, just constant. To check the consistency of the mixture, lift the pot from the heat and then lift the spoon, letting the mixture drip back into the pan. If a mixture should thicken too quickly, remove the pan from the heat and beat vigorously. A cooked custard can always be strained through a sieve to improve smoothness. This technique will not, however, save a sauce badly curdled from overcooked eggs.

Most custard recipes suggest that butter and flavoring be added off heat, after cooking. Do this with a gentle touch to avoid breaking down the mixture from one that is smooth to one that is watery. Stir custards gently from time to time while cooling to prevent a film from forming on top. I don't recommend covering a custard with anything until cooled to room temperature. If you cover a hot or warm liquid, you take a chance of souring the mixture before it cools.

MASTERING MERINGUE TOPPINGS   Old-fashioned meringues are not hard to make. The bowl and beaters used should be clean and dry, to avoid contaminating the egg whites with either fat or water. The egg whites will beat to greater volume if they are allowed to warm to room temperature before use. Beat them slowly until they begin to thicken, then speed the beating until they form firm, but not quite stiff, peaks when the beaters are stopped and raised. Then add the sugar, at medium speed, one tablespoon at a time, allowing at least 10 seconds between additions for it to dissolve. Undissolved sugar could cause weeping of the baked meringue. When all the sugar has been added, speed up the beating again until stiff peaks form when the beaters are stopped and raised.

Cool the pie filling to room temperature before covering it with meringue. If meringue covers a hot filling, the steam that is not allowed to escape collects on the underside of the meringue, causing an unsightly mess. Seal the meringue to the crust all the way around the pie to keep it from shrinking while baking. Bake as directed. Cool completely to room temperature before covering or chilling the finished pie.

STEAMING PUDDINGS   Steam your pudding in any mold that will withstand a hot-water bath. A special pudding mold has its own tight-fitting lid. If you improvise, fit a lid of foil, line it with buttered wax paper, and bind it to the mold tightly with string. Choose a mold ample enough to allow for expansion of the batter as it cooks, and never fill a mold more than half to two-thirds full. The sides should slant to allow the pudding to release. The steaming kettle should be large enough to allow room around the mold.

Fit the bottom of the kettle with a trivet or rack to hold the mold off the bottom. I use my large pasta cooker with the perforated insert in place. Steam the pudding in water that comes half to two-thirds up the sides of the mold. Measure this level with the empty mold. Then bring the water almost to boiling before you lower the filled mold into the pot.

If the water level drops during the steaming, add boiling water to bring it up to the original level.

It will take a pudding two to four times as long to steam as the same mixture would take to bake in dry heat. Reheat cold cooked puddings by steaming for 45 to 60 minutes.

CHURNING OLD-FASHIONED ICE CREAM   Homemade ice creams are so very fresh tasting because they do not have the emulsifiers and stabilizers of the commercial varieties. This also means that they may become icy with long-term storage. It's best to make only what you will eat in a matter of days.

Never try to freeze a warm mixture. Always chill first. A warm mix that contains a high butterfat content will freeze with an unpleasant buttery taste.

Recipes that contain alcohol, such as bourbon or rum, take much longer to freeze, and may remain somewhat softer, even in storage. Sugar also retards freezing, and a very sweet mixture will be slow to harden. Try churning, followed by still-freezing, if churning alone is not enough.

Leave about one-quarter to one-third of the freezing canister unfilled to allow for expansion during churning. Machines vary greatly in how much air they incorporate into their freezing mixtures, making the yields given in the recipes approximations. Double or triple small recipes for larger machines. Freeze large recipes in successive batches in smaller ones.

The usual ratio of salt to ice is 1:5. More salt will cause faster freezing; less salt, the opposite. If the mix is frozen too quickly, the ice cream will be coarse with large ice crystals. If churning continues for an extended time without freezing, you may whip the cream into butter. Your machine's manual should give you an idea of recommended amounts and expected freezing times.

Freshly churned ice cream is so soft it will melt rapidly in your spoon or bowl. That's when I like to enjoy my first mouthful. Firm freshly churned cream for an hour or two for the best serving texture. Either pack fresh ice around the canister and insulate with papers or cloth, or transfer to freezer containers and firm in the freezer.

Ice cream that has been stored long enough to become hard can stand on the counter for 15 to 30 minutes to soften before dipping.

Recipes intended for churning can be still-frozen if the mixture is stirred frequently while freezing. Reserve whipping cream to be whipped separately and folded into a partially frozen mix to improve the texture.

TURNING OUT CANDY   My collection of candy recipes is uncomplicated. I leave the tempering of chocolate to the confectioner. It does help to learn the stages in the cooking of syrups. The reading of a thermometer and a cold-water test can both be used to determine the stage of your bubbling pot.

Soft-Ball Stage (234–240°F): Syrup forms a soft ball in cold water that flattens when it is picked up.
Firm-Ball Stage (244–249°F): Syrup forms a firm ball in cold water that holds its shape unless pressed.
Hard-Ball Stage (250–265°F): Syrup forms a hard ball in cold water, but is pliable when removed.
Soft-Crack Stage (270–290°F): Syrup separates into hard strands that are brittle in cold water, but soft and pliable when removed.
Hard-Crack Stage (300–310°F): Syrup forms brittle strands in cold water that remain brittle when removed from the water, and are not sticky.

The candy-making pot should have a heavy bottom to minimize the danger of scorching. Allow ample room for boil-up during cooking. You will need a 1- to 2-quart capacity for every cup of sugar used. Use a wooden spoon for stirring, as a metal spoon dissipates the heat in the mixture.

Sugar crystallization is the major fault of poorly prepared candy. Dissolve the sugar early in the cooking process with thorough mixing and stirring. To prevent the forming of sugar crystals on the sides of the pan, you can do one or all of the following: cover the pan to cook for several minutes, allowing steam to wash down any crystals that form; dip a pastry brush into water and use it to brush the crystals down; butter a pan before beginning to help prevent the forming of crystals.

Temperature and humidity work together in candy making. If the atmosphere is a little humid, cook your candy to a slightly higher temperature to offset its effect. If the humidity is high, put off your candy making until a drier day.

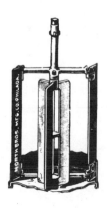

High and Handsome Layer Cakes

Frosted and filled in a multitude
of ways

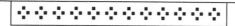

Some of these practically make themselves. Some take a little work. But all will make you proud.

Fresh Coconut Cake

Mother's Easy Chocolate Cake

Banana Layer Cake

Hurry-up Caramel Cake

Burnt Sugar Cake

Black-Walnut Buttercream Cake

Illinois Jam Cake

Toasted-Butter-Pecan Cake

Fresh Coconut Cake

❖ ❖ ❖

This is grand and glorious for special occasions. The moist cake is made more so by a buttery, sugary coconut filling. A scrumptious, soft marshmallowy icing tops it off. The coconut can be prepared a day or two ahead of baking and kept in the refrigerator. The cake, filling, and frosting should be made the day it is to be served.

Prepare fresh coconut (see opposite page) and Coconut Milk (see p. 18). Preheat the oven to 350°F. Grease and lightly flour three 9-inch round layer pans. Sift, stir, or whisk together and set aside

3 cups cake flour, sifted before measuring
¾ teaspoon salt
1 tablespoon baking powder

In a large bowl, gradually adding the sugar, cream together

1 cup shortening
2 cups granulated sugar

Add, blending well

1½ teaspoons pure vanilla extract

Add, one at a time, beating well after each

4 large eggs

Add alternately (4 parts dry, 3 parts coconut milk), blending after each addition

reserved dry ingredients
1 cup plus 2 tablespoons Coconut Milk

Spoon and scrape the thick batter into the prepared pans. Spread as smoothly as possible, using a rubber spatula, taking care not to leave a hump in the middle. Bake at 350°F for 30 minutes, or until the cake springs back when lightly touched in the center and is beginning to pull away from the sides of the pan. Cool in pans elevated on wire racks for 8 minutes, then turn out to cool completely, again on wire racks. Trim away rounded tops, if any, on two of the layers. Lightly brush away any crumbs. Turn the first two layers upside down (these are the layers you trimmed), and the top layer right side up. Cover the first two layers with

Coconut Filling (see opposite page)

Frost top and sides with

Boiled Vanilla Icing (see page 18).

Makes 16 servings.

COCONUT FILLING

In a large, heavy saucepan, cook over medium heat, stirring constantly, until the sugar dissolves, the butter melts, and the mixture begins to bubble

1 cup granulated sugar
4 tablespoons unsalted butter
2 tablespoons water
pinch (¹⁄₁₆ teaspoon) salt

Remove from the heat. In a side bowl beat until smooth

2 large egg yolks

Stir about one-half the sugar mixture into the beaten yolks. Stir the warmed yolks into the sugar mixture. Continue to cook, stirring constantly, until the mixture bubbles and begins to thicken. It will thicken more as it cools. Remove from the heat. Stir in

¼ teaspoon pure vanilla extract

Cool to lukewarm. Beat well and then stir in

2 cups grated fresh coconut

Spread on cooled cake layers while still slightly warm.

Makes about 1½ cups filling.

TO PREPARE FRESH COCONUT

Coconuts are available at most supermarkets, with the husks removed. Pick out a medium to large one and shake it before you buy. Listen for a sloshing sound, indicating it is full of liquid.

Drive an ice pick or screwdriver into the three holes at the end of the coconut. Shake out the liquid and discard. Wrap the coconut in old toweling and place it on a hard surface, such as concrete. Whack it with a heavy mallet or the side of a hammer until it cracks into several pieces. Pry out the pieces of coconut meat. Pare the brown skin from the meat with a sharp knife or vegetable peeler. Rinse away any fiber that remains and pat the meat dry with paper toweling. Cut the meat into chunks and grate with a coarse hand grater or the medium grating disk of a food processor. One coconut will yield about 3 cups grated coconut. Freshly grated coconut may be stored, covered, in the refrigerator for up to 2 days. It does not freeze well.

Combine

1 cup grated fresh coconut
1¼ cups hot scalded milk

Let stand until lukewarm, about 20 minutes. Strain through a sieve, pressing on the coconut to get out all the goodness you can. Cool the milk completely before use. The coconut can be added to your morning muffin batter.

BOILED VANILLA ICING

This is a wonderful icing, billowy-soft, and not too sweet, but you need perfect timing to make it. If you cook the syrup too long, boiling it to a temperature that is higher than specified, it can clump into hard candy on the bottom of the bowl containing the beaten whites. If you don't cook the syrup long enough, boiling it to a temperature that is lower than specified, the icing will not thicken. If your icing does not thicken, you can, as a last resort, gradually add confectioners' sugar until it does. If you have cooked the syrup too long, there is no remedy except starting over. Read the recipe carefully before beginning, to ensure your success.

Use a heavy 2-quart saucepan, with a shape that is tall rather than flat. If the pan is too broad-based, the syrup will not come up high enough on your thermometer to register heat. Cook over medium heat, stirring occasionally, until the sugar is dissolved

1 cup granulated sugar
⅓ cup water
1 tablespoon light corn syrup
⅛ teaspoon cream of tartar
⅛ teaspoon salt

Cover and cook 3 minutes to wash down any sugar crystals that may remain on the sides of the pan. Uncover and cook, without stirring, until a candy thermometer reads 240°F. While the syrup is cooking, in the small bowl of a mixer (be sure the beaters are clean and dry), beat at medium speed until soft peaks form when the beaters are raised

2 large egg whites

You will want to time the whites so that they are ready just about the same time as the syrup. When the syrup has reached the right temperature, remove it from the heat. Turn the mixer to high speed and add the hot syrup to the whites in a slow but steady stream, taking care not to pour it directly onto the beaters. Do not scrape the last of the syrup from the pan. Continue to beat at high speed until the mixture is thickened enough to form stiff peaks when the beaters are stopped and raised, about 5 minutes. Remove the bowl from the mixer and fold in

1 teaspoon pure vanilla extract

Spread the slightly warm icing on the cooled cake.

Makes about 3 cups icing.

Mother's Easy Chocolate Cake

This was one of Mother's basic cakes—easy on both cook and pocketbook. She kept the ingredients on hand so she could whip it up whenever she pleased.

Preheat the oven to 350°F. Grease two 9-inch round layer pans. Stir together and use to dust the pans, knocking out any excess

1 tablespoon unbleached all-purpose flour
1 tablespoon cocoa

Stir together in a large bowl, pressing out any lumps with the back of a spoon

2 cups unbleached all-purpose flour
1½ cups granulated sugar
½ cup cocoa
1 teaspoon salt
2 teaspoons baking powder
¼ teaspoon baking soda

Add

2 large eggs
2 teaspoons pure vanilla extract
½ cup vegetable oil
1 cup milk

Stir together until all dry ingredients are damp and the batter is smooth. Stir in

½ cup boiling water

The batter will be thin. Pour into the prepared pans. Quickly raise the pans, one at a time, about 1 inch above the countertop and drop. This deflates some of the larger bubbles in the batter. Immediately place in the oven. Bake at 350°F for 30 to 35 minutes, or until the cake springs back when lightly touched in the center. Cool the pans elevated on wire racks for 5 minutes. Turn out to cool completely, right side up. Frost and fill the cooled cake with Seven-Minute White Icing, as Mother did (page 37), or my Easy Chocolate Frosting (see opposite page).

Makes 10 servings.

EASY CHOCOLATE FROSTING

Stir together and have ready (if lumpy, stir through a sieve)

3¾ cups (1 pound) confectioners' sugar
½ cup cocoa

In small mixer bowl beat together until light and fluffy

8 tablespoons unsalted butter
1 tablespoon pure vanilla extract

At low speed, add alternately

confectioners' sugar mixture
⅓ cup milk, more or less

Stop the mixer to scrape the beaters and bowl. Beat at high speed for 1 minute.

Makes about 2 cups frosting.

Banana Layer Cake

Use sweet, ripe bananas that are still suitable for eating for a moist, flavorful cake. Pecans add crunch between the layers.

Preheat the oven to 350°F. Grease two 9-inch layer pans. Line the bottoms of the pans with wax paper, and then grease the paper. Dust the paper-lined pans with flour. Sift, stir, or whisk together and set aside

2 cups unbleached all-purpose flour
½ teaspoon salt
¾ teaspoon baking powder
¾ teaspoon baking soda
1 teaspoon ground cinnamon
¼ teaspoon ground nutmeg

In a large bowl cream together, adding the sugar gradually

½ cup shortening
1½ cups granulated sugar

Add, one at a time, blending well after each

2 large eggs

Add, in this order, blending after each addition

1 teaspoon pure vanilla extract
1 cup mashed bananas
½ reserved dry ingredients
¼ cup buttermilk
remaining dry ingredients

Spoon and scrape into the prepared pans, spreading evenly. The batter will be thick. Bake at 350°F for 30 minutes. Cool in pans on wire racks 8 minutes. Turn out on wire racks. Remove the wax paper. Invert the layers to cool right side up. Frost and fill with Pecan-Cheese Frosting (see opposite page).

Makes 10 to 12 servings.

PECAN-CHEESE FROSTING

Beat together until soft and fluffy

4 tablespoons unsalted butter
8 ounces cream cheese
1½ teaspoons pure vanilla extract

Gradually add, beating well

3½ cups confectioners' sugar

Add additional confectioners' sugar, if needed to make the mixture spreadable. Thin, if necessary with milk. Frost the top of the first layer. Sprinkle over the frosting

½ cup chopped pecans

Cover with the second layer. Frost the sides and top with the remaining frosting. Place in a circle on the outer edge of the top of the cake

16 pecan halves

Makes about 2 cups frosting

Hurry-up Caramel Cake

The light texture and flavor of this southern quick-mix cake make it a Sunday favorite. The cake is equally at home at a backyard barbecue or with a full-fledged fried-chicken dinner.

Be sure all ingredients are at room temperature (about 70°F) before beginning. Preheat the oven to 350°F. Grease and lightly flour two 9-inch round layer pans. Stir together in a large mixer bowl, pressing out any lumps with the back of a spoon

½ cup granulated sugar
1 cup light brown sugar

Stir into the sugars, again pressing out any lumps

2¼ cups unbleached all-purpose flour
1 teaspoon salt
1 tablespoon baking powder

Add and mix at low speed until the dry ingredients are moistened, then beat at medium speed until smooth

8 tablespoons soft unsalted butter
1 cup milk

Stop to scrape the bowl and beaters. Add and beat at low speed until the eggs are blended, and then beat at medium speed until smooth

2 large eggs
1½ teaspoons pure vanilla extract

Stop to scrape the bowl and beaters. Beat again at medium speed until smooth. Spoon and scrape the batter into the prepared pans, spreading evenly. Bake at 350°F for 30 minutes, or until the cake begins to pull away from the sides of the pan. Cool in the pans 8 minutes. Turn out to cool completely on wire racks. Fill and frost with Hurry-Up Caramel Frosting (see opposite page).

Makes 10 to 12 servings.

HURRY-UP CARAMEL FROSTING

In a large, heavy saucepan, stir over medium heat until the butter is melted, the sugar is dissolved, and the surface of the mixture is covered with bubbles

8 tablespoons soft unsalted butter
1 cup light brown sugar
⅛ teaspoon salt
5 ounces evaporated milk

Remove from the heat. Stir in.

1 teaspoon pure vanilla extract

Beat in, ½ cup at a time, to make frosting spreadable

4 cups confectioners' sugar, more or less

Work quickly to fill and frost the cake, as this tends to harden and "sugar up" like pralines.

Makes about 2½ cups frosting.

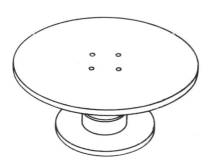

Burnt Sugar Cake

My friend Molly Culbert has been waiting for this since the book began. The burnt sugar syrup that flavors both the cake and frosting reminds her of the things she enjoyed growing up on the bluffs at Clarksville, Missouri. This one's for you, Molly.

Make one recipe Burnt Sugar Syrup (see opposite page). Preheat the oven to 350°F. Grease two 9-inch round layer pans. Line the bottoms with wax paper, and grease the paper. Lightly flour the pans, knocking out excess flour. Sift, stir, or whisk together and set aside

2 cups unbleached all-purpose flour
½ teaspoon salt
2½ teaspoons baking powder

In a large bowl, beat until light and fluffy

8 tablespoons unsalted butter

Gradually add, creaming well

1 cup granulated sugar

Add, one at a time, beating well after each

2 large eggs

Blend in, in this order

1 teaspoon pure vanilla extract
4 tablespoons Burnt Sugar Syrup

Add alternately (three parts dry, two parts milk), blending after each addition

reserved dry ingredients
¾ cup milk

Spoon and scrape into the prepared pans. Bake at 350°F for 25 to 30 minutes, or until the cake springs back when lightly touched in the center. Cool in the pans 8 minutes. Turn out on wire racks. Carefully remove the wax paper, and then cool the layers completely, right side up. Frost and fill the cooled cake with Burnt Sugar Buttercream Icing (see opposite page).

Makes 10 to 12 servings.

BURNT SUGAR BUTTERCREAM ICING

In a large bowl, beat until smooth

8 tablespoons unsalted butter
4 tablespoon Burnt Sugar Syrup (see below)

Add alternately, blending well after each addition (four parts sugar, three parts cream)

3¾ cups (1 pound) confectioners' sugar
6 tablespoons whipping (heavy) cream

Add additional cream, by the spoonful, if needed to make the frosting spreadable.

Makes about 2 cups icing.

BURNT SUGAR SYRUP

They used to say, "Cook the sugar till it smokes." The flavor is more palatable short of that point, however. Despite the name, you want a dark, rich flavor, not a burned one.

Spread in an 8- or 10-inch cast-iron skillet

1 cup granulated sugar

Cook over medium heat until it melts and turns a rich caramel color. Don't stir until it starts melting, and then stir constantly, using a wooden spoon. When the desired color is reached, remove from the heat. Protect your hands and stand back for the next step. It may spatter hot syrup, so be careful. Stirring constantly, slowly add

1 cup boiling water

Return to the heat and continue to stir until any remaining lumps are dissolved and the mixture thickens slightly.

Makes almost ¾ cup syrup.

Black-Walnut Buttercream Cake

Mmmmm. Black walnuts. Hard to describe, these American nuts are haunt-
ingly different from the English variety. The trees are easy to grow. One day
when our children were small, they came home proudly lugging a large grocery
sack filled with black walnuts. I looked at the green-and-brown-splotched husk-
covered nuts, and at the children's already stained, very black hands, and I
knew I couldn't let them keep their treasure in their closets. I drew a line near
the field that bordered our yard, and told the kids to throw their walnuts out
toward that field. My youngest son had not yet developed a pitching arm, and
the next spring an irregular row of trees sprang up along the lot line. Although
you can husk and crack your own black walnuts, I buy mine recipe-ready,
leaving the ones from our trees for the squirrels.

Preheat the oven to 350°F. Grease two 9-inch round layer pans. Line
the bottoms with wax paper, and grease the paper. Lightly flour the
pans, knocking out excess. Sift, stir, or whisk together and set aside

2½ cups cake flour, sifted before measuring
½ teaspoon salt
2½ teaspoons baking powder

In a large bowl cream until soft and fluffy

8 tablespoons unsalted butter

Gradually add, creaming well

1¼ cups granulated sugar

Add one at a time, beating well after each

3 large eggs

Blend in

1½ teaspoons pure vanilla extract

Add alternately (three parts dry, two parts cream), blending well after
each addition

reserved dry ingredients
¾ cup whipping (heavy) cream

Gently fold in

¾ cup chopped black walnuts

Spoon and scrape into the prepared pans, spreading evenly. Bake at 350°F for 30 to 35 minutes, or until the cake springs back when lightly touched in the center. Cool in the pans 8 minutes. Turn out on wire racks. Remove wax paper and then reinvert to cool right side up. Frost and fill with Black-Walnut Buttercream Frosting (see below).

Makes 10 to 12 servings.

BLACK-WALNUT BUTTERCREAM FROSTING

Beat together until smooth

8 tablespoons soft unsalted butter
1½ teaspoons pure vanilla extract

Add alternately, beginning and ending with confectioners' sugar

4 cups confectioners' sugar
¼ cup whipping (heavy) cream

Add additional cream or sugar, if needed to make the frosting spreadable. (If you're out of cream, use milk.) After the cake is frosted, sprinkle around the edge of the top

¼ cup chopped black walnuts

Makes about 2 cups frosting.

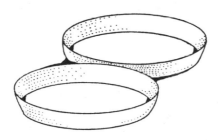

Illinois Jam Cake

This is prairie-farm jam cake—a takeoff on the blackberry-jam cake so popular in Kentucky. Although I make my own strawberry jam, I used store-bought for recipe testing, so that my results can be repeated in your kitchen.

Preheat the oven to 350°F. Grease and flour two 9-inch round layer pans. Sift, stir, or whisk together and set aside

2 cups unbleached all-purpose flour
¼ teaspoon salt
1 teaspoon baking soda
1 teaspoon ground cinnamon
¼ teaspoon ground nutmeg
¼ teaspoon ground allspice

In a large bowl, beat until soft and fluffy

10 tablespoons unsalted butter

Gradually add, creaming well

1 cup granulated sugar

Add, one at a time, beating well after each

3 large eggs

Add in this order, blending after each addition

1 cup strawberry jam
½ sifted dry ingredients
½ cup buttermilk
remaining dry ingredients

Pour and scrape the batter into the prepared pans. Bake at 350°F for 35 to 40 minutes, or until the cakes spring back when lightly touched in the center. Cool in the pans 8 minutes. Turn out to cool, right side up, on wire racks. Frost and fill the cooled cake with Strawberry Icing (see opposite page).

Makes 10 servings.

STRAWBERRY ICING

The jam gives this a lovely pink color.

Beat together until light and fluffy

**4 tablespoons unsalted butter
3 ounces cream cheese**

Blend in

**3 tablespoons strawberry jam
2 tablespoons fresh lemon juice**

Gradually add

3¾ cups (1 pound) confectioners' sugar

Add additional lemon juice, if needed, to make the icing spreadable.

Makes about 2 cups icing.

Toasted-Butter-Pecan Cake

Pecans are always good. Toasting makes them even better.

Preheat the oven to 350°F. Grease and flour two 8-inch round layer pans. Place in a shallow baking pan (a small cookie sheet is perfect)

1½ cups chopped pecans

Dot the pecans with slivers of

3 tablespoons unsalted butter

Bake at 350°F for 15 minutes, stirring every 5 minutes. Remove from the oven to cool. Sift, stir, or whisk together and set aside

2 cups cake flour, sifted before measuring
½ teaspoon salt
2 teaspoons baking powder

In a large bowl, beat until light and fluffy

8 tablespoons unsalted butter
1½ teaspoons pure vanilla extract

Add, ⅓ cup at a time, beating well after each addition

1⅓ cups granulated sugar

Add, one at a time, beating well after each

2 large eggs

Add alternately (three parts dry ingredients, two parts half-and-half), blending after each addition

sifted dry ingredients
⅔ cup half-and-half

Fold in

1 cup of the toasted pecans (reserve remainder for frosting)

Pour and scrape the batter into the prepared pans. Spread evenly with a spatula. Bake at 350°F for 30 to 35 minutes, or until the cake springs back when lightly touched in the center. Cool in the pans elevated on wire racks for 8 minutes. Turn out to cool completely, right side up. Frost the cooled cake with Toasted-Butter-Pecan Frosting (see opposite page).

Makes 8 to 10 servings.

TOASTED-BUTTER-PECAN FROSTING

Beat together until soft and fluffy

4 tablespoons unsalted butter
3 ounces cream cheese
1 teaspoon pure vanilla extract

Add alternately

3¾ cups (1 pound) confectioners' sugar
2 tablespoons half-and-half

Stir in

remaining toasted pecans from cake recipe

Add additional half-and-half, if needed, to make the mixture spreadable.

Makes about 2 cups frosting.

Delicate Cakes

Light and luscious for special occasions

These look impressive, but they aren't hard to make.

French Cream Cake

Chocolate Angel Food

Heavenly Angel Food Cake

Sunshine Sponge Cake

Classic Chiffon Cake

Raspberry Cream Cake

Company Dessert Cake

Perfect Cheesecake

Chocolate Mousse Cake

French Cream Cake

The idea for this cake originated with Ella Scharlach, who delighted two generations with her catered dinners and desserts. Because of the elaborate preparation, it was usually reserved for special occasions and birthdays, and hostesses always mentioned if it was Ella's. Here is my version of that popular cake.

Make one recipe Light Milk Sponge Cake (see below). When completely cooled, slice the cake into 3 layers.
Make one recipe of Sweetened Whipped Cream (page 270) and spread between the layers. Chill the cake while preparing the icing.
Make one recipe of Seven-Minute White Icing (see page 37) and frost the top and sides of the assembled cake. Chill the cake while preparing Chocolate Coating.
Make one recipe of Chocolate Coating for Cake (see page 38). Drizzle the coating over the top of the cake in a zig-zag pattern until the top is almost covered with chocolate. Using the back of a metal spoon, smooth out the coating to cover the top. Allow some coating to drip down the sides of the cake. Chill until ready to serve.

Makes 12 to 16 servings.

LIGHT MILK SPONGE CAKE

Only four eggs are needed for this delicate sponge cake. It's especially good for layering with fruits, custards, or creams.

Preheat the oven to 325°F. Sift, stir, or whisk together and set aside

1½ cups cake flour, sifted before measuring
¼ teaspoon salt
1½ teaspoons baking powder

In the large bowl of a mixer beat at high speed until thick

4 large egg yolks

Add

½ cup granulated sugar

Beat at high speed until light. Slowly add, beating in well at low speed, in this order

½ cup skim milk
1 teaspoon pure vanilla extract
sifted dry ingredients

With clean beaters and bowl, beat until foamy and just beginning to thicken

4 large egg whites
¼ teaspoon cream of tartar

Gradually add, beating until soft mounds form

1 cup granulated sugar

Gradually, and very gently, fold the beaten egg whites into the batter. Turn into an ungreased 10-inch tube pan. Bake at 325°F for about 1 hour, or until the cake springs back when lightly touched in the center. Invert the cake in the pan to cool. Remove the cool cake, loosening with a long slender knife or spatula. Frost and fill as described above.

Makes 12 to 16 servings.

SEVEN-MINUTE WHITE ICING

This makes a light and fluffy icing. Although considered no-fail, it may falter on a hot, humid day. Best made when the weather is cool and clear.

Be certain all utensils are well washed and fat free. Make sure not a speck of the egg yolk gets into the whites. In the top of a double boiler, beat until thoroughly blended

2 large egg whites
1½ cups granulated sugar
5 tablespoons cold water
¼ teaspoon cream of tartar
1 teaspoon light corn syrup

Heat over rapidly boiling water for a full 7 minutes, beating constantly with a wire whisk or hand-held beater. No fudging on time allowed. Remove from the heat. Stir in

½ teaspoon pure vanilla extract

Continue beating as before, or transfer to the small bowl of an electric mixer. Beat until the icing is a spreading consistency. Don't give up. It will thicken as it cools. Spread on a completely cooled cake.

Makes about 2 cups icing.

CHOCOLATE COATING FOR CAKE

Mix together in the top of a double boiler

1 ounce unsweetened chocolate, chopped
2 ounces semisweet chocolate, chopped
1 teaspoon vegetable oil

Heat over simmering, not boiling, water until melted, stirring constantly as the chocolate melts. Remove from the heat as soon as melted. Dry the bottom of the pan. One drop of water could ruin the chocolate. Drizzle or spread over the top of a frosted cake. Use quickly before the chocolate begins to set up.

Makes enough to coat the top of one 9-inch cake.

Chocolate Angel Food

❖ ❖ ❖

We have a club in Hoopeston called the Mary Hartwell Catherwood Club, founded at the instigation of Frances Trego, first wife of one of our early mayors, A. H. Trego. In her words:

"It may seem somewhat egotistical, I fear, when I tell you that so far as I know, the idea of our Tea Club came to me first. One exceedingly stormy day, as I sat sewing at a window, it broke upon my mind suddenly, like an inspiration, that a society that would call immediate neighbors together once a week for friendly visit and interchange of thought would be a good thing. I thought of it as an entirely informal affair where we could bring our thimbles and fancy work, stocking mending, or whatever, while one could read to us a part of the time as we kept our fingers busy. Then there should be a cup of tea with a cracker or sandwich and an early getting home for those who felt the need of being there.

"So impressed was I with the possible benefit in it that I donned waterproof and rubbers and waded over to Mrs. Mary Catherwood's to talk it over with her. She quite agreed in the desirability of doing it and kindly wished me to push ahead in organizing it. Of course, being modest and not given to leadership, I as kindly urged her to take initiatory steps. As a consequence, neither moved, although every now and then she wanted to know of me when I was going to lead out in the good direction. She probably talked of the idea with others as I did, but it was more than a year before talk shaped into action."

And so it was in January 1895 that Mrs. Catherwood called a group of neighbors together and founded the club named after her. (Mary Hartwell Catherwood was one of the first women in the Midwest to make a living by writing. Her best-known work was *Lazarre*, published in 1901.) At the first meeting tea was served, and the ladies decided to meet every Monday afternoon.

The club was not without its crises in those early years. During the first year or two, hostesses served just tea and plain crackers. Then some began to step out of line. One lady served not only crackers and tea, but coffee; another one provided doughnuts; still another went so far as to serve hot biscuits and butter. Then strawberries and cream were offered, and the next hostess came up with strawberries and cream and sandwiches and cake. Obviously steps had to be taken. At the next meeting, it was voted that refreshments be limited to four solids. An amendment was passed that two kinds of cake be classed as one solid. It was then voted that the hostess should be fined ten cents for each additional dish. Modern hostesses find that one dessert, flanked with nuts and mints, suffices.

A limit on membership became necessary so that members could continue to entertain in their homes, and twenty-five was settled upon. In 1896 the limit was raised to thirty and that is the way it stands today. Openings are *usually offered first to daughters or daughters-in-law of members, should they happen to live in town, and I was one of the lucky daughters-in-law. The understated elegance of this cake makes it appropriate for serving at a "Mary Hartwell" meeting.*

Preheat the oven to 300°F. Sift together or stir through a sieve four times and set aside

¾ cup granulated sugar
¾ cup confectioners' sugar
1 cup cake flour
¼ cup cocoa

Place in a mixing bowl

1½ cups egg whites, from 10 to 12 large eggs

Sprinkle through a sieve, over the egg whites

¼ teaspoon salt
1 teaspoon cream of tartar

Beat or whip until soft mounds form. Do not overbeat. There should not be stiff peaks. Sift over the beaten whites, using only one-quarter at a time, and gently fold in

sifted dry ingredients

Sprinkle over the batter and gently fold in

1 teaspoon pure vanilla extract

Turn into an ungreased 10-inch tube pan and bake at 300°F for 1 hour and 5 minutes, or until the cake springs back when lightly touched in the center. Cool the cake in the pan, elevated and upside down, for at least 1 hour. Loosen the cake from the sides and tube with a long, slender knife or spatula. Cool completely on a wire rack. Slice the cooled cake into 4 layers. Fill between layers and frost the top with Chocolate Whipped Cream (see page 270). You will need a double recipe. Chill until ready to serve.

Makes 12 servings.

Heavenly Angel Food Cake

❖ ❖ ❖

A classic cake. It contains no fat or egg yolks and can be eaten unadorned or sauced simply with fruit. It can also be scooped out and filled with custard, whipped cream, or ice cream, for a more elegant presentation.

Place an oven rack in the lower third of the oven and preheat to 350°F. Sift or stir through a sieve three times and then set aside

1 cup cake flour, sifted before measuring
½ cup confectioners' sugar

In the large bowl of a mixer, beat until foamy

1½ cups egg whites, from 10 to 12 large eggs

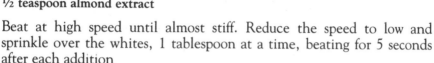

Sprinkle over the whites

¼ teaspoon salt
1½ teaspoons cream of tartar
1 tablespoon cold water
1½ teaspoons pure vanilla extract
½ teaspoon almond extract

Beat at high speed until almost stiff. Reduce the speed to low and sprinkle over the whites, 1 tablespoon at a time, beating for 5 seconds after each addition

1 cup granulated sugar

Return to high speed and beat again until almost stiff. Remove the bowl from the mixer. Add the reserved flour mixture, about 2 heaping table-spoons at a time, first sprinkling it over the whites, and then gently folding it in. Spoon and scrape the batter into a clean and dry 10-inch tube pan. Bake at 350°F for 45 minutes, or until the crust is golden brown and cracks are very dry. Cool in the pan, elevated and upside down, for 1½ hours. Use a thin knife or spatula to help release the cake and cool it completely on a wire rack. Cut the cake by tearing it apart into pieces with two forks, or use a gentle sawing motion with a serrated knife.

Makes 12 servings.

Sunshine Sponge Cake

Make this with the egg yolks that are left after making an angel food cake.

Preheat the oven to 350°F. Sift, stir, or whisk together and set aside

2 cups cake flour, sifted before measuring
2 teaspoons baking powder
¼ teaspoon salt

Heat together just until the milk is hot and the butter is completely melted

1 cup milk
4 tablespoons unsalted butter

Set the milk mixture aside to cool slightly. In the large bowl of a mixer beat at high speed until thick

11 large egg yolks

Gradually add, beating continuously while adding,

2 cups granulated sugar

Add alternately to the egg yolk–sugar mixture, mixing in at low speed (three parts dry, two parts milk)

sifted dry ingredients
heated milk-butter mixture

Add and mix just until blended

2 teaspoons pure vanilla extract

Spoon and scrape into an ungreased 10-inch tube pan. Bake at 350°F for 1 hour or until the cake springs back when lightly touched in the center. Cool in the pan elevated and inverted on a wire rack for at least 1 hour. Loosen the cake from the sides and tube with a long slender knife or spatula. Cool completely on a wire rack. Serve slices of the cake with sugared berries in season and top with whipped cream.

Makes 12 servings.

Classic Chiffon Cake

Before chiffon's introduction, there were basically two kinds of cake. Butter cakes were made with a firm fat, such as butter or shortening, and foam cakes were made with beaten egg whites and yolks. Chiffon cakes, developed by Harry Baker in the early twenties, and introduced to the world by Betty Crocker in 1948, combined the lightness of a foam with the richness of a butter cake. The secret ingredient, now shared by all, was vegetable oil. Using more whites than yolks adds to the lightness of this delicious cake.

Preheat the oven to 325°F. In a mixing bowl, whisk together until well mixed

2¼ cups cake flour
1½ cups granulated sugar
1 teaspoon salt
1 tablespoon baking powder

Separate, reserving the yolks in a small bowl and the whites in a measuring cup

6 large eggs

Add enough whites to the measuring cup to fill to the 1-cup line. (If you have frozen whites, they can be defrosted and used.) Place the egg whites in the large bowl of a mixer and press through a sieve into them

½ teaspoon cream of tartar

Beat the whites at high speed until stiff. Remove bowl from mixer stand. Make a well in the center of the dry ingredients, and in that well place in this order

½ cup vegetable oil
reserved egg yolks
½ cup cold water
¼ cup fresh orange juice
1 teaspoon pure lemon extract
grated zest of 1 lemon

Beat with a whisk until smooth. Pour the egg-yolk mixture in a thin stream over the beaten whites, using about one-quarter at a time. Fold the two mixtures together gently after each addition, taking care not to overmix. Pour and scrape the batter into an ungreased 10-inch tube pan. Bake at 325°F for 75 minutes, or until the top springs back when lightly touched in the center. Cool in the pan, inverted on its funnel, until completely cool, about 2 hours. Use a thin knife or spatula to loosen the sides and base. Frost with Classic Cream Cheese Frosting (see page 44).

Makes 12 to 16 servings.

CLASSIC CREAM CHEESE FROSTING

In a mixing bowl, cream together

3 ounces cream cheese
4 tablespoons unsalted butter
1 tablespoon fresh lemon juice
1 tablespoon fresh orange juice
grated zest of 1 lemon

Stir through a sieve and then gradually beat into the creamed mixture

3 cups confectioners' sugar

Add additional confectioners' sugar, if needed to make the frosting spreadable. Add additional lemon juice if the frosting is too thick. Spread on cooled cake.

Makes about 1¾ cups frosting.

Raspberry Cream Cake

This is an easily made, quick-mix white cake. The layers are split and spread with raspberry jam, and the whole thing is put together with a smooth cream cheese frosting. Fresh raspberries finish it off.

Preheat the oven to 350°F. Grease and flour two 8-inch round layer pans. Sift, stir, or whisk together in a large mixer bowl

2 cups unbleached all-purpose flour
1¼ cups granulated sugar
1 tablespoon baking powder
½ teaspoon salt

Add to the dry ingredients

½ cup shortening
1 teaspoon pure vanilla extract
½ teaspoon almond extract
½ cup whipping cream
7 tablespoons water

Beat at low speed, scraping the bowl as you beat, for 1 minute, or until the dry ingredients are damp. Stop to scrape the beaters. Add

3 large egg whites

Beat at medium speed 1 minute, or until smooth, scraping the bowl often. Stop to scrape the beaters. Beat at medium speed 1 minute longer, or until thick and smooth. Pour and scrape the batter into the prepared pans. Spread evenly with a rubber spatula. Bake at 350°F for 25 to 30 minutes, or until the cake springs back when lightly touched in the center. Cool in pans 8 minutes. Turn out on wire racks to cool right side up. When the layers are completely cool, slice them horizontally, making 4 layers in all. Stir until smooth

1 jar (12 ounces) seedless red raspberry jam

Spoon half of the jam on one cut side of each layer, spreading almost to the edge with the back of the spoon. Reassemble the cut layers. Frost and fill with Special Cream Cheese Frosting (see below). Decorate the top of the cake with

fresh red raspberries

Pass a bowl of the raspberries at the table.

Makes 10 servings.

SPECIAL CREAM CHEESE FROSTING

Beat together until smooth and creamy

4 tablespoons unsalted butter
3 ounces cream cheese
1 teaspoon pure vanilla extract

Add alternately, beating well after each addition

3¾ cups (1 pound) confectioners' sugar
¼ cup whipping (heavy) cream

Add additional cream, if needed, to make the frosting spreadable.

Makes about 2 cups frosting.

Company Dessert Cake

My cousin Bernice sent this to me, saying it was a long-time favorite of the Fresno Eastern Star. Imagine my surprise when I found an identical cake in a fifty-year-old Hoopeston (my hometown) fundraiser. Don't tell me good recipes don't get around.

Preheat the oven to 325°F. Grease and flour two 8-inch round layer pans. Sift, stir, or whisk together and set aside

1 cup unbleached all-purpose flour
1 teaspoon baking powder
¼ teaspoon salt

In a large bowl cream together

½ cup shortening
½ cup granulated sugar

Add, in this order, beating well after each addition,

1 teaspoon pure vanilla extract
3 large egg yolks

Add alternately, beginning and ending with dry ingredients (three parts dry, two parts milk)

reserved dry ingredients
6 tablespoons milk

The batter will be stiff, which is O.K. Spread evenly in the prepared pans. In the small bowl of a mixer, beat at high speed until firm, almost stiff, peaks form

4 large egg whites

Reduce speed to medium and add, 1 tablespoonful at a time, allowing 10 seconds between additions

1 cup granulated sugar

Return to high speed and beat until stiff peaks form. Spread half the egg-white mixture evenly over each of the layers. Sprinkle over each layer half of

1 cup chopped pecans or walnuts

Gently press the nuts into the egg whites. Bake at 325°F for 30 minutes. Let cool in the pans 6 minutes. Loosen the edges, if necessary, with a slender knife or spatula. Turn out very carefully and cool upright on wire racks. When cooled completely, keep the meringue sides up, and fill between the layers with Custard Filling (see below). Chill the cake for several hours before cutting to allow the flavors to marry and mellow. Be sure to refrigerate leftovers.

Makes 8 servings.

CUSTARD FILLING

Stir together in a small saucepan

2 tablespoons granulated sugar
4 teaspoons (1 tablespoon plus 1 teaspoon) cornstarch
pinch (about ¹⁄₁₆ teaspoon) salt

In a side bowl beat until smooth

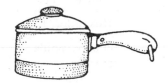

1 large egg yolk

Gradually stir into the yolk

1 cup milk

Gradually stir the yolk mixture into the sugar mixture. Cook over medium heat, stirring constantly, until it thickens, 5 to 7 minutes. Turn the heat to low and cook 1 minute longer, stirring briskly. Remove from the heat and continue to stir gently for about 1 minute. Gently fold in

¹⁄₂ teaspoon pure vanilla extract

Let cool to room temperature, stirring gently from time to time, to prevent a film from forming on top.

Makes about 1 cup filling.

Perfect Cheesecake

This is creamy without being heavy, light without being dry, with just enough crust to remember without being overdone.

Preheat the oven to 325°F. Assemble a 10-inch springform pan. Lightly butter the sides only. Mix together to form a crust mixture

1½ cups graham-cracker crumbs (about 24 squares)
2 tablespoons granulated sugar
6 tablespoons melted unsalted butter

Press a thin layer of the mixture three-quarters of the way up the sides of the buttered pan. Press the remainder evenly across the bottom. Avoid a buildup where the sides and bottom meet. Chill while preparing the filling. In a large bowl of an electric mixer, beat until light and fluffy

4 packages (8 ounces each) cream cheese

Beat in, ½ cup at a time

1½ cups granulated sugar

Add, one at a time, beating well after each

6 large egg yolks

Blend in, in this order

¼ teaspoon salt
1 tablespoon unbleached all-purpose flour
1 tablespoon cornstarch
1 tablespoon pure vanilla extract
3 tablespoons fresh lemon juice

Stir until smooth and then blend in

2 cups sour cream

With clean bowl and beaters, beat until soft peaks form

6 large egg whites

Fold and stir one-fourth of the beaten egg whites into the batter at a time. Be thorough, mixing until no white lumps remain. Be less gentle than when folding whites into a cake batter. Pour the batter into the prepared pan. Bake at 325°F for 1 hour. Turn the oven off and let the cake remain in the oven without opening the door for 1 hour. Remove from the oven. Cool at room temperature on a wire rack for 3 to 4 hours. Loosely cover and refrigerate for 12 to 24 hours before serving. Remove the sides from the springform pan and place the cake on a serving plate. Dip a knife in hot water before using it to cut the cake. Clean the knife between slices. Serve unadorned or with Pineapple Sauce (page 272), Blueberry Sauce (page 223), or Montmorency Cherry Sauce (page 275).

Makes 16 servings.

Chocolate Mousse Cake

This flourless cake is decadently rich and very chocolate. Don't tell anyone how easy it is. Let them be impressed.

Preheat the oven to 350°F. Butter a 9- or 9½-inch springform pan. (The 9½-inch fits a tad better, but may be hard to find.) Batter will be thin. If the pan is known to leak, line it with foil and butter the foil. In a heavy saucepan, cook over low heat, stirring often, until melted and smooth

1 pound (4 sticks) soft unsalted butter
1 cup granulated sugar
¼ teaspoon salt
16 squares (1 ounce each) semisweet chocolate, coarsely chopped
1 cup freshly brewed coffee

Meanwhile, in a large mixer bowl, beat until thick and lemon-colored

8 large eggs

With the mixer at medium speed, pour the chocolate mixture into the beaten eggs, in a thin and steady stream. As soon as the batter is even-colored, with no light streaks, pour it into the prepared pan. Bake at 350°F for 50 to 55 minutes, or until a wooden pick inserted in the center comes out clean. Cool at room temperature for 3 to 4 hours. Expect the cake to fall in the center as it cools. Remove the sides of the pan. Cover loosely and refrigerate for at least 4 hours before serving. Spoon 2 table-spoons of Raspberry Sauce (see below) onto each serving plate. Place slices of cake on the sauce. Offer a choice of Sweetened Whipped Cream (page 270) or Chocolate Whipped Cream (page 270). Fresh raspberries are the perfect garnish.

Makes 16 servings.

RASPBERRY SAUCE

Partially thaw

2 packages (10 ounces each) frozen red raspberries in light syrup

Purée in a food processor or blender. Strain through a sieve to remove seeds. Cover and refrigerate until serving time. Right before serving, stir in

1 to 2 teaspoons kirsch or light rum (optional)

Makes 2 cups sauce.

Tender Cakes

*With mouth-watering sour cream
and buttermilk flavor*

It is the lactic acid in sour cream and buttermilk that
gives these cakes such a tender crumb. Delicious!

Devilish Dump Cake

Sour-Cream Chocolate Cake

Rum-Flavored Spice Cake

Golden State Orange Cake

Grandma Martha's Crumb Cake

Lemon Buttermilk Cake

White Buttermilk Cake

Sour-Cream Poundcake

Devilish Dump Cake

❖ ❖ ❖

This easy-mix cake is dark and delicious. One of my family's birthday favorites.

Preheat the oven to 350°F. Grease two 9-inch round layer pans. Line the bottoms of the pans with wax paper. Grease the paper. Mix together and use to dust pans, knocking out any excess

1 tablespoon unbleached all-purpose flour
1 tablespoon cocoa

Place in a large sieve over a large mixer bowl, in this order

1¾ cups unbleached all-purpose flour
¾ teaspoon salt
1½ teaspoons baking soda
⅔ cup cocoa
1½ cups granulated sugar

Stir through the sieve into the bowl. Remove the sieve. (A large sifter can be used in place of a sieve, if you prefer.) Add, in this order

½ cup shortening
1 teaspoon pure vanilla extract
2 large eggs (be sure these are at room temperature)
1½ cups buttermilk

Beat at low speed, scraping the bowl as you beat, for 1 minute, or until the dry ingredients are damp. Stop to scrape beaters. Beat at medium speed 2 minutes, or until smooth, scraping the bowl often. Stop to scrape the beaters. Beat at medium speed 1 minute longer, or until thick and smooth. Pour and scrape the batter into the prepared pans. Spread evenly with a rubber spatula. Bake at 350°F for 30 to 35 minutes, or until the cake springs back when lightly touched in the center. Cool in pans 8 minutes. Turn out on wire racks. Carefully remove the paper and invert to cool completely, right side up. Frost and fill the cooled cake with Devilish Frosting (see opposite page).

Makes 10 to 12 servings.

DEVILISH FROSTING

This is so devilishly good you could eat it with a spoon.

Place in a large sieve over a large mixer bowl, in this order

3¾ cups (1 pound) confectioners' sugar
½ cup cocoa
⅛ teaspoon salt

Stir through the sieve into the bowl. Remove the sieve. Add, in this order

8 tablespoons soft unsalted butter
1 teaspoon pure vanilla extract
4 tablespoons buttermilk (plus more, as needed)

Beat at low speed until smooth. Add additional buttermilk, 1 tablespoon at a time, until the mixture is spreadable. The amount varies with the thickness of the buttermilk, averaging 6 tablespoons.

Makes about 2 cups frosting.

Sour-Cream Chocolate Cake

❖ ❖ ❖

This is rich and moist old-fashioned Devil's Food. The baking soda reacts with the chocolate to give the cake a reddish color.

Preheat the oven to 350°F. Grease two 9-inch round layer pans. Stir together and use to dust the pans, knocking out any excess

1 tablespoon cocoa
1 tablespoon cake flour

Sift together and set aside

2¼ cups cake flour, sifted before measuring
½ teaspoon salt
2 teaspoons baking soda

Melt in a double boiler over hot, not boiling, water

3 squares (1 ounce each) unsweetened chocolate

Set aside to cool. In a large bowl, cream until light and fluffy

8 tablespoons unsalted butter

Stir together, pressing out any lumps with the back of a spoon, and gradually add, creaming well

1 cup granulated sugar
1 cup light brown sugar

Add, one at a time, beating well after each

3 large eggs

Blend in, in this order,

cooled chocolate
1 teaspoon pure vanilla extract

Add alternately (three parts dry, two parts sour cream), blending after each addition

reserved dry ingredients
1 cup sour cream

Stir in with a wooden spoon, about ½ cup at a time

1 cup boiling water

The batter will be thin. Pour it into the prepared pans. Quickly raise the pans, one at a time, about 1 inch above the countertop and drop. This will deflate some of the larger bubbles in the batter. Immediately place in the oven. Bake at 350°F for 30 to 35 minutes, or until the cake springs back when lightly touched in the center. Cool in pans elevated on wire racks for 8 minutes. Turn out to cool completely on wire racks, making sure the layers are right side up. Frost when cool with Sour-Cream Chocolate Frosting (see below).

Makes 10 to 12 servings.

SOUR-CREAM CHOCOLATE FROSTING

Press through a sieve and have ready

1¾ cups confectioners' sugar

Melt in the top of a double boiler over hot, not boiling, water

12 ounces semisweet chocolate morsels

Remove from the heat and cool slightly. Stir in, in this order,

1 cup sour cream
sieved confectioners' sugar (you may not need it all)

Makes about 2½ cups frosting.

Rum-Flavored Spice Cake

All my favorite flavors are here: brown sugar, buttermilk, cocoa, and rum. With just enough spice to keep it interesting.

Preheat the oven to 350°F. Grease and flour three 9-inch round layer pans. Sift, stir, or whisk together and set aside

3 cups unbleached all-purpose flour
1 teaspoon salt
1 teaspoon baking powder
1 teaspoon baking soda
1 teaspoon ground cinnamon
1 teaspoon ground allspice
1 teaspoon ground cloves
1 tablespoon cocoa

In a large bowl, cream until light and fluffy

2 sticks unsalted butter

Stir together, pressing out any lumps with the back of a spoon, and then gradually add, creaming well

1 cup granulated sugar
1 cup light brown sugar

Add, one at a time, beating well after each

4 large eggs

Blend in

1 tablespoon dark rum

Add alternately (four parts dry, three parts buttermilk), blending after each addition

reserved dry ingredients
1⅓ cups buttermilk

Spoon and scrape into the prepared pans, spreading evenly. Bake at 350°F for 30 to 35 minutes, or until the cake springs back when lightly touched in the center. Cool in the pans 8 minutes, and then turn out to cool on wire racks. Frost and fill the cooled cake with Rum-Flavored Frosting (see opposite page).

Makes 16 servings.

RUM-FLAVORED FROSTING

In a large bowl, beat together until smooth

12 tablespoons soft unsalted butter
11 ounces cream cheese (one 8-ounce and one 3-ounce package)
1 tablespoon dark rum
1 tablespoon fresh lemon juice

Gradually add, until the frosting is speadable

6½ cups confectioners' sugar, more or less

Makes about 4 cups frosting.

Golden State Orange Cake

I love the combination of oranges, raisins, and walnuts. All from California, of course. These are generous layers. Note the special pan size.

Preheat the oven to 350°F. Grease and flour two 9 x 1¾-inch round layer pans. Sift, stir, or whisk together and set aside

2¾ cups cake flour, sifted before measuring
¾ teaspoon salt
1½ teaspoons baking soda

In a large bowl beat together until light and fluffy

¾ cup shortening
grated zest of 1 orange
1 teaspoon pure orange extract

Stir together, pressing out any lumps with the back of a spoon, and then gradually add to the shortening mixture, creaming well

¾ cup granulated sugar
¾ cup light brown sugar

Add, one at a time, beating well after each

3 large eggs

Add alternately (four parts dry, three parts buttermilk), blending after each addition

reserved dry ingredients
1½ cups buttermilk

Stir together and then stir in

¾ cup chopped raisins
¾ cup chopped walnuts

Spoon and scrape into the prepared pans. Spread evenly with a spatula. Bake at 350°F for 35 to 40 minutes, or until the cake springs back when lightly touched in the center. Cool in the pans elevated on wire racks for 8 minutes. Turn out to cool completely, right side up. Fill and frost the cooled cake with Orange Cream-Cheese Frosting (see opposite page). Place in a circle on the outer edge of the top of the cake.

16 walnut halves

Makes 10 to 12 servings.

ORANGE CREAM-CHEESE FROSTING

Beat together until soft and fluffy

4 tablespoons soft unsalted butter
3 ounces cream cheese
grated zest of 1 orange

Add alternately

3¾ cups (1 pound) confectioners' sugar
2 tablespoons fresh orange juice

Add additional orange juice, if needed, to make the mixture spreadable

Makes about 2 cups frosting.

Grandma Martha's Crumb Cake

This is rich with butter and sour cream, altogether better than any crumb cake I have seen recorded. Martha Mervis of Danville, Illinois, gave me hers in a 9-inch-square pan, but I love the ease of turning it out of the springform.

Preheat the oven to 350°F. Grease a 9-inch-square baking pan or an 8-inch springform pan. Line the bottom of the pan with wax paper and grease the paper. Flour the lined pan, knocking out any excess. Stir together in a large mixer bowl

1 cup unbleached all-purpose flour
1 cup cake flour, sifted before measuring
1 cup granulated sugar
1 cup light brown sugar

Add and beat at low speed until the mixture turns to fine crumbs

8 tablespoons soft unsalted butter

Lightly spoon out ½ cup of the crumbs and reserve for topping. Add to the remaining crumbs

1 cup sour cream
2 large eggs
½ teaspoon salt
½ teaspoon baking soda
1 teaspoon pure vanilla extract

Beat at low speed, scraping the bowl constantly, until the dry ingredients are moistened. Stop to scrape the beaters. Beat at medium speed, scraping the bowl often, until smooth and thick, about 2 more minutes. Scrape the batter into the prepared pan. Tilt and shake the pan gently to smooth out the top. Sprinkle the reserved crumbs evenly over the batter. Bake at 350°F for 45 minutes, or until a wooden pick inserted in the center comes out clean. Cool in the pan elevated on a wire rack. If using a springform pan, release and remove the sides after about 10 minutes. Serve warm or cold.

Makes 8 to 10 servings.

Lemon Buttermilk Cake

*Here's a quick little lemon cake, easy enough to make for tonight's supper.
The frosting is soft and, when spread on the warm cake, gives the whole cake
a lemon flavor.*

Preheat the oven to 350°F. Grease an 8 x 8 x 2-inch baking dish. Sift,
stir, or whisk together and set aside

1¼ cups unbleached all-purpose flour
¼ teaspoon salt
¼ teaspoon baking powder
¼ teaspoon baking soda

In a large bowl, beat together until well blended

5 tablespoons soft unsalted butter
10 tablespoons granulated sugar
grated rind of 1 lemon

Add, beating well

1 large egg

Add and blend well

reserved dry ingredients
½ cup buttermilk

Spoon and scrape the batter into the prepared pan. Spread evenly with
a spatula. Bake at 350°F for 30 to 35 minutes, or until the cake springs
back when lightly touched in the center. Cool in the pan elevated on a
wire rack. Frost the slightly warm cake with Soft Lemon Frosting (see
below). Serve warm or cold.

Makes 9 servings.

SOFT LEMON FROSTING

In a medium-size bowl, beat together until creamy

1 cup confectioners' sugar
1 tablespoon soft unsalted butter
2 tablespoons fresh lemon juice

Spread over the entire surface of the warm cake

Makes about ½ cup frosting.

White Buttermilk Cake

This is the best "plain old cake" you can make. The frosting is old-fashioned fudge.

Preheat the oven to 350°F. Grease and flour two 9-inch round layer pans. Sift, stir, or whisk together and set aside

2 cups unbleached all-purpose flour
½ teaspoon salt
½ teaspoon baking soda
1 teaspoon baking powder

Beat together until light and fluffy

⅔ cup shortening
1 teaspoon pure vanilla extract

Add, ½ cup at a time, beating well after each addition

1½ cups granulated sugar

Add, one at a time, beating well after each

3 large eggs

Add alternately (three parts dry ingredients, two parts buttermilk), blending after each addition

reserved dry ingredients
1 cup buttermilk

Spoon and scrape into the prepared pans. Spread evenly with a rubber spatula. Bake at 350°F for 30 to 35 minutes, or until the cake springs back when lightly touched in the center. Cool in the pans elevated on a wire rack for 8 minutes. Turn out to cool completely, right side up. Fill and frost the cooled cake with Cocoa Fudge Frosting (see opposite page).

Makes 10 to 12 servings.

COCOA FUDGE FROSTING

This will stiffen as you work with it, so spread between the layers and on the top of the cake while it is still a little soft. Do the sides last as the frosting stiffens.

Stir through a sieve and have ready

1¾ cups confectioners' sugar

In a heavy saucepan, stir together over medium heat until everything is melted and smooth

1 cup granulated sugar
⅛ teaspoon salt
¼ cup cocoa
4 tablespoons soft unsalted butter
½ cup whipping (heavy) cream
2 tablespoons light corn syrup

Continue to cook, stirring often, until the mixture begins to boil. Boil for 3 minutes, stirring constantly. During the last minute or so, you should have a boil that you can't stir down. Remove from the heat.

Place the pan in a sink filled with cold water up to the level of the mixture in the pan. When the pan is cool enough to feel just lukewarm on the bottom (it doesn't take long), remove it from the sink and dry the bottom of the pan. Beat in

1 teaspoon pure vanilla extract

Add, about ½ cup at a time

sieved confectioners' sugar (you may not need it all)

Beat vigorously with a wooden spoon until thick enough to spread, but still soft enough to almost pour. If it takes too long to suit you, put the pan back in the cold water and beat it there. If the frosting gets too thick to spread, add a drop or two of hot water to thin it. Spread on the cooled cake while the frosting is still warm. Apply more thinly than a buttercream. Work quickly once you start. Do not rework areas you have already frosted.

Makes about 1½ cups frosting.

Sour-Cream Poundcake

A poundcake keeps well. Made with sour cream, it keeps even better. Don't doctor this up with flavoring. It needs none.

Preheat the oven to 300°F. Grease and flour a large fluted tube pan. Sift before measuring

3 cups unbleached all-purpose flour

Resift with

¼ teaspoon salt
¼ teaspoon baking soda

In a large mixer bowl, beat until light and fluffy

2 sticks unsalted butter

Gradually add, creaming well

3 cups granulated sugar

Add one at a time, beating well after each

6 large egg yolks

Gradually add, in this order

1 cup sour cream
sifted dry ingredients

With clean beaters and bowl, beat until stiff

6 large egg whites

Stir one-quarter of the egg whites into the batter, then fold in the remainder. Spoon and scrape into the prepared pan. Bake at 300°F for 1½ to 1¾ hours, or until a wooden pick inserted in the center comes out clean. Cool in the pan elevated on a wire rack for 10 minutes. Turn out to cool completely on a wire rack. Serve thin slices with hot coffee or tea.

Makes 12 to 16 servings.

Granny's Cakes

Recipes from generations past

These old-fashioned cakes are so good, you'll get hungry just reading through the recipes.

Rotation Cake

Hot-Water Gingerbread

Mayonnaise Chocolate Cake

Mayonnaise Lemon Cake

Mystery Cake

Spirited Fruitcake

Pineapple Upside-Down Cake

Old-Fashioned Jelly Roll

Traditional Poundcake

Rotation Cake

This is sometimes called 1-2-3-4 Cake, with the order of ingredients being: 1 cup butter, 2 cups sugar, 3 cups flour, 4 eggs. It forms the basis for most butter cakes made today. I have combined all-purpose and cake flour, and used half-and-half instead of milk, to come closer to the flour and "top milk" my grandmother would have used.* I found the frosting in my mother-in-law's handwritten recipes.

Grease and lightly flour three 8-inch round layer pans. Preheat the oven to 350°F. Sift, stir, or whisk together and set aside

1 cup cake flour, sifted before measuring
2 cups unbleached all-purpose flour
3 teaspoons baking powder
1 teaspoon salt

In a mixing bowl, cream together until light and fluffy, adding sugar gradually

1 cup (2 sticks) soft unsalted butter
2 cups granulated sugar

Add, one at a time, beating well after each

4 large eggs

Blend in

1 teaspoon pure vanilla extract

Add alternately (three parts dry, two parts half-and-half), blending after each addition

reserved dry ingredients
1 cup half-and-half

Spoon and scrape the batter into the prepared pans. Spread evenly with a spatula. Bake at 350°F for 30 to 35 minutes, or until the cake springs back when lightly touched in the center. Cool in the pans elevated on wire racks for 8 minutes. Turn out to cool completely, right side up. Fill and frost with Hungarian Frosting (see opposite page).

Makes 12 servings.

---

*Before milk was homogenized, the cream rose to the top. The milk bottle had a narrowed neck below the cream to trap it. We used a special silver spoon to scoop it out. If the remaining milk was not disturbed, the top milk was richer than the rest.

HUNGARIAN FROSTING

Be sure to read about eggs (page 2) before beginning. Use only clean Grade A eggs with no cracks.

In the top of a double boiler melt over hot, not boiling, water

4 squares (1 ounce each) unsweetened chocolate

Set aside to cool. In the small bowl of a mixer beat together at low speed

**2½ cups confectioners' sugar
⅛ teaspoon salt
¼ cup freshly brewed coffee**

With the mixer running, add the melted chocolate in a steady stream. Add, one at a time, beating well after each

4 large egg yolks

Raise the speed to medium and beat in, about 1 tablespoon at a time

5½ tablespoons soft unsalted butter

Continue beating until thick enough to spread.

Makes about 2 cups frosting.

Hot-Water Gingerbread

This is an old-time homey dessert. We like it best with Vinegar Sauce.

Preheat the oven to 350°F. Grease an 8 x 8 x 2-inch baking dish. Sift, stir, or whisk together and set aside

1¾ cups unbleached all-purpose flour
¼ teaspoon salt
1 teaspoon baking soda
1 teaspoon ground ginger
½ teaspoon ground cinnamon

Cream together in a mixing bowl

⅓ cup shortening
½ cup granulated sugar

Add, in this order, blending well after each addition (if using a mixer, scrape the beaters often)

1 large egg
½ cup unsulphured molasses
½ reserved dry ingredients
⅓ cup hot water
remaining dry ingredients
⅓ cup hot water

Pour and scrape into the prepared baking dish. Use a spatula to push the batter into the corners of the dish. Bake at 350°F for 30 minutes, or until the cake springs back when lightly touched in the center. Serve squares of the cake warm, topped with Vinegar Sauce (page 276), or Tart Lemon Sauce (page 272).

Makes 9 servings.

Mayonnaise Chocolate Cake

This is a dark, moist cake—very popular in the fifties, but not seen much today. It deserves a revival.

Preheat the oven to 350°F. Grease and lightly flour a 9 x 12-inch pan. Sift, stir, or whisk together and set aside

2 cups unbleached all-purpose flour
4 tablespoons cocoa
¼ teaspoon salt
1 teaspoon baking soda

In a mixing bowl beat together

1 cup mayonnaise (use regular, not diet)
1 teaspoon pure vanilla extract
1 cup granulated sugar

Add alternately (three parts dry, two parts coffee), blending after each addition

reserved dry ingredients
1 cup cold coffee

Spoon the batter into the prepared pan. Bake at 350°F for 30 to 35 minutes, or until the cake springs back when lightly pressed in the center. Cool in the pan elevated on a wire rack. Frost with Quick Mocha Icing (see below).

Makes 12 servings.

QUICK MOCHA ICING

This is enough icing for the top of one 9 x 12-inch cake. Double the recipe to frost and fill one 9-inch 2 layer cake.

With the back of a wooden spoon, rub through a sieve into a mixing bowl

1½ cups confectioners' sugar
1 tablespoon cocoa

Add

4 tablespoons soft unsalted butter
pinch salt (about ¹⁄₁₆ teaspoon)
½ teaspoon pure vanilla extract
2 tablespoons hot coffee

Beat well. Add additional coffee, if needed, to make the icing spreadable.

Makes about ¾ cup icing.

Mayonnaise Lemon Cake

Most recipes for mayonnaise cakes call for cocoa in the batter, but the flavor can be other than chocolate.

Preheat the oven to 350°F. Grease and lightly flour two 8-inch round layer pans. Sift, stir, or whisk together and set aside

2 cups unbleached all-purpose flour
¼ teaspoon salt
1 teaspoon baking soda

In a mixing bowl beat together

1 cup mayonnaise (use regular, not diet)
1 teaspoon pure lemon extract
1 cup granulated sugar

Add alternately (three parts dry, two parts milk), blending after each addition

sifted dry ingredients
¾ cup milk

Spoon the batter into the prepared pans. Bake at 350°F for 25 to 30 minutes, or until the cake springs back when lightly pressed in the center. Cool in the pans elevated on wire racks 8 minutes. Turn out to cool, right sides up. Frost with Quick Lemon Icing (see below).

Makes 8 to 10 servings.

QUICK LEMON ICING

The touch of rum used here takes away the raw taste found in some quick lemon icings.

With a wooden spoon, rub through a sieve into a mixing bowl

3 cups confectioners' sugar

Add

6 tablespoons soft unsalted butter
grated zest of 1 lemon
1 tablespoon light rum
3 tablespoons fresh lemon juice

Beat well. Add additional lemon juice, if needed to make the icing spreadable.

Makes about 1½ cups icing.

Mystery Cake

This moist, spicy cake dates from the 1920s when canned condensed tomato soup first became available. It seems ordinary the day it is made, but if kept for a day before serving, it is delicious.

Preheat the oven to 350°F. Grease and lightly flour two 8-inch layer pans. Sift, stir, or whisk together and set aside

2 cups unbleached all-purpose flour
¼ teaspoon salt
1 teaspoon baking powder
1 teaspoon baking soda
1 teaspoon ground cinnamon
½ teaspoon ground nutmeg
½ teaspoon ground cloves

In a large bowl cream together

½ cup shortening
grated zest of 1 lemon

Gradually add, creaming well

1½ cups granulated sugar

Add, one at a time, beating well after each

3 large eggs

Blend in, in this order

½ reserved dry ingredients
1 can (10¾ ounces) condensed tomato soup
remaining dry ingredients

The batter will be thick. That is O.K. Spoon into the prepared pans, carefully spreading it with a spatula. Bake at 350°F for 35 to 40 minutes, or until the cake springs back when lightly touched in the center. Cool in the pans elevated on wire racks for 8 minutes. Turn out to cool completely, right side up. Frost and fill with Easy Cream Cheese Frosting (see page 72).

Makes 8 to 10 servings.

EASY CREAM CHEESE FROSTING

Beat together until light and fluffy

**8 ounces cream cheese
2 tablespoons soft unsalted butter
1 tablespoon fresh lemon juice**

Press through a sieve and then blend into the cream-cheese mixture

4 cups confectioners' sugar

Makes about 2 cups frosting.

Spirited Fruitcake

If you like fruitcake, do try this one, with its rich poundcake base, packed with home-candied fruit. One to give, and one to keep.

One or two days before baking day, make and have ready

**1 recipe Candied Orange Peel (see page 262)
1 recipe Candied Lemon Peel (see page 263)**

Early on baking day, allowing 1 hour of preparation time, and 1 hour or longer of cooling time, make and have ready

Candied Pineapple (see opposite page)

When ready to bake, preheat the oven to 275°F. Butter two 9 x 5-inch loaf pans. Line the bottoms of the pans with wax paper and then butter the paper. Dust the pans with flour (about 1 tablespoon each), tilting the pans to coat all surfaces. Knock out the excess. Chop the candied orange and lemon peel into ¼-inch dice. Toss it in a bowl with

**2½ cups golden raisins
2 cups coarsely chopped pecans
5 tablespoons unbleached all-purpose flour**

In another bowl, sift, stir, or whisk together

**1¾ cups unbleached all-purpose flour
¼ teaspoon salt
¼ teaspoon baking soda
¼ teaspoon ground ginger
¼ teaspoon ground mace**

In a third bowl (be sure this one is large) cream together

2 sticks unsalted butter
1 teaspoon pure lemon extract

Gradually cream into the butter mixture

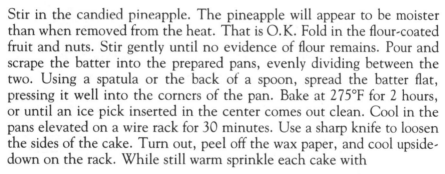

1 cup granulated sugar

Add, one at a time, beating well after each

4 large eggs

Add, in this order, blending after each addition

½ flour-spice mixture
¼ cup light rum
remaining flour-spice mixture

Stir in the candied pineapple. The pineapple will appear to be moister than when removed from the heat. That is O.K. Fold in the flour-coated fruit and nuts. Stir gently until no evidence of flour remains. Pour and scrape the batter into the prepared pans, evenly dividing between the two. Using a spatula or the back of a spoon, spread the batter flat, pressing it well into the corners of the pan. Bake at 275°F for 2 hours, or until an ice pick inserted in the center comes out clean. Cool in the pans elevated on a wire rack for 30 minutes. Use a sharp knife to loosen the sides of the cake. Turn out, peel off the wax paper, and cool upside-down on the rack. While still warm sprinkle each cake with

2 tablespoons light rum

When completely cool, wrap each cake in plastic wrap. Overwrap with foil, sealing tightly. Store at least 24 hours before slicing the first piece. Once or twice a week, unwrap and sprinkle with additional rum. It is best if used within two weeks.

Makes two 2¼-pound fruitcakes.

CANDIED PINEAPPLE

Drain, reserving juice

1 can (20 ounces) pineapple tidbits, packed in juice

Place in a small (about 1-quart) nonreactive saucepan

⅓ cup reserved juice from pineapple
⅔ cup sugar

Cook over medium heat, stirring frequently, until the sugar dissolves. Add the drained pineapple. Boil gently until all but about 1 teaspoon of the syrup is absorbed. Stir frequently at first, constantly as the level of syrup drops, to prevent scorching. Remove from the heat and cool.

Pineapple Upside-Down Cake

The Dole Pineapple Company on the island of Lanai, Hawaii, first introduced us to sliced pineapple in cans, and then to an old-fashioned skillet cake with pineapple as its base. Inventive cooks have come up with many variations, using pineapple and/or other canned fruits. My favorite features pineapple, lightly touched with the compatible flavor of rum.

Preheat the oven to 325°F. Sift, stir, or whisk together and set aside

1 cup cake flour, sifted before measuring
1 teaspoon baking powder
⅛ teaspoon salt

Drain, reserving juice

1 can (20 ounces) pineapple slices, packed in their own juice

In a 10-inch cast-iron skillet, over medium heat, stir together until melted

4 tablespoons unsalted butter
¾ cup light brown sugar

Remove from the heat and stir in

1 tablespoon light rum

Tilt the pan to coat the sides. Carefully place 1 pineapple slice in the center of the pan. Arrange 6 more slices evenly around that one in a circle. Save the remaining slices for another use. Tuck into the centers and in between the pineapple in the empty spaces

19 pecan halves

Set the skillet aside while preparing the batter. In a large mixer bowl beat until thick

3 large egg yolks

Add, 1 tablespoon at a time, beating well after each addition

1 cup granulated sugar

Reduce the speed to low and gradually blend in, in this order

¼ cup reserved pineapple juce
1 tablespoon light rum
reserved dry ingredients

Remove the bowl from the mixer. Wash and dry the beaters. In the small bowl of the mixer combine

3 large egg whites
¼ teaspoon cream of tartar

Beat at high speed until stiff. Fold the beaten egg whites into the batter, one-quarter at a time. Carefully pour and scrape the batter over the fruit and nuts in the skillet. Bake at 325°F for 40 to 45 minutes, or until the cake springs back when lightly touched in the center. Cool on a wire rack 15 minutes. If necessary, loosen the sides of the cake with a spatula or knife. Cover with a large plate or platter and carefully invert. Lift the skillet slowly to allow time for all the juices to drip onto the cake. Serve slightly warm or at room temperature with Rum-Flavored Whipped Cream (see below).

Makes 10 to 12 servings.

RUM-FLAVORED WHIPPED CREAM

Using chilled beaters and bowl, whip together until the cream begins to thicken

1 cup whipping (heavy) cream
2 tablespoons confectioners' sugar

Add, and then beat until soft peaks form

1 tablespoon light rum

Makes about 2 cups whipped cream.

Old-Fashioned Jelly Roll

Jelly rolls are impressive to serve, yet simple to make. If you have never made one, read through the recipe carefully before beginning, and you should have success. To be sure the eggs are at room temperature, leave them out on the counter for 2 hours before beginning.

Preheat the oven to 400°F. Grease a 15½ x 10½ x 1-inch jelly-roll pan. Line the pan with wax paper, letting it extend slightly beyond the ends, and then grease the paper. Dust the paper lightly with flour, knocking out any excess. Sift together twice and set aside

⅔ cup cake flour, sifted before measuring
1½ tablespoons cornstarch
¼ teaspoon salt
¾ teaspoon baking powder

In the small bowl of a mixer, beat at low speed until smooth

4 large eggs

Turn the speed to high and beat until thick and lemon-colored, about 3 minutes. Return to low speed and add, 1 tablespoon at a time

¾ cup granulated sugar

Return to high speed and beat for a full 8 minutes. The mixture should become light-colored and creamy, and will almost threaten to overflow the bowl. Return to low speed and gradually add

1 teaspoon pure vanilla extract

Transfer the batter to the large bowl of the mixer, using a rubber spatula to get every last bit. Scatter the sifted dry ingredients over the batter. Beat at low speed, constantly scraping the sides of the bowl with the spatula, just until the dry ingredients are incorporated. Do not overbeat. Pour and scrape into the prepared pan, first pouring two strips of batter down the length of the pan. Spread evenly with a spatula, gently working it into the corners of the pan. Bake at 400°F for 12 to 14 minutes, or until the cake springs back when lightly touched in the center. Take care not to overbake. While the cake is baking, spread a clean kitchen towel on the counter. Sift through a sieve, back and forth over the cloth, for a generous dusting

¼ cup confectioners' sugar

When the cake is done, hold the ends of the wax paper along with the pan and invert the pan over the dusted cloth. Remove the pan. If the paper is stuck to the pan, you can use the ends of the paper to help the release. Carefully remove the wax paper. Release the long sides first, then one short end. Gently pull one end of the cake away from the paper and then gently pull the paper down the cake to release. Quickly but gently roll the cake from a narrow end, with the cloth included in the rolling. Leave it rolled, on a wire rack, for about 1 minute. Stir with a fork until smooth

1 cup tart jelly, such as currant

Unroll the cake on the counter. Spread the jelly over the cake, stopping ½ inch short of one narrow end. Reroll the cake, without the cloth, working toward the end that is short of jelly, and place the roll seam side down on a serving plate. Let it cool completely. Right before serving, cut a thin slice from each end of the cake to remove any crisp edges that may remain. Strain through a sieve over the top of the cake

2 tablespoons confectioners' sugar

Cut into thin slices. Make a fan of several slices on each dessert plate. Garnish with sprigs of fresh basil. A scoop of sherbet can be served with it, but is not necessary.

Makes 8 to 10 servings.

Traditional Poundcake

Have all ingredients at room temperature before beginning this cake. Select the largest eggs from a dozen. If you measure your flour, rather than weigh it, spoon it gently into the cup.

Preheat the oven to 325°F. Grease and lightly flour a 10-inch tube pan. Sift together three times and set aside

1 pound (about 3⅓ cups) unbleached all-purpose flour
½ teaspoon salt
1 teaspoon baking powder
1 teaspoon ground mace

In the large bowl of a mixer, beat until light and fluffy

1 pound (4 sticks) unsalted butter

Gradually add, beating until light in both texture and color

1 pound (about 2⅓ cups) superfine sugar (sometimes called "bar sugar")

Add, one at a time, beating well after each

8 large eggs

Blend in

1 tablespoon pure vanilla extract
1 tablespoon cognac or rum

Remove the bowl from the mixer. Fold in the dry ingredients, ½ cup at a time, only until well blended, taking care not to overmix. Spoon and scrape the batter into the prepared pan, smoothing the top with the back of a spoon. Bake at 325°F for 70 to 75 minutes, or until a wooden pick inserted in the center comes out clean, and the cake is beginning to pull away from the sides of the pan. Cool in the pan elevated on a wire rack 10 minutes. Turn out on the rack to cool completely. Thin slices are good plain, or topped with ice cream and/or a fruit sauce.

Makes 16 servings.

Carrying Cakes

Cooled and frosted right in the pan

These easily made cakes are perfect for picnics and potlucks.

California Carrot Cake

Prairie State Sheet Cake

Meringue-Topped Spice Cake

Persimmon-Pecan Picnic Cake

Pumpkin Spice Cake

Disappearing Cake

Crazy Cake

Super Sundae Cake

California Carrot Cake

This is the best of carrot cakes. The flavor improves if it is made a day ahead of serving.

Preheat the oven to 350°F. Grease and lightly flour a 9 x 13-inch baking pan. Drain and set aside, reserving 1 tablespoon juice for the frosting

1 can (8 ounces) crushed pineapple, packed in pineapple juice

In the large bowl of a mixer beat until light and lemon-colored

4 large eggs

Stir together, pressing out any lumps with the back of a spoon, then gradually beat into the eggs

1 cup granulated sugar
1 cup light brown sugar

Add in a thin stream, beating all the while

1 cup vegetable oil

Sift, stir, or whisk together and then blend into the egg mixture, ¼ cup at a time

2 cups unbleached all-purpose flour
1 teaspoon salt
1 teaspoon baking powder
1 teaspoon baking soda
2 teaspoons ground cinnamon

Stir in, in this order

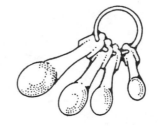

drained pineapple
2 cups grated carrots
½ cup chopped pecans

Spread the batter in the prepared pan. Bake at 350°F for 55 to 60 minutes, or until the cake springs back when lightly touched in the center. Cool in the pan elevated on a wire rack. Frost the top of the cooled cake with Pineapple Cream Cheese Frosting (see opposite page).

Makes 12 to 16 servings.

PINEAPPLE CREAM CHEESE FROSTING

Beat together until light and fluffy

3 ounces cream cheese
4 tablespoons unsalted butter
1 tablespoon reserved pineapple juice

Press through a sieve and then blend into the cream cheese mixture

2½ cups confectioners' sugar

Makes about 1½ cups frosting.

Prairie State Sheet Cake

This folk recipe, passed around by word of mouth, rarely appears in print. I know it's fudgy-good enough for my collection. The state is Illinois, of course, which is as prairie-flat as the cake itself.

Preheat the oven to 400°F. Grease and flour a 15½ x 10½ x 1-inch jelly-roll pan. Stir together in a large mixing bowl, pressing out any lumps with the back of a spoon

2 cups unbleached all-purpose flour
2 cups granulated sugar
⅓ cup cocoa
½ teaspoon salt
1 teaspoon baking soda

In a heavy saucepan heat to boiling

1 cup water
8 tablespoons soft unsalted butter
½ cup vegetable oil

Pour the boiling mixture over the dry ingredients and mix well. Stir in, in this order, blending after each addition

½ cup buttermilk
2 large eggs
1 teaspoon pure vanilla extract

Pour the mixture into the prepared pan. Carefully tilt the pan so that the batter flows into the corners. Bake at 400°F for 20 minutes. During the last 5 minutes of baking time, prepare Cocoa Icing (see below). When the cake comes from the oven, place it on a wire rack to cool in the pan, and immediately spread with hot icing. Serve warm or cold.

Makes 18 to 24 servings.

COCOA ICING

In a large bowl stir together, pressing out any lumps with the back of a spoon

3¾ cups (1 pound) confectioners' sugar
⅓ cup cocoa
⅛ teaspoon salt

Stir into the sugar-cocoa mixture

1 cup chopped walnuts

In a heavy saucepan bring to a boil

8 tablespoons soft unsalted butter
⅓ cup plus 1 tablespoon milk

Pour the boiling mixture over the dry ingredients and mix well.

Makes about 2 cups icing.

Meringue-Topped Spice Cake

This is so easy to make and to carry. Just right for a picnic in the park.

Preheat the oven to 350°F. Grease an 8 x 8 x 2-inch baking dish. Stir together in a large mixer bowl, pressing out any lumps with the back of a spoon

1 cup granulated sugar
½ cup light brown sugar

Remove ½ cup of the sugar mixture and reserve for Meringue Topping (see page 84). Stir into the remainder

1¼ cups unbleached all-purpose flour
½ teaspoon salt
1½ teaspoons baking powder
1 teaspoon ground cinnamon
½ teaspoon ground cloves
¼ teaspoon ground nutmeg

Add to the stirred ingredients

½ cup shortening
1 large egg
1 large egg yolk (save white for Meringue Topping)
½ cup milk

Beat at low speed until the dry ingredients are moistened, about 1 minute. Stop to scrape the beaters and bowl. Beat at medium speed for 2 minutes, scraping the bowl continuously. Spread the batter in the prepared pan. Spread Meringue Topping (see page 84) evenly over the batter. Bake at 350°F for 35 to 40 minutes, or until the top is nicely browned. Cool in the pan elevated on a wire rack.

Makes 9 servings.

MERINGUE TOPPING

With clean and dry bowl and beaters, beat at medium-high speed until almost stiff

1 large egg white

Add, 1 tablespoonful at a time, beating all the while at medium-low speed

reserved sugar mixture (see page 83)

Fold in

½ cup chopped pecans

Makes about 1 cup topping.

Persimmon-Pecan Picnic Cake

Two southern favorites, persimmons and pecans, are a complementary team in this moist, flavorful cake.

Read about persimmons (page 4). Preheat the oven to 325°F. Grease and flour a 9 x 13-inch baking pan. Stir together and then set aside

1 cup wild persimmon pulp (page 205)
1½ teaspoons fresh lemon juice

Sift, stir, or whisk together and set aside

2 cups unbleached all-purpose flour
1 teaspoon salt
1 teaspoon baking soda
1 teaspoon ground cinnamon
¼ teaspoon ground nutmeg

In a large bowl beat

3 large eggs

Add to the eggs, in this order, blending after each addition

2 cups granulated sugar
1 cup vegetable oil
1 teaspoon pure vanilla extract
1 cup sour cream

reserved dry ingredients
reserved persimmon pulp
1 cup coarsely chopped pecans

Pour and scrape the batter into the prepared pan. Use a spatula to spread the batter evenly into the corners of the pan. Bake at 325°F for 55 to 60 minutes, or until the cake springs back when lightly touched in the center. Cool in the pan on a wire rack. Frost the cooled cake with Zesty Cream Cheese Frosting (see below).

Makes 12 servings.

ZESTY CREAM CHEESE FROSTING

In a mixing bowl, cream together

3 ounces cream cheese
4 tablespoons unsalted butter
2 tablespoons fresh lemon juice
grated zest of 1 lemon

Stir through a sieve and then gradually beat into the creamed mixture

2½ cups confectioners' sugar

Add additional confectioners' sugar, if needed to make the frosting spreadable. Spread on the cooled cake. Sprinkle over the frosting

3 tablespoons chopped pecans

Gently press the pecans into the frosting.

Makes about 1½ cups frosting.

Pumpkin Spice Cake

The fall of the year is great for picnics. Warm days cooled with gentle breezes suggests an afternoon hike, a portable feast, and an evening bonfire. This is the cake to take.

Preheat the oven to 350°F. Grease a 9 x 13-inch baking pan. In the large bowl of a mixer beat until light and lemon-colored (start at low speed, end at high)

4 large eggs

Gradually beat into the eggs

2 cups granulated sugar

Add in a thin stream, beating all the while

1 cup vegetable oil

Turn the speed to low and blend in

1 can (16 ounces) pumpkin purée

Sift, stir, or whisk together and then blend into pumpkin mixture, ½ cup at a time

2 cups unbleached all-purpose flour
¾ teaspoon salt
2 teaspoons baking powder
1 teaspoon baking soda
2 teaspoons ground cinnamon
¼ teaspoon ground ginger
¼ teaspoon ground cloves

Stir in

¾ cup raisins

Pour and scrape the mixture into the prepared pan. Bake at 350°F for 45 to 50 minutes, or until the cake springs back when lightly touched in the center. Cool in the pan elevated on a wire rack. Frost the cooled cake with Ginger Cream Cheese Frosting (see opposite page). Sprinkle over the frosting

¾ cup chopped walnuts

Makes 12 servings.

GINGER CREAM CHEESE FROSTING

Beat together until light and fluffy

3 ounces cream cheese
4 tablespoons unsalted butter
⅛ teaspoon ground ginger

Add alternately

2½ cups confectioners' sugar
2 tablespoons fresh lemon juice

Makes about 1½ cups frosting.

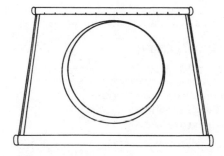

Disappearing Cake

This is usually called Lazy Daisy Cake, but we changed the name. A boarder in our household always ate more than his share. When the man of the house would come home for a snack, he would spy the empty pan and say, "I see you made Disappearing Cake again!"

Preheat the oven to 350°F. Butter an 8 x 8 x 2-inch baking dish. Sift, stir, or whisk together and set aside

1 cup unbleached all-purpose flour
1 teaspoon baking powder
¼ teaspoon salt

Heat in a small saucepan until the milk is hot and the butter is melted

½ cup milk
1 tablespoon unsalted butter

Set the saucepan off the heat. In the large bowl of a mixer, beat until thick

2 large eggs

Add gradually, beating all the while

1 cup granulated sugar

Blend into the egg-sugar mixture, in this order

1 teaspoon pure vanilla extract
reserved dry ingredients
hot milk mixture

Pour the batter into the prepared dish and bake in a preheated 350°F oven for 30 to 35 minutes, or until the cake springs back when lightly touched in the center. Remove the hot cake from the oven. Set the thermostat to broil. Spread the cake with the topping opposite. Toast under the broiler until the sugar is caramelized. Watch closely. This can burn if you turn your back. Serve warm or cold.

Makes 9 servings.

TOPPING FOR DISAPPEARING CAKE

Mix together in a medium-size bowl

**½ cup light brown sugar
4 tablespoons melted unsalted butter
¼ cup whipping (heavy) cream
1 cup packaged sweetened flaked coconut**

Crazy Cake

This cake is mixed right in the pan, without an egg to help it rise. The crazy part is that it turns out so well.

Preheat the oven to 350°F. Stir together in an ungreased 8 x 8 x 2-inch baking dish

**1½ cups unbleached all-purpose flour
1 cup sugar
3 tablespoons cocoa
½ teaspoon salt
1 teaspoon baking soda**

Make three depressions in the stirred ingredients. Into these place

**6 tablespoons oil
1 tablespoon cider vinegar
1 teaspoon vanilla extract**

Pour over all

1 cup cold milk, water, or coffee

Mix with a fork just until all ingredients are well blended. Bake at 350°F for 25 to 30 minutes, or until the cake springs back when lightly pressed in the center. Cool in the pan. Serve warm or cold with Vanilla Sauce (page 273) or Fast Fudge Sauce (page 270).

Makes 9 servings.

Super Sundae Cake

Not too sweet, this unfrosted cake is a good base for vanilla ice cream and a coating of hot fudge.

Grease and lightly flour an 8 x 8 x 2-inch baking dish. Preheat the oven to 350°F. Sift, stir, or whisk together and set aside

1⅓ cups unbleached all-purpose flour
2 teaspoons baking powder
½ teaspoon baking soda
¼ teaspoon salt

In a small saucepan, mix together

¼ cup cocoa
¼ cup sugar

Press out any lumps with the back of a spoon. Stir into the cocoa mixture

¼ cup water

Cook over medium heat for 1 minute, stirring constantly. Set aside. In a mixing bowl, cream together

¼ cup shortening
½ cup granulated sugar

Add and beat until light and fluffy

1 large egg

Add in this order, blending after each addition

cooked cocoa mixture
½ flour mixture
6 tablespoons milk
remaining flour mixture
1 teaspoon vanilla extract

Transfer the batter to the prepared dish, using a spatula to gently push it evenly into corners. Bake at 350°F for 25 to 30 minutes, or until the cake begins to shrink away from the sides of the pan. Cool in the pan elevated on a wire rack. Serve squares of this cake, warm or cold, topped with a scoop of vanilla ice cream and homemade Fast Fudge Sauce (page 270).

Makes 9 servings.

All But Forgotten Icebox Cakes

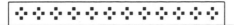

Chilled confections to delight
the taste buds

These old-fashioned delights are as good as they ever
were.

Chocolate Icebox Cake

Raspberry Angel Cake

Maple Mousse Cake

Tipsy Parson

Quick Refrigerator Cheesecake

Chocolate Icebox Cake

This is easy to make and delicious. Use only clean Grade A eggs, free from cracks. Read about eggs (page 2) before beginning.

Make Heavenly Angel Food Cake (page 41) or use store-bought. You will need 12 to 16 ounces of cake. In a large mixer bowl beat until soft and fluffy

8 tablespoons unsalted butter

In a side bowl, stir together (if lumpy, stir through a sieve)

¾ cup cocoa
1 cup granulated sugar
1 cup confectioners' sugar

Add the cocoa mixture to the butter alternately with

¼ cup cold coffee

Add one at a time, beating well after each

3 large egg yolks

In a small mixer bowl, with clean beaters, beat until almost stiff

3 large egg whites

Add to the whites and then beat until stiff but not dry

2 tablespoons granulated sugar

Gently fold the beaten whites into the chocolate mixture. Rinse and dry a small bowl and beaters, and then use to beat until the cream will mound slightly

2 cups whipping (heavy) cream

Gently fold the cream into the chocolate mixture. Tear the angel food cake into 1-inch chunks. Place a layer of chunks in a 9 x 12-inch glass baking dish. Spoon about half of the chocolate mixture over the cake pieces. Repeat each layer once, making four layers in all. Cover with plastic wrap and refrigerate for 12 to 24 hours. Cut into squares to serve.

Makes 12 to 16 servings.

Raspberry Angel Cake

This is pretty and pink. It makes me think of flowered hats and white gloves. A delight from a gentler time.

Make Heavenly Angel Food Cake (page 41) or use store-bought. You will need 8 to 10 ounces of cake. In a large bowl, stir together to dissolve the gelatin

1 box (3 ounces) raspberry-flavored gelatin
1¼ cups boiling water

Add and stir until the raspberries thaw

1 box (10 ounces) frozen raspberries

Refrigerate until partially set. The mixture should mound slightly in a spoon. While waiting for the mixture to jell, cut the cake into 1-inch cubes and put them in a 9 x 12-inch baking dish. When the gelatin is ready, with chilled beaters and bowl, beat until the cream will mound slightly

1 cup whipping (heavy) cream

Whip the gelatin with a wire whisk, and then gently fold in the whipped cream. Spoon the gelatin mixture over the cake. Press down any cake squares that float. Cover with plastic wrap and chill until firm, 4 to 8 hours. Cut into squares to serve.

Makes 12 servings.

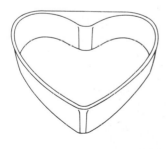

Maple Mousse Cake

This is light and luscious, with the marvelous flavor of pure maple syrup. Be sure to read about eggs (page 2) before beginning.

Bake Heavenly Angel Food Cake (page 41), or use store-bought. You will want 8 to 10 ounces of cake. Sprinkle the gelatin over the water, and combine to soften

¼ cup cold water
1 envelope unflavored gelatin

Meanwhile, in a heavy saucepan, whisk until smooth

3 large egg yolks

Add in this order, whisking constantly

pinch salt
½ cup pure maple syrup
¾ cup scalded milk

Cook over low to medium heat, stirring constantly, until the mixture thickens enough to coat a metal spoon. It should look like very thin gravy. Remove from the heat. Add the softened gelatin, stirring until dissolved. Chill, stirring occasionally, until the mixture mounds in a spoon. While waiting, cut or tear the cake into 1-inch squares. When the maple mixture is ready, beat in a large mixer bowl until almost stiff

3 large egg whites

Beat in a small mixer bowl until the cream will mound slightly

1 cup whipping (heavy) cream

Gently fold the maple mixture into the egg whites. Fold in the whipped cream. Fold in the cake cubes. Spoon into a 9 x 12-inch glass baking dish, spreading evenly. Cover with plastic and refrigerate to firm, 6 to 24 hours. Cut into squares and serve. Top with Sweetened Whipped Cream (page 270). Sprinkle Maple Praline (see opposite page) over the cream.

Makes 12 servings.

MAPLE PRALINE

There's not enough liquid here to make it practical to use a candy thermometer. You'll have to rely on your eyesight and instincts. Things can get hot, so wear protective mitts on both hands and use a wooden spoon throughout.

Rub a small baking sheet with oil and set it on the counter in a convenient place. In a heavy saucepan, cook over high heat until the syrup surface is covered with bubbles

½ cup pure maple syrup

Stir in

⅔ cup slivered almonds

Continue to cook and stir until the syrup darkens slightly. Be watchful. You don't want it to smoke and burn. Quickly remove it from the heat and transfer to the oiled baking sheet, spreading the nuts as best you can. When cool, break apart into individual nuts. If preferred, process briefly in a food processor or blender to chop coarsely. Be careful not to overprocess.

Makes about 1 cup praline.

Tipsy Parson

This is a variation of the old English trifle. It earned its name because parishioners noticed that the parson, though he forswore the drinking of spirits, never refused a piece of the cake. I make mine as individual servings. You could, of course, layer the cake and custard in a trifle bowl, for a more traditional presentation.

Make Pouring Custard (see opposite page) up to the point where the custard is chilled. Preheat the oven to 350°F. Grease and flour a 9 x 12-inch baking pan. Sift, stir, or whisk together in a large mixer bowl

2 cups unbleached all-purpose flour
1¼ cups granulated sugar
1 tablespoon baking powder
½ teaspoon salt

Add to the dry ingredients

½ cup shortening
1 teaspoon pure vanilla extract
¼ teaspoon almond extract
¾ cup cool water

Beat at low speed, scraping the bowl as you beat, for 1 minute, or until the dry ingredients are damp. Stop to scrape the beaters. Add

4 large egg whites

Beat at medium speed 1 minute, or until the batter is lump-free, scraping the bowl often. Stop to scrape the beaters. Beat at medium speed 1 minute longer, or until thick and creamy. Pour and scrape the batter into the prepared pan. Spread evenly with a rubber spatula. Bake at 350°F for 30 to 35 minutes, or until the cake springs back when lightly touched in the center. Cool in the pan elevated on a wire rack. When the cake is cool, cut it into twelve 3-inch squares. Split each square in half horizontally. Spread one cut side of each square with

1 tablespoon raspberry jam or jelly

(You will use one 12-ounce jar in all.) Reassemble the squares of cake and place each, upside down, in a glass dessert dish. Sprinkle each with

1 tablespoon medium-dry sherry

(You will use ¾ cup in all.) Finish the custard with the whipping cream. Spoon ⅓ cup of the custard over each serving. Cover and chill until ready to serve. Garnish with silvered almonds right before serving.

Makes 12 servings.

POURING CUSTARD

In a large bowl, beat until lemon-colored

4 large egg yolks

Stir together and then gradually stir into the egg yolks

¾ cup granulated sugar
2 tablespoons cornstarch
⅛ teaspoon salt

Scald and then gently stir into the egg mixture

2 cups half-and-half
1 cup milk

Transfer the mixture to a heavy saucepan and cook over low to medium heat, stirring constantly, just until the mixture thickens. Do not allow to boil. Remove from the heat. Stir gently for a few minutes to allow steam to escape. Gently stir in

2 teaspoons pure vanilla extract

Let cool to room temperature, stirring gently from time to time to prevent a film from forming on top. Cover with plastic wrap and refrigerate to chill. When ready to assemble the cake, beat with chilled beaters in a chilled bowl just until the cream will mound slightly

1 cup whipping (heavy) cream

Gently fold the whipped cream into the chilled custard.

Makes 4 cups custard.

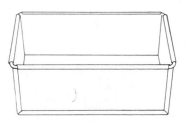

Quick Refrigerator Cheesecake

When we were young with three toddlers underfoot, our main form of entertainment was two tables of bridge. This was always my dessert. Super easy and always well received. I still make it when time is short.

In an 8 x 8 x 2-inch glass baking dish combine

1 cup graham-cracker crumbs (about 16 squares)
2 tablespoons granulated sugar

Stir into the crumb-sugar mixture

4 tablespoons melted unsalted butter

Remove 2 tablespoons of the crumb mixture for topping. Press the remaining mixture evenly over the bottom of the dish. Chill while preparing the filling. In a large bowl, beat together until smooth and fluffy

8 ounces cream cheese
grated zest of 1 lemon

Gradually add, in this order, beating until smooth after each addition

1 can (14 ounces) sweetened condensed milk
1½ teaspoons pure vanilla extract
⅓ cup fresh lemon juice

Gently pour the filling over the chilled crumb crust. Sprinkle the reserved crumbs on top. Cover the dish with plastic wrap and refrigerate to chill and firm, 4 to 24 hours. Cut into squares to serve. Serve plain or with Sweetened Whipped Cream (page 270), Pineapple Sauce (page 272), or Montmorency Cherry Sauce (page 275).

Makes 8 servings.

Pie Doughs and Crusts

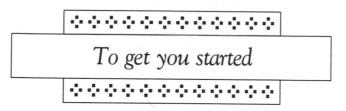

To get you started

My collection of pie doughs is limited, but it's all you need.

Foolproof Pie Dough

Foolproof Pie Shell

Old-Fashioned Pie Dough

Easy Egg Pastry

No-Roll Pie Crust

Foolproof Pie Dough

This is an adaptation of a recipe that appeared on the back of a shortening label when I was a young bride. I use this more than any other crust for my pies. There are directions for both traditional and rustic shaping. The latter is good for fruit pies where the casual look is most attractive.

Mix together in a bowl

2 cups unbleached all-purpose flour
1 teaspoon salt

Cut into the flour until the particles are uniform and the texture is that of very coarse cornmeal

¾ cup shortening

Sprinkle over the flour mixture, 1 tablespoon at a time, tossing with a fork after each addition

4 to 6 tablespoons cool water

Use only as much water as needed to bring the dough together. Too much water will make a crust tough. Continue stirring with a fork to work into a firm ball. For traditional shaping, divide the dough in half. Well, almost in half. The larger of the two pieces will make the bottom crust; the smaller, the top. Shape each half into a ball and flatten it slightly, keeping the edges smooth. Cover with plastic and chill in the refrigerator for 10 minutes, or up to 2 days. If the dough has chilled more than an hour, let it warm slightly at room temperature before uncovering and shaping. Shape (see below), and bake as directed in recipes for filled pies.

 Traditional Shaping: Roll out the larger of the two balls of dough on a lightly floured surface. First pat and press the dough gently to enlarge the circle. Turn the dough over and repeat the patting and pressing. Then use the rolling pin to roll from the center to the edge, lifting the rolling pin as you approach the edge so as not to make it too thin. Turn the dough a quarter turn and repeat. Keep turning the dough and repeating the rolling. As the circle expands, you will have to turn your body rather than the dough, as it will become thin and fragile. When you have about a 12-inch circle, fold the dough in quarters and transfer it to a pie pan. Unfold, easing it into the pan. Trim about ¼ inch beyond the edge of the pan. Fill with pie filling. Roll out the second half of the dough in the same way to about an 11-inch circle. Center over the filling. Trim off any excess edges. Fold the top crust under the bottom and press gently to seal. Rotate the pie as you flute the edge by pressing from the inside with one finger and the outside with thumb and forefinger. Cut vents and bake as directed in pie recipes.

 Rustic Shaping: Shape the dough into one large ball, rather than two.

Roll out to about a 15-inch circle. Fold the dough as before and transfer to a pie pan. Unfold and ease into the pan. Fill with pie filling. Gently ease the sides up over the filling in 5 or 6 places. Do not pull the dough up tightly. The center of the pie should be left open. You will not need to flute the edges or cut steam vents. Bake as directed in pie recipes.

Makes enough dough for one 9-inch double-crust pie.

Foolproof Pie Shell

This is just slightly more than half the above recipe. The little extra ensures enough dough to make a high fluted edge for your one-crust pies.

Mix together in a bowl

1⅓ cups unbleached all-purpose flour
½ teaspoon salt

Cut into the flour mixture until the particles are uniform and the texture is that of very coarse cornmeal

½ cup shortening

Sprinkle over the flour mixture, 1 tablespoon at a time, tossing with a fork after each addition

3 to 4 tablespoons cool water

Use only as much water as needed to bring the dough together. Too much water will make a crust tough. Continue stirring with a fork to work the dough into a ball. Flatten the ball slightly, keeping the edges smooth. On a lightly floured surface, roll out to a slightly larger than 12-inch circle. Fold the circle in half and gently transfer it to a 9-inch pie pan. Unfold and work your way around the pan, lifting the edges and easing the dough into the pan so that it is not stretched at any point. Trim the dough about ½ inch beyond the edge of the pan. Use scraps to add to the dough anywhere it may be lacking. Turn the edge of the dough under, forming a double thickness, and turn this dough up around the edge of the pan. Flute by using one finger to press along the inside edge, and your thumb and forefinger of the other hand to press from the outside. This will form a high fluted edge to contain generous fillings.

If the pie is to be filled before baking, refrigerate the shaped dough while preparing that filling. If the filling is intended for a baked pie shell, prick the dough with a fork generously all over the bottom and sides. Gently line the shell with regular-weight aluminum foil. This will keep the edges from collapsing, and the bottom from bubbling up. Bake in a preheated 425°F oven for 6 minutes. Remove the foil. Bake for 7 to 9 minutes longer, or until lightly browned.

Makes one 9-inch pie shell.

Old-Fashioned Pie Dough

The small amount of cider vinegar used in this dough contributes to its flaky texture.

Place in a medium-size bowl

2 cups unbleached all-purpose flour

Rub into the flour with your fingers, or cut in with a pastry blender

¾ cup shortening

Mix together in a side bowl

¼ cup cold water
1 teaspoon salt
1 teaspoon cider vinegar

Add the water mixture to the flour mixture, 1 tablespoon at a time, tossing with a fork, until it becomes somewhat pliable like clay. Stop adding liquids before the mixture becomes pasty. If needed to prevent a crumbly texture, add additional water in small amounts, until the desired texture is achieved. Divide the dough in half. With lightly floured hands, gently pat each half into a slightly flattened ball. Wrap each half in plastic wrap and chill in the refrigerator for at least 20 minutes, or up to 2 days. Shape as directed in Foolproof Pie Dough (page 100).

Makes enough dough for one 9-inch double-crust pie.

Easy Egg Pastry

The egg waterproofs this dough, making it the choice for juicy fillings.

Mix together in a medium-size bowl

2¼ cups unbleached all-purpose flour
1 teaspoon salt

Cut into the flour, until the largest lumps are the size of small peas

¾ cup shortening

Beat together in a side bowl

1 egg
4 tablespoons cold water
4 teaspoons fresh lemon juice

Add the egg mixture to the flour mixture, 2 tablespoons at a time, stirring lightly with a fork after each addition. When all the liquid has been added, continue to stir and turn the dough until it comes together. Pat it together with your hands. Cover and chill for 20 minutes, or up to 2 days. Shape as directed in Foolproof Pie Dough (page 100).

Makes enough dough for one 9-inch double-crust pie.

No-Roll Pie Crust

If you don't share my enthusiasm for rolling out pie crust, try this. It works best as a prebaked shell.

Use a fork for stirring throughout. Directly in a pie pan, stir together

1½ cups plus 1 tablespoon unbleached all-purpose flour
1½ teaspoons granulated sugar
¾ teaspoon salt

In a measuring cup, stir together vigorously until the mixture is an opaque white

½ cup vegetable oil
2 tablespoons cold milk

Pour the oil mixture over the flour mixture and mix lightly until all dry ingredients are moistened. Pat pieces of the dough onto the sides of the pan and then pat the remainder over the bottom. Take care to press the dough evenly as thin spots will burn easily when baked. Keep pressing out and up until a ⅜- to ½-inch ridge is formed at the top edge. Flute the edge. Chill for 30 minutes. Meanwhile, preheat the oven to 425°F. Prick the chilled crust all over with a fork. Bake at 425°F for 10 to 15 minutes, or until lightly browned. Cool on a wire rack.

Makes 1 baked pie shell.

Fresh Fruit Pies

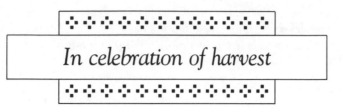

In celebration of harvest

Goodness knows we can't have pie every day, but I try to have at least one for every fruit in season.

American Apple Pie

Peaches and Cream Pie

Rhubarb Pie

Rhubarb-Strawberry Pie

Fresh Blueberry Pie

Cold Blueberry Pie

Glazed Strawberry Pie

Two-Crust Strawberry Pie

Red Raspberry Pie

Sour Cherry Pie

Green Gooseberry Pie

Concord Grape Pie

American Apple Pie

There is nothing more American than apple pie, and this is one of the best. McIntosh apples do not store well and are only good for pie right after harvest, but any tart cooking apple that will not cook up into mush can be substituted. Read about apple varieties (page 4).

Prepare one recipe of Old-Fashioned Pie Dough (page 102). Chill the dough while preparing the filling. Place an oven rack in the bottom third of the oven and preheat to 450°F. Peel, quarter, and core

3 pounds firm, crisp McIntosh apples, or enough to make 6 cups sliced

As you work, drop the quartered apples into acidulated water.* When all are prepared, drain and slice them into ¼-inch slices. In a large bowl, toss the sliced apples with

2 tablespoons fresh lemon juice

In a side bowl combine and mix well

½ cup granulated sugar
½ cup brown sugar
2 tablespoons unbleached all-purpose flour
¾ teaspoon ground cinnamon
¼ teaspoon ground nutmeg

Roll out one-half the dough and use to line a 9-inch pie pan. Trim off the excess. Roll out and have ready the second half for the top crust. Brush the bottom of the dough in the pan with

1 tablespoon melted unsalted butter

Transfer the apples to the sugar mixture using a slotted spoon, leaving behind excess liquid. Toss the apples and sugar mixture to coat the apples, and transfer all to the lined pie pan. Arrange the slices so that their flat sides are horizontal. Otherwise, they will mound up too high in the center. Use all the apples. They will compact as they cook. Dot the top with slivers of

2 teaspoons firm unsalted butter

Top with the rolled-out top crust. Trim so that it extends just a little beyond the bottom crust. Fold this extra rim under the bottom crust, gently working your way around the pie. Press gently but firmly around

---

* Acidulated water: To 1 quart water add 1 tablespoon lemon juice or cider vinegar.

this edge, sealing the crusts together. Flute the edge and cut vents in the top crust. Brush the crust with

1 teaspoon melted unsalted butter

Sprinkle with

¼ teaspoon granulated sugar

Bake in a preheated 450°F oven for 10 minutes. Reduce the heat to 350°F and bake for an additional 35 to 40 minutes. Cool on a wire rack. Serve à la mode with vanilla ice cream or top with slices of sharp Cheddar cheese.

Makes 6 to 8 servings.

Peaches and Cream Pie

We celebrate the harvest of the Illinois peach crop with this pie's delicately spiced, creamy custard filling.

Place an oven rack on the bottom third of the oven and preheat to 425°F. Prepare one recipe of Foolproof Pie Dough (page 100). Chill the dough while preparing the filling. Place in a large bowl

5 cups peeled, sliced firm-ripe peaches (about 10 small)

Mix together and then gently mix into the peaches

½ cup granulated sugar
2 tablespoons unbleached all-purpose flour
⅛ teaspoon ground nutmeg
⅛ teaspoon ground ginger

In a side bowl beat together and set aside

1 large egg
1 tablespoon granulated sugar
½ cup whipping (heavy) cream
¼ teaspoon pure vanilla extract

Roll out one-half the chilled pie dough and line a 9-inch pie pan. Roll out and have ready the second crust. Gently stir the peach mixture and spoon into the pastry-lined pan. Pour the cream mixture over the peaches. Top with the rolled-out crust. Cut several slits in the top crust. Fold the top edge over the bottom edge of the crust and seal and flute the edge. Bake at 425°F for 15 minutes. Reduce the heat to 350°F and bake 25 to 30 minutes longer, or until the crust is golden-brown and the filling is bubbling hot. Cool on a wire rack. Serve warm or cold. Be sure to refrigerate leftovers.

Makes 6 to 8 servings.

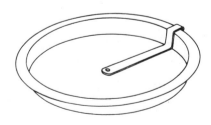

Rhubarb Pie

One taste and you will know why rhubarb is affectionately called "pieplant."

Prepare one recipe of Foolproof Pie Dough (page 100). Cover and chill the dough while preparing the filling. Place an oven rack in the bottom third of the oven and preheat to 450°F. Cut in ½-inch slices enough rhubarb to make

4 cups sliced rhubarb

Mix together and then stir into the sliced rhubarb to coat

1½ cups granulated sugar
6 tablespoons unbleached all-purpose flour
⅛ teaspoon salt

Roll out one-half the pie dough and line a 9-inch pie pan. Transfer the rhubarb filling to the pastry-lined pan. Dot the top with slivers of

2 tablespoons unsalted butter

Roll out the second half of the dough and cut into ½-inch-wide strips. Weave the strips into a lattice pattern to cover the filling. Seal and flute the edges. If preferred, use Rustic Shaping (pages 100–101), rolling top and bottom crust at one time. Bake in the 450°F oven for 20 minutes. Reduce the heat to 350°F and bake 20 to 25 minutes longer, or until the crust is golden-brown and the filling is bubbling hot. Cool on a wire rack. Serve chilled or at room temperature.

Makes 6 to 8 servings.

Rhubarb-Strawberry Pie

Substitute 1 to 2 cups strawberries for 1 to 2 cups sliced rhubarb. Proceed as for Rhubarb Pie (above).

Makes 6 to 8 servings.

Fresh Blueberry Pie

A great recipe for celebrating fresh blueberry season.

Place an oven rack in the bottom third of the oven and preheat to 450°F. Use Foolproof Pie Dough (page 100). Cover and chill the dough while preparing the berries. Wash and drain

6 cups fresh blueberries

Dry the berries on toweling until ready to use. Roll out one-half the dough and line a 9-inch pie pan. Roll out and have ready the second half of the dough. In a small bowl, mix together

1 cup granulated sugar
6 tablespoons unbleached all-purpose flour
⅛ teaspoon salt
¼ teaspoon ground cinnamon

Spoon 2 tablespoonfuls of the sugar mixture into the pastry-lined pan. Top with half the blueberries. Sprinkle half the remaining sugar mixture over these berries. Repeat with the remaining berries and sugar mixture. Sprinkle with

1 tablespoon fresh lemon juice

Dot with slivers of

1 tablespoon unsalted butter

Top with the second rolled-out piece of dough. Fold the top edge over the bottom edge of the crust, and seal and flute the edge. Cut vents in the top for escape of steam. Bake at 450°F for 20 minutes. Reduce the heat to 375°F and bake for 40 minutes longer, or until the filling is bubbling hot and the crust is well browned. This pie requires a full hour's cooking, so expect the crust to brown a little more than usual. Cool on a wire rack. Chill in the refrigerator until cold before serving. Otherwise the pie may be runny. Serve with or without vanilla ice cream.

Makes 6 to 8 servings.

Cold Blueberry Pie

This chilled berry pie, topped with freshly whipped cream, is refreshing and delicious.

Prebake one Foolproof Pie Shell (page 101) and allow time to cool. In a heavy nonreactive saucepan, stir together

¾ cup granulated sugar
2 tablespoons cornstarch
¼ teaspoon ground cinnamon

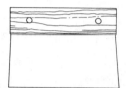

Stir in, in this order

2 tablespoons cold water
1 tablespoon fresh lemon juice
4 cups fresh blueberries

Cook over medium-high heat, stirring frequently, until the mixture begins to boil. Reduce the heat to medium-low and continue to cook, stirring constantly, just until the juice thickens and loses its cloudy appearance. Remove from the heat. Stir in

1 tablespoon soft unsalted butter

Cool to just slightly warm, stirring occasionally as it cools. Spoon into the baked pie shell. Chill at least 6 hours, or as long as overnight. Top each serving with a generous dollop of Sweetened Whipped Cream (page 270).

Makes 6 to 8 servings.

Glazed Strawberry Pie

This popular pie is easy enough to make often when strawberries are in season. Some cooks strain the crushed berries for a clearer glaze. I prefer this fruitier version.

Prebake one Foolproof Pie Shell (page 101), and allow time to cool. Gently wash and hull

6 cups fresh strawberries

Using the smallest berries, crush enough to make

1 cup crushed strawberries

Cover and refrigerate the remaining strawberries. In a heavy saucepan stir together

1 cup granulated sugar
3 tablespoons cornstarch

Stir into the cornstarch mixture, in this order

½ cup water
crushed strawberries

Cook over medium heat, stirring constantly, until the mixture thickens and is clear. Remove from the heat. Add, stirring until the butter is melted

1 tablespoon fresh lemon juice
2 tablespoons unsalted butter

Cool to room temperature. Slice or quarter the reserved berries and fold them gently into the cooled glaze. Spoon into the pie shell. Refrigerate the pie until ready to serve. Serve topped with Sweetened Whipped Cream (page 270).

Makes 6 to 8 servings.

Two-Crust Strawberry Pie

I don't know why most cooks neglect this pie. Its distinctive strawberry flavor always wins applause at our house.

Prepare one recipe Foolproof Pie Dough (page 100). Cover and chill the dough while preparing the filling. Place an oven rack in the bottom third of the oven and preheat to 425°F. In a large bowl place

4 cups washed, hulled, sliced strawberries (about 6 cups whole berries)

Mix together and then mix gently into the berries

1 cup granulated sugar
¼ cup unbleached all-purpose flour

Roll out half the pie dough and line a 9-inch pie pan. Stir the berries gently and spoon into the pastry-lined pan. Dot the berries with slivers of

1 tablespoon unsalted butter

Roll out the top crust and place it over the filling. Fold the top edge over the bottom edge of the crust, and seal and flute the edge. Make several slashes in the top crust with a sharp knife. Bake at 425°F for 15 minutes. Reduce the heat to 350°F and bake 25 to 30 minutes longer, or until the crust is golden-brown and the filling is bubbling hot. Cool on a wire rack. Serve at room temperature, plain or with cream.

Makes 6 to 8 servings.

Red Raspberry Pie

We don't mow the yard where the fruit trees are planted, allowing the area underfoot to grow up in wildflowers and bramble bushes. This is where the raspberries are, and picking them is rather like taking a walk in the woods. Our bushes provide a bowl of berries at breakfast every morning and an occasional Red Raspberry Pie.

Place an oven rack in the bottom third of the oven and preheat to 450°F. Prepare one recipe of Foolproof Pie Dough (page 100). Chill the dough while preparing the filling. Gently wash and drain the berries and measure into a bowl

5 cups fresh raspberries

Mix together and then gently stir into the berries

1 cup granulated sugar
⅓ cup unbleached all-purpose flour

Roll out one-half the dough and line a 9-inch pie pan. Roll out and have the second half ready. Or use Rustic Shaping (pages 100–101). Spoon the berry mixture into the pastry-lined pan. Sprinkle over the berries

2 teaspoons fresh lemon juice

Top with slivers of

1 tablespoon unsalted butter

Cover with the second half of the pastry. Fold the top edge over the bottom edge of the crust, and seal and flute the edge. Cut several vents in the top for escape of steam. Bake at 450°F for 15 minutes. Reduce the heat to 350°F and bake for 25 to 30 minutes longer, or until the top is golden-brown and the filling is bubbling hot. Serve slightly warm or cold, topped with vanilla ice cream.

Makes 6 to 8 servings.

Sour Cherry Pie

Sour cherries will darken if stored between picking and cooking. The filling for this pie is made when the cherries are freshly picked. The pie can wait until the following day, if you prefer.

Place in a heavy saucepan

4¾ cups pitted sour cherries

Sprinkle over the cherries

1½ cups granulated sugar
5 tablespoons unbleached all-purpose flour

Cook on medium-high heat, stirring almost constantly at first, not as often when juices begin to flow. Continue to cook, stirring, until well thickened. Remove from the heat. Stir in until melted

2 tablespoons unsalted butter

Cool the filling to room temperature. It may be stored, chilled, overnight. Prepare one recipe of Foolproof Pie Dough (page 100) and chill until ready to use. When ready to bake, place an oven rack in the bottom third of the oven and preheat the oven to 425°F. Roll out one-half the pie dough and line a 9-inch pie pan. Spoon the cooled filling into the pastry-lined pan. Roll out the top crust. Using a sharp knife, cut three small circles in the center of the rolled-out dough to resemble a cluster of cherries. Cut several oblong slits around the cherries to resemble leaves. Place the top crust over the filling. Fold the edge of the top crust over the bottom crust edge. Seal and flute the edge. Bake at 425°F for 15 minutes. Reduce the heat to 350°F and bake for 20 to 25 minutes longer, or until the crust is golden-brown. Cool on a wire rack. Serve chilled or at room temperature.

Makes 6 to 8 servings.

Green Gooseberry Pie

Use berries that are still green for this tart gooseberry pie. Some pink ones can be thrown in, but reserve the red-ripe ones for eating out of hand.

If you don't grow your own gooseberries, you may have trouble finding them. There is an annual Gooseberry Festival in Watseka, Illinois, usually held on the last Sunday in June, where one can buy fresh and fresh-frozen gooseberries. Dorothy Christian, the driving force behind this event, promises never to run out, but it wouldn't hurt to go early in the day to avoid disappointment. For dates and times of this year's festival, call the Old Courthouse Museum, Watseka, 815-432-2215.

Use Old-Fashioned Pie Dough (page 102). Chill the dough while preparing the filling. Place an oven rack in the bottom third of the oven and preheat to 450°F. Wash and trim the tops and tails from enough gooseberries to make

4 cups trimmed gooseberries

Stir together

1¼ cups granulated sugar
6 tablespoons unbleached all-purpose flour

Reserve ½ cup of this sugar-flour mixture, and toss the remainder with the berries to coat. Roll out half the dough and line a 9-inch pie pan. Sprinkle over the bottom of the pastry-lined pan

4 tablespoons reserved sugar-flour mixture

Spoon the gooseberry mixture over the sugar-flour-coated pastry. Sprinkle the remaining sugar-flour mixture over all. Dot the top with

1 tablespoon unsalted butter

Roll out the second half of the dough and cover the berries. Fold the top edge over the bottom edge of the crust, and seal and flute the edge. Cut vents in the top crust for escape of steam. Bake at 450°F for 15 minutes. Reduce the heat to 350°F and bake 35 to 40 minutes longer, or until the crust is golden-brown and the filling is bubbling hot. Cool on a wire rack. Serve at room temperature or chilled. Good with vanilla ice cream.

Makes 6 to 8 servings.

Concord Grape Pie

Concords are the juiciest of grapes, and they make a most delicious pie. I suggest a rustic shaping of the crust for this juicy pie.

Prepare one recipe of Old-Fashioned Pie Dough (page 102), or Easy Egg Pastry (page 102). Cover and chill the dough while preparing the filling. Place the oven rack in the bottom third of the oven and preheat to 450°F. Pinching the grapes between thumb and forefinger, squeeze into a saucepan the pulp from

6 cups washed and stemmed Concord grapes

Reserve the skins in a side bowl. Bring the pulp to a boil over medium heat, stirring constantly. Remove from the heat and press through a sieve to remove seeds. Stir the strained pulp into the reserved skins along with

1 tablespoon fresh lemon juice

Roll out the dough into one large circle and transfer to a 9-inch pie pan. Stir together in a side bowl

1¼ cups granulated sugar
6 tablespoons unbleached all-purpose flour

Sprinkle about ¼ cup of the sugar mixture over the bottom of the crust. Stir the remainder into the grape mixture, and spoon into the crust. Dot with slivers of

1 tablespoon unsalted butter

Gently pull the edges of the crust over the filling, leaving the center open. Sprinkle the top of the crust with

granulated sugar

Bake in a preheated 450°F oven for 15 minutes. Reduce the heat to 350°F and continue to bake for 30 minutes. Cool on a wire rack. Serve slightly warm with a scoop of vanilla ice cream.

Makes 6 to 8 servings.

Simple Sugar Pies

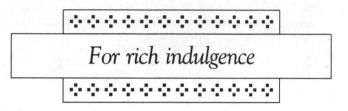

For rich indulgence

These are good winter pies, to make when fresh fruits are not available.

Simple Sugar Pie

Dixie Pecan Pie

Chocolate Lover's Pecan Pie

Wet-Bottom Shoofly Pie

Southern Chess Pie

Northern-Maple Nut Pie

Peanut Pie

Sugared Coconut Pie

Simple Sugar Pie

This has to be the grandmother of all sugar pies. Its richness belies a humble past. The cream and butter were once considered free, being provided by the family Jersey cow.

Preheat the oven to 450°F. Line a 9-inch pie pan with dough for Foolproof Pie Shell (page 101). Trim and flute the edge. Chill while preparing the filling. In a mixing bowl cream

6 tablespoons unsalted butter

Adding the sugar gradually, cream into the butter in this order

1 cup granulated sugar
1 teaspoon pure vanilla extract
⅛ teaspoon salt

Spread the creamed-butter mixture in the bottom of the chilled pastry in the pan. Sprinkle evenly with

6 tablespoons unbleached all-purpose flour

Gently pour over all

2 cups whipping (heavy) cream

A little of the flour may float to the surface. It is O.K. Dust the top with

freshly grated nutmeg (about ⅛ teaspoon)

Bake at 450°F for 10 minutes. Reduce the heat to 350°F and bake 50 to 55 minutes longer, or until the filling is thickened and well browned on top. Cool on a wire rack. If it does not appear firm after cooling, chill slightly before cutting. Refrigerate leftovers.

Makes 8 to 10 servings.

Dixie Pecan Pie

A wickedly rich southern favorite. Rum replaces the usual vanilla to mellow that richness. Use the freshest whole pecans you can find and chop or break them right before use.

Preheat the oven to 425°F. Line a 9-inch pie pan with dough for Fool-proof Pie Shell (page 101). Trim and flute the edge. Place the pastry-lined pan in the refrigerator to chill while preparing the filling. In a mixing bowl beat

3 large eggs

Add, in this order, blending well after each addition

1 cup granulated sugar
¼ teaspoon salt
4 tablespoons melted unsalted butter
1 cup dark corn syrup
1 tablespoon dark rum

Remove the pie shell from the refrigerator. Place in the shell

1½ cups coarsely chopped or broken pecans

Stir the filling once more and gently pour over the pecans. Bake in the 425°F oven for 15 minutes. Reduce the heat to 350°F and bake an additional 20 to 25 minutes. Do not overbake. The filling should be just slightly soft in the very center. It will continue to firm after removal from the oven. Cool on a wire rack. Serve slightly warm, or at room temperature, with hot coffee or tea. No topping needed. Refrigerate leftovers.

Makes 8 to 10 servings.

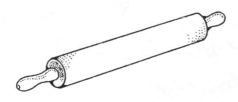

Chocolate Lover's Pecan Pie

If you prefer chocolate for dessert, you will want to make this your pecan pie.

Preheat the oven to 350°F. Line a 9-inch pie pan with dough for Fool-proof Pie Shell (page 101). Trim and flute the edge. Place the pastry-lined pan in the refrigerator to chill while preparing the filling. In a mixing bowl beat

3 large eggs

Add, in this order, blending well after each addition

½ cup granulated sugar
¼ teaspoon salt
1 cup light corn syrup
3 squares (1 ounce each) semisweet chocolate, melted
3 tablespoons unsalted butter, melted
1 teaspoon pure vanilla extract

Remove the pie shell from the refrigerator. Place in the shell

1½ cups coarsely chopped or broken pecans

Stir the filling once more and gently pour over the pecans. Bake in the 350°F oven for 50 to 55 minutes. Do not overbake. The filling should be just slightly soft in the very center. It will continue to firm after removal from the oven. Cool on a wire rack. Serve warm or at room temperature with hot coffee or tea. No topping needed. Refrigerate leftovers.

Makes 8 to 10 servings.

Wet-Bottom Shoofly Pie

Molasses-flavored caramel flavors a butter-rich topping to give this pie its quaint name. The ingredients can be divided roughly into thirds and layered into the pie shell, sometimes called Gravel Pie. I much prefer this "wet-bottom" version.

Preheat the oven to 375°F. Line a 9-inch pie pan with dough for Fool-proof Pie Shell (page 101). Trim and flute the edge. Place the pastry-lined pan in the refrigerator to chill while preparing the filling. In a mixing bowl stir together, pressing out any lumps with the back of a spoon

1 cup unbleached all-purpose flour
⅔ cup brown sugar
½ teaspoon ground cinnamon
⅛ teaspoon ground cloves
⅛ teaspoon ground ginger
⅛ teaspoon ground nutmeg

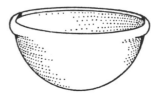

Cut in until the texture is mealy

8 tablespoons unsalted butter

In another bowl stir together

¼ teaspoon salt
½ cup hot water
½ cup dark corn syrup
½ cup unsulphured molasses

Remove the pie shell from refrigerator and have ready to fill. Stir together and then stir into the molasses mixture

½ cup hot water
1 teaspoon baking soda

Gently pour the molasses mixture into the waiting pie shell. Sprinkle the crumb topping evenly over the molasses mixture. Bake in a 375°F oven for 35 to 40 minutes, or until the filling is firm and the topping is nicely browned. Cool on a wire rack. Serve warm or at room temperature. Be sure to refrigerate leftovers.

Makes 8 to 10 servings.

Southern Chess Pie

❖ ❖ ❖

There are as many ways to make Chess Pie as there are cooks to bake them, some more complicated than others. This simplified version has the rich, tart flavor and the thin, crisp crusting that one looks for in a true chess pie. If asked what you are baking, answer, "Jes' pie."

Place an oven rack in the lower third of the oven and preheat to 350°F. Line a 9-inch pie pan with dough for Foolproof Pie Shell (page 101). Trim and flute the edge. Chill the pastry-lined pan while preparing the filling. Adding the sugar 4 tablespoons at a time, in a mixing bowl cream

8 tablespoons unsalted butter
2 cups granulated sugar

Add to the creamed butter-sugar mixture in this order, mixing well after each addition

2 tablespoons unbleached all-purpose flour
⅛ teaspoon salt
grated zest of 2 lemons

Add one at a time, beating well after each

4 large eggs

Add, 1 tablespoonful at a time, beating well after each

4 tablespoons fresh lemon juice

Pour and scrape the filling into the chilled pie shell. Bake in the lower third of the oven at 350°F for 40 to 45 minutes, or until the filling appears set and a thin brown crust forms on top. Cool on a wire rack. Serve slightly warm or at room temperature. Refrigerate leftovers.

Makes 6 to 8 servings.

Northern-Maple Nut Pie

❖ ❖ ❖

The flavor of this pie comes from pure maple syrup, cooked down from the sap of northern maple trees. They say the further north the trees are grown, the better flavored the syrup.

Preheat the oven to 425°F. Line a 9-inch pie pan with dough for Foolproof Pie Shell (page 101). Trim and flute the edge. Place the pastry-lined pan in the refrigerator to chill while preparing the filling. In a mixing bowl beat

3 large eggs

Add, in this order, beating well after each addition

⅓ cup granualted sugar
⅛ teaspoon salt
3 tablespoons melted unsalted butter
1 cup pure maple syrup

Remove the pie shell from the refrigerator. Place in the shell

1¼ cups coarsely chopped walnuts or pecans

Stir the filling once more and gently pour over the nuts. Bake at 425°F for 15 minutes. Reduce the heat to 350°F and bake an additional 20 to 25 minutes. Do not overbake. The filling should be just slightly soft in the very center. It will continue to firm after removal from the oven. Cool on a wire rack. Serve slightly warm or at room temperature. Refrigerate leftovers.

Makes 8 to 10 servings.

Peanut Pie

This combines the richness of a pecan pie with the addictive flavor of peanuts.

Place an oven rack just below the middle and preheat the oven to 425°F. Line a 9-inch pie pan with dough for Foolproof Pie Shell (page 101). Trim and flute the edge. Chill the pastry-lined pan while preparing the filling. In a mixing bowl beat

3 large eggs

Add, in this order, blending well after each addition

⅔ cup granulated sugar
⅓ cup creamy peanut butter
1 cup dark corn syrup
1 teaspoon pure vanilla extract

Remove the pie shell from the refrigerator. Toss in a sieve to remove excess salt, and then place in the shell

1 cup salted dry-roasted peanuts

Stir the filling once more and gently pour over the peanuts. Bake in the 425°F oven for 15 minutes. Reduce the heat to 350°F and bake an additional 20 to 25 minutes. Do not overbake. The filling should be just slightly soft in the very center. It will continue to firm after removal from the oven. Cool on a wire rack. Serve warm or at room temperature. I know it sounds excessive, but I like to top my piece with a scoop of vanilla ice cream. Be sure to refrigerate leftovers.

Makes 8 to 10 servings.

Sugared Coconut Pie

This sweet indulgence is confection in a crust.

Preheat the oven to 425°F. Line a 9-inch pie pan with dough for Foolproof Pie Shell (page 101). Trim and flute the edge. Place the pastry-lined pan in the refrigerator to chill while preparing the filling. In a mixing bowl beat

3 large eggs

Add, in this order, blending well after each addition

½ cup granulated sugar
¼ teaspoon salt
4 tablespoons melted unsalted butter
1 cup light corn syrup
1 teaspoon pure lemon extract

Remove the pie shell from the refrigerator. Place in the shell

1½ cups packaged, sweetened flaked coconut

Stir the filling once more and gently pour over the coconut. Bake in a 425°F oven for 15 minutes. Reduce the heat to 350°F and bake an additional 20 to 25 minutes. Do not overbake. The filling should be just slightly soft in the very center. It will continue to firm after removal from the oven. Cool on a wire rack. Serve warm or at room temperature. Refrigerate leftovers.

Makes 8 to 10 servings.

Creamy Custard Pies

With old-fashioned goodness

My mother made soft pies and custards more than any other kind of dessert. Perhaps that's why I think they are so special.

Mile-High Lemon Meringue Pie

Lime Meringue Pie

Homestead Buttermilk Pie

Classic Coconut Cream Pie

Mother's Coconut Meringue Pie

Soft Vanilla Pie

Old-Fashioned Chocolate Cream Pie

Sour-Cream Lemon Pie

My Best Banana Cream Pie

Butterscotch Cream Pie

Chocolate Silk Pie

Country Custard Pie

Old-Fashioned Pumpkin Pie

Cottage Cheese Pie

Mile-High Lemon Meringue Pie

Most lemon meringue pies are not lemony or high enough to suit me. By using four eggs instead of the usual three, and a full one-half cup of juice, you can have a pie that is worth making up.

Prebake one Foolproof Pie Shell (page 101) and allow time to cool. Separate, placing whites in the small bowl of a mixer, and yolks in a side bowl

4 large eggs

In a large, heavy nonreactive saucepan, stir together, pressing out any lumps with the back of a spoon

1½ cups granulated sugar
6 tablespoons cornstarch
¼ teaspoon salt

Gradually stir in, in this order

½ cup cold water
½ cup strained fresh lemon juice
reserved egg yolks, beaten until smooth

When the mixture is smooth, gradually stir in

1½ cups boiling water

Place over medium heat and cook, stirring constantly, until the mixture begins to thicken and bubble. Continue to cook, stirring briskly, until thick and bubbly, about 1 minute longer. It should drop from the spoon in thick, smooth sheets (lift the pot to stop the cooking while you check). Remove from the heat. Gently stir in until melted

2 tablespoons soft unsalted butter

Stir with a gentle folding motion for a minute or two to partially cool, then pour and scrape the filling into the cooled crust. Let the filling cool to room temperature before beginning the meringue. Meanwhile preheat the oven to 425°F. In the small bowl of an electric mixer, beat at high speed until firm, almost stiff, and peaks form when the beaters are stopped and raised

reserved egg whites

Continue beating at high speed and add, 1 teaspoon at a time, beating for one or two seconds after each addition

½ cup superfine sugar

Continue to beat until stiff, pointy peaks form that are *almost* dry. It is easy to go from stiff to dry—try to stay just short of dry. Spoon some of the meringue around the edge of the filling. With the back of a spoon, spread this meringue so that it touches the inner edge of the crust all around. Spoon the remaining meringue into the center and spread to cover the filling completely. Leave the meringue in natural swirls and mounds. Bake in a 425°F oven for 4 to 6 minutes, or until a delicate brown. Cool on a wire rack, away from any drafts. When the pie has cooled to room temperature, refrigerate to chill. Although this may be eaten at room temperature, the flavor will be improved and the cutting made easier if it is chilled before serving. Best eaten the day it is made. Be sure to refrigerate any leftovers.

Makes 6 to 8 servings.

Lime Meringue Pie

❖ ❖ ❖

Make this when the greengrocer's limes are plump and juicy.

Substitute ½ cup strained fresh lime juice for the ½ cup lemon juice in Mile-High Lemon Meringue Pie (opposite page). Proceed as before. The egg yolks will color the filling a soft yellow. If you want it to look more lime like, add 2 or 3 drops of green food coloring after adding the butter.

Makes 6 to 8 servings.

Homestead Buttermilk Pie

The piquant flavor of buttermilk is enhanced by lemon tartness in this creamy custard pie.

Prepare one unbaked Foolproof Pie Shell (page 101). Chill while preparing the filling. Preheat the oven to 350°F. In the large bowl of a mixer beat until light and lemon-colored

3 large eggs

Gradually add, beating until thick

1 cup granulated sugar

Blend in, in this order

⅛ teaspoon salt
3 tablespoons unbleached all-purpose flour
3 tablespoons melted unsalted butter
3 tablespoons fresh lemon juice

With the machine running at low speed, slowly add

1¼ cups buttermilk

Pour the filling into the chilled pie shell. Bake at 350°F for 40 to 45 minutes, or until the top is golden-brown and a table knife inserted midway between center and edge of the pie comes out clean. Cool on a wire rack. Serve chilled or at room temperature. Refrigerate any leftovers.

Makes 6 to 8 servings.

Classic Coconut Cream Pie

This recipe is a lot of work, and it messes up everything in the kitchen, but, oh my, it is good.

Prebake one Foolproof Pie Shell (page 101) and allow time to cool. Preheat the oven to 350°F. Spread on an ungreased baking sheet

1½ cups packaged, sweetened flaked coconut

Bake at 350°F for 8 to 10 minutes, or until just beginning to brown. Stir the coconut after the first 4 minutes of baking, and then watch carefully after that, stirring once every minute. Do not overtoast or the coconut will begin to lose flavor. Set aside to cool. In a large heavy saucepan stir together

½ cup unbleached all-purpose flour
⅔ cup granulated sugar
¼ teaspoon salt

Gradually add, stirring all the while

1 cup milk

When you are sure the mixture is lump-free, heat to scalding and then stir in

2 cups half-and-half

Cook over medium-high heat, stirring constantly, until thickened. The mixture should resemble a thick white sauce or béchamel. Remove from the heat. Beat in a side bowl

4 large egg yolks

Stir about 1 cup of the hot milk mixture into the beaten egg yolks, and then stir the warmed egg yolks into the hot milk mixture. Cook over medium heat, stirring constantly, until thick enough to drop from a spoon in sheets, followed by a couple of plops. The spoon should begin to leave a path as you stir. Remove from the heat. Press through a sieve into a side bowl, to ensure complete smoothness. Stir in, in this order

1½ teaspoons pure vanilla extract
reserved toasted coconut, except for ¼ cup

Let the filling cool to just slightly warm, stirring gently now and then to prevent a film from forming on top. Pour and scrape the almost-cooled filling into the baked pie shell. Refrigerate to chill and firm the filling. Top each serving with a generous dollop of Sweetened Whipped Cream (page 270). Sprinkle with a little of the reserved toasted coconut. Be sure to refrigerate leftovers.

Makes 8 servings.

Mother's Coconut Meringue Pie

This was my favorite pie when I was growing up. The filling is quick and easy. It's topped with a simple meringue.

Prebake one Foolproof Pie Shell (page 101) or No-Roll Pie Crust (page 103) and allow time to cool. Separate, placing whites in the small bowl of a mixer and yolks in a side bowl

3 large eggs

In a large heavy saucepan, stir together, pressing out any lumps with the back of a spoon

½ cup granulated sugar
4 tablespoons cornstarch
¼ teaspoon salt

In the side bowl, beat the reserved egg yolks until smooth and then gradually stir in

½ cup cold milk

Gradually stir the yolk mixture into the sugar mixture and then slowly stir in

2 cups scalded milk

Cook over medium heat, stirring constantly, until the mixture begins to thicken, 5 to 7 minutes. Turn the heat to low and continue to cook and stir, until thick and bubbly, about 1 minute. Remove from the heat and gently fold in, in this order

1 tablespoon soft unsalted butter
1 teaspoon pure vanilla extract
1 cup packaged, sweetened flaked coconut

Gently stir the filling for a minute or two to let steam escape, then pour and scrape into the cool pie shell. Let the filling cool to room temperature before beginning the meringue. Then set the oven at 425°F. It does not need to fully preheat before you bake meringue. Measure out and have ready

6 tablespoons superfine sugar

In the small bowl of an electric mixer, beat at high speed until firm points form when beaters are stopped and raised

reserved egg whites

Reduce the speed to medium and add, 1 teaspoon at a time, beating for three seconds after each addition (count: one hundred, two hundred, three hundred)

reserved superfine sugar

Return to high speed and beat until stiff, glossy peaks form. It should be quite stiff—almost dry, but not quite. Spoon some of the meringue around the edge of the filling. With the back of a spoon, spread this meringue so that it touches the inner edge of the crust all around. Spoon the remaining meringue into the center and spread to cover the filling completely. Leave some ripples in the top, but make no decorative swirls. Sprinkle over the meringue

¼ cup packaged, sweetened flaked coconut

Bake in the 425°F oven for 5 minutes, or until a delicate brown. Cool on a wire rack, away from any drafts. The pie can be chilled after it has cooled completely and can be eaten either chilled or at room temperature. Best eaten the day it is made. Be sure to refrigerate any leftovers.

Makes 6 to 8 servings.

Soft Vanilla Pie

As simple as this pie is, it is one of my most popular. It must take folks back to mother's kitchen.

Follow directions for Mother's Coconut Meringue Pie, leaving the coconut out of both filling and meringue.

Makes 6 to 8 servings.

Old-Fashioned Chocolate Cream Pie

This is serious chocolate. Choose a simple topping of whipped cream and grated chocolate, or glorify it with Macaroon Meringue (see below). Either one is delicious.

Prebake one Foolproof Pie Shell (page 101) and allow time to cool. Melt in the top of a double boiler over hot, almost simmering water

3 tablespoons unsalted butter
3 squares (1 ounce each) semisweet chocolate

While chocolate and butter melt, stir together in a large saucepan, pressing out any lumps with the back of a spoon

1 cup granulated sugar
4 tablespoons cornstarch
3 tablespoons cocoa
¼ teaspoon salt

In a side bowl beat until smooth

3 large egg yolks

Slowly stir into the yolks

½ cup milk

Slowly stir the yolk mixture into the sugar mixture and then slowly stir in

2 cups scalded milk

Cook over medium heat, stirring constantly, until thick and bubbly, 5 to 7 minutes. Cook and stir 1 minute longer. The mixture should drop from the spoon in thick, but smooth, sheets (lift the pot to stop the cooking while you check). Remove from the heat. Continue to stir the mixture off the heat for about 3 minutes, as it has a tendency to continue cooking. Stir the chocolate-butter mixture until smooth and then gently stir into the cooked mixture. Stir again for about 3 minutes. Gently fold in

1 teaspoon pure vanilla extract

Gently stir for another minute or two and then spoon and scrape into the pie crust. Cool to room temperature. Chill until set, about 3 hours. Top with Sweetened Whipped Cream (page 270) and garnish with grated semisweet chocolate. Refrigerate leftovers. If you prefer meringue topping, prepare Macaroon Meringue (see below) after the filling has cooled to room temperature. Top and bake as directed below.

Makes 8 servings.

MACAROON MERINGUE

Preheat the oven to 425°F. In the small bowl of a mixer beat at high speed until firm, almost stiff, peaks form when beaters are stopped and raised

3 large egg whites

Reduce the speed to medium and add, 1 teaspoonful at a time, allowing a second or two between additions

6 tablespoons superfine sugar

Return to high speed and beat until stiff, pointy peaks form when the beaters are stopped and raised. Remove the bowl from the mixer and gently fold in

½ cup packaged, sweetened flaked coconut

Drop the meringue by spoonfuls onto the cooled filling. Spread gently to cover completely and press gently with the back of a spoon to seal the meringue to the edge of the crust all the way around. Bake at 425°F for 5 to 7 minutes, or until a delicate brown. Cool on a wire rack, away from all drafts. When the pie is completely cool, it may be refrigerated without damaging the meringue.

Makes enough meringue to cover one 9-inch pie.

Sour-Cream Lemon Pie

The delicate tartness of sour cream is a flawless complement to the lemon in this pie filling. It can be made a day ahead of serving, making it perfect party food.

Prebake one 9-inch Foolproof Pie Shell (page 101) or No-Roll Pie Crust (page 103) and allow time to cool. Mix together in a heavy nonreactive saucepan, pressing out any lumps with the back of a spoon

1 cup granulated sugar
¼ cup cornstarch

Stir together, then gradually stir into the sugar mixture

3 large egg yolks
1 cup milk

Stir in

½ cup fresh lemon juice

Cook over medium heat, stirring constantly, until thick, 5 to 7 minutes. Remove from the heat. Fold in gently, 1 tablespoon at a time, until melted and smooth

4 tablespoons unsalted butter

Cool to room temperature, stirring occasionally to prevent a film from forming on top. Stir in, blending well

1 cup sour cream

Spoon and scrape into the baked pie shell. Chill until firm, at least 4 hours. Garnish with Sweetened Whipped Cream (page 270) and twists made from thin slices of lemon. Refrigerate leftovers.

Makes 6 to 8 servings.

My Best Banana Cream Pie

Ripe bananas nestled in a rich milk custard wrapped in a vanilla crumb crust. These are the flavors that'll take you back home.

Preheat the oven to 350°F. Mix together

1¾ cups vanilla-wafer crumbs (about 55 wafers)
3 tablespoons granulated sugar
5 tablespoons melted unsalted butter

Remove ¼ cup of the crumb mixture and reserve. Press the remaining mixture evenly over the bottom and up the sides of a 9-inch pie pan. Bake at 350°F for 8 to 10 minutes, or until golden-brown. Cool on a wire rack. In a heavy saucepan stir together, pressing out any lumps with the back of a spoon

½ cup granulated sugar
¼ cup cornstarch
⅛ teaspoon salt

Stir in, in this order

¼ cup cold milk
3 large egg yolks, beaten

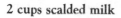

When the mixture is smooth, stir in

2 cups scalded milk

Cook over medium heat, stirring constantly. As soon as the mixture begins to thicken, turn the heat to low and continue to cook, stirring constantly, until thick and bubbly, about 1 minute longer. If the mixture threatens to become lumpy, remove it from heat at once and stir vigorously until smooth. When thick, remove from the heat and gently stir in, in this order

2 tablespoons soft unsalted butter
1 teaspoon pure vanilla extract

Let cool 10 minutes, stirring occasionally to prevent a film from forming on top. Spoon one-third of the filling into the cooled crust. Peel and slice into ¼-inch slices over this filling

2 ripe bananas

Spoon and scrape the remaining filling over the bananas. Sprinkle the reserved crumb mixture over the top. Chill until firm, at least 3 hours. Serve plain or topped with Sweetened Whipped Cream (page 270). Be sure to refrigerate leftovers.

Makes 6 to 8 servings.

Butterscotch Cream Pie

This is butterscotch-rich without being cloying. Toasted pecans add a tasty crunch.

Prebake one Foolproof Pie Shell (page 101) or No-Roll Pie Crust (page 103), and allow time to cool. Spread out on a baking sheet

¾ cup coarsely chopped or broken pecans

Bake in a 350°F oven for about 6 to 8 minutes, or until lightly browned. Stir them halfway through baking. Cool in the pan on a wire rack. In a heavy 3-quart saucepan, melt together over low heat, stirring frequently

6 tablespoons butter
1¼ cups light brown sugar

Continue to cook, stirring, until the mixture bubbles and begins to darken, about 5 minutes. It should smell like butterscotch. Remove from the heat. Protect your hands and avert your face (the mixture will bubble up and cause steam), while you stir in

1¼ cups boiling water

Continue to stir until smooth. In a side bowl, stir together

5 tablespoons cornstarch
¼ teaspoon salt

Stir into the cornstarch mixture, in this order, blending well after each

¼ cup cold water
1 can (12 ounces) evaporated milk

Slowly add the evaporated-milk mixture to the brown-sugar mixture, stirring constantly. Cook over medium heat, stirring, until the mixture begins to bubble, about 5 minutes. Continue to cook and stir until thick, about 1 minute. Remove from the heat. In a side bowl, beat until smooth

3 large egg yolks

Stir about 1 cup of the hot mixture into the beaten egg yolks, and then stir the warmed yolks into the hot mixture. Return to the heat and cook, stirring constantly, until thickened, about 1 more minute. Remove from the heat. Stir in

1½ teaspoons pure vanilla extract

Let cool 5 minutes, stirring gently all the while. Scatter toasted pecans over the bottom of the baked pie crust. Pour partially cooled filling through a sieve to ensure smoothness and then carefully pour over the pecans. Chill for at least 2 hours before cutting. This is so rich and creamy it needs no topping. Be sure to refrigerate leftovers.

Makes 8 servings.

Chocolate Silk Pie

This is silky-smooth and about as chocolate as you can get. Use only clean, Grade A, perfect eggs, with nary a crack to mar their shells. Be sure to read about eggs (page 2) before beginning.

Prebake one Foolproof Pie Shell (page 101), and allow time to cool. For the filling, use the large bowl of an electric mixer at low speed throughout, stopping occasionally to scrape the beaters and bowl. Beat until soft and creamy

12 tablespoons unsalted butter

Add, 2 tablespoons at a time, beating until light and fluffy after each addition

1¼ cups granulated sugar

Blend in, in this order

⅛ teaspoon salt
1½ teaspoons pure vanilla extract
3 squares (1 ounce each) unsweetened chocolate, melted and slightly cooled

Add, one at a time, beating for a full 2 minutes after each

3 large eggs

Spoon into the baked pie shell, spreading as evenly as possible. Cover lightly with plastic film and chill until set, about 2 hours. Serve topped with Sweetened Whipped Cream (page 270). Garnish with a little grated semisweet chocolate. Be sure to refrigerate leftovers.

Makes 8 servings.

Country Custard Pie

Creamy custard—delicately flavored with brown sugar, vanilla, and nutmeg —a real country pie. Stir ingredients thoroughly, but avoid making bubbles, so the mixture stays smooth.

Prepare one unbaked Foolproof Pie Shell (page 101). Chill while preparing the filling. Preheat the oven to 450°F. In a large bowl beat with a wire whisk just until smooth

4 large eggs

Switch to a spoon. Stir together in a side bowl, pressing out any lumps with the back of a spoon, and then stir into the eggs

⅓ cup granulated sugar
⅓ cup brown sugar
¼ teaspoon salt

Add, in this order, while gently stirring

1 teaspoon pure vanilla extract
2½ cups scalded half-and-half

Pour into the chilled pie shell. Sprinkle over the top

¼ teaspoon freshly grated nutmeg

Bake at 450°F for 10 minutes. Reduce the heat to 325°F and bake 30 to 40 minutes longer, or until a knife inserted halfway between center and edge comes out clean. Cool on a wire rack. Serve at room temperature or chilled. Be sure to refrigerate leftovers.

Makes 6 to 8 servings.

Old-Fashioned Pumpkin Pie

Every fall, on the last weekend in October, Hoopeston hosts the Pumpkin Family Reunion. In addition to hundreds of painted and carved pumpkins for competition and display, there is a pumpkin-cooking contest. In helping judge that contest, I have tasted more ways to make pumpkin pie than I had ever before imagined. Despite that exposure, my favorite remains this old-fashioned custard version.

Prepare one unbaked Foolproof Pie Shell (page 101). Chill the shell while preparing the filling. Preheat the oven to 450°F. In a large bowl beat

3 large eggs

Add and mix well

1 can (16 ounces) solid-pack pumpkin

Mix together, pressing out any lumps with the back of a spoon, and then stir into the pumpkin mixture

⅞ cup (¾ cup plus 2 tablespoons) brown sugar
½ teaspoon salt
1½ teaspoons ground cinnamon
½ teaspoon ground ginger
¼ teaspoon ground cloves
⅛ teaspoon ground mace

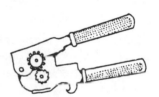

Stir in

1⅓ cups half-and-half

Pour and scrape the filling into the chilled pie shell. Bake in the pre-heated 450°F oven for 15 minutes. Reduce the heat to 325°F and bake for 30 to 35 minutes longer, or until the pie is set except for 1 inch in the center. It will continue to set up after removal from the oven. Cool on a wire rack. Serve at room temperature or chilled, topped with Sweetened Whipped Cream (page 270). Refrigerate any leftovers.

Makes 6 to 8 servings.

Cottage Cheese Pie

This delightful pie will remind you of cheesecake. You can cream the cheese and then mix in the remainder of the ingredients in a food processor, if you wish, but you will lose the fine-grained texture of the sieved cheese.

Preheat the oven to 350°F. Mix together

1½ cups graham-cracker crumbs
¼ cup granulated sugar
4 tablespoons melted unsalted butter

Press evenly over the bottom and up the sides of a 9-inch pie pan. Chill while preparing the filling. Press through a sieve into a large bowl

2 cups (1-pound carton) cottage cheese

Blend into the cheese, in this order, adding the eggs one at a time

3 large eggs
½ cup granulated sugar
⅛ teaspoon salt
¼ cup milk
¼ cup fresh lemon juice

Gently pour the filling into the chilled crust. Bake at 350°F for 45 to 50 minutes, or until the outer half of the filling is set. The center will still be somewhat soft. Cool completely on a wire rack. Chill for several hours before cutting to serve. Serve plain or with Pineapple Sauce (page 272). Refrigerate any leftovers.

Makes 8 servings.

Ordinary Pies

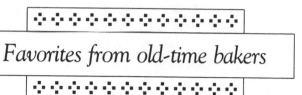

Time was when a farm housewife wouldn't call her family to supper until she had a pie cooling on the shelf. Meeting such a deadline led to some mighty tasty ideas.

Southern Sweet Potato Pie

Raisin Pie

Marmalade Pie

Green Tomato Pie

Dried Apricot Pie

Josephine's Grape Juice Pie

Vinegar Pie

Old-Fashioned Oatmeal Pie

Country Applesauce Pie

Mock Apple Pie

Schnitz Apple Pie

Southern Sweet Potato Pie

Folks who try my Sweet Potato Pie are surprised when I tell them what it's made of.

Prepare an unbaked Foolproof Pie Shell (page 101). Chill while preparing the filling. Preheat the oven to 450°F. In a large bowl beat

2 large eggs

Add and mix well

1½ cups cooked, mashed sweet potatoes
1 tablespoon soft unsalted butter

Mix together, pressing out any lumps with the back of a spoon, and then stir into the sweet potato mixture

¾ cup brown sugar
¼ teaspoon salt
½ teaspoon ground cinnamon
½ teaspoon ground nutmeg

Stir in

1 can (12 ounces) evaporated milk
1 teaspoon pure vanilla extract

Pour the filling into the prepared pie shell. Bake in the preheated 450°F oven for 15 minutes. Reduce the heat to 300°F and bake for 20 to 25 minutes longer, or until the pie is set except for 1 inch in the center. It will continue to set up after removal from the oven. Cool on a wire rack. Serve at room temperature, plain or with Sweetened Whipped Cream (page 270). Refrigerate any leftovers.

Makes 6 to 8 servings.

Raisin Pie

With an extra box of raisins in the pantry, a prairie farmwife has always been able to whip up a pie for unexpected company or for a family mourning the loss of a loved one. This one has a not-too-sweet filling, perfectly balanced with the fresh, tart flavor of oranges and lemons.

Prepare one recipe Easy Egg Pastry (page 102). Chill the dough while preparing the filling. In a medium-size saucepan combine

one 15-ounce box raisins (about 2½ cups)
2 cups water

Simmer, covered, for 5 minutes. Uncover and remove from the heat. In a large nonreactive saucepan, stir together

¾ cup granulated sugar
3½ tablespoons cornstarch
⅛ teaspoon salt

Stir in, in this order

¼ cup fresh orange juice
¼ cup fresh lemon juice
cooked raisin mixture

Cook over medium heat, stirring constantly, until thickened. Remove from the heat. Stir in until melted

2 tablespoons unsalted butter

Let cool until you can comfortably touch the bottom of the pan without protection. Meanwhile preheat the oven to 400°F. Roll out half the chilled pie dough and line a 9-inch pie pan. Stir the filling and then pour and scrape into the bottom crust. Roll out the second half of the dough for the top crust. Cut a ½-inch circle out of the center of the top and several smaller circles a short distance from the first one. Cover the filling with the top dough. Fold the top edge over the bottom edge of the crust, and seal and flute the edge. Cut and pinch several pieces of scrap dough to form shapes like leaves. Wet them slightly on the bottom and stick them around the circles for decoration. Bake at 400°F for 30 to 35 minutes, or until the crust is lightly browned. Cool on a wire rack. Serve at room temperature or chilled. Though not as rich as most raisin pies, this is still very filling. Slim slices will suffice.

Makes 8 to 10 servings.

Marmalade Pie

I like a bit more marmalade than most recipes call for.

Prepare one unbaked Foolproof Pie Shell (page 101). Chill while preparing the filling. Preheat the oven to 350°F. In a mixing bowl cream together

4 tablespoons unsalted butter
½ teaspoon pure lemon extract

Add gradually, creaming well

½ cup granulated sugar

Add, one at a time, beating well after each

3 large eggs

Stir in

1 cup orange marmalade

Spoon the filling into the prepared pie shell. Bake in a preheated 350°F oven for 35 to 40 minutes, or until a knife inserted in the center comes out clean. Cool on a wire rack. Serve at room temperature. Refrigerate leftovers.

Makes 6 to 8 servings.

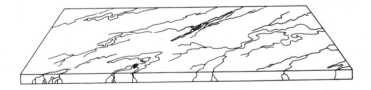

Green Tomato Pie

This spicy old-fashioned pie puts frost-threatened tomatoes to good use. Use the medium-size green fruits, before they begin to color. Very small dark-green tomatoes are unsuitably bitter.

Place an oven rack in the bottom third of the oven and preheat to 425°F. Prepare Old-Fashioned Pie Dough (page 102). Chill the dough while preparing the filling. Remove stem and blossom ends, and then chop, as fine as if making slaw, enough green tomatoes to make

4 cups chopped green tomatoes

Mix together, pressing out any lumps with the back of a spoon

½ cup granulated sugar
¾ cup brown sugar
6 tablespoons unbleached all-purpose flour
⅛ teaspoon salt
⅛ teaspoon ground white pepper
1 teaspoon ground cinnamon

Roll out half the pie dough and line a 9-inch pie pan. Sprinkle 2 tablespoons of the sugar-flour mixture over the pastry-lined pan. Drain any accumulated juice from the chopped tomatoes, and then toss them with the remaining sugar-flour mixture to coat. Spoon this mixture into the pan. Sprinkle over the filling

1 tablespoon fresh lemon juice

Dot the top with slivers of

2 tablespoons unsalted butter

Roll out the remaining dough and cover the pie. Fold the top edge over the bottom edge of the crust, and seal and flute the edge. Cut vents in the top for escape of steam. Bake at 425°F for 40 to 45 minutes, or until the top is golden-brown and the filling is bubbling hot. Cool on a wire rack. Serve at room temperature or chilled.

Makes 6 to 8 servings.

Dried Apricot Pie

Fresh apricots are a real treat, but the fruit does not ship well, often going from slightly underripe to soft, without developing any real flavor. For those who live far from the orchard, the answer is this reliable pie made with dried fruit.

Prepare one recipe Foolproof Pie Dough (page 100). Chill the dough while preparing the filling. Place in a heavy nonreactive 3-quart saucepan

1 pound (about 2¾ cups) dried apricot halves, each half snipped into four
    pieces
3 cups water

Bring to a boil. Regulate to a simmer and cook, covered, for 25 minutes, or until the apricots are tender. Drain the apricots, reserving the juice. Rinse and dry the saucepan, and in it stir together

1½ cups granulated sugar
3 tablespoons quick-cooking tapioca
⅛ teaspoon salt
¼ teaspoon ground mace (optional)

Stir in, in this order

1 cup reserved liquid from apricots
2 tablespoons fresh lemon juice
2 tablespoons unsalted butter
drained apricots

Cook over high heat, stirring occasionally, until the mixture begins to boil. Reduce the heat to medium and cook, stirring frequently, for 5 minutes. Remove from the heat and cool until you can comfortably touch the bottom of the pan without protection. Meanwhile, preheat the oven to 350°F. Roll out half the chilled pie dough and line a 9-inch pie pan. Stir the filling and then pour and scrape into the bottom crust. Roll out the second half of the dough for the top crust. Fold the dough twice, forming a triangle, and cut across the point of the triangle. Unfold over the pie and cut 8 short slashes radiating out from the hole in the center. Fold the top edge over the bottom edge of the crust, and seal and flute the edge. Sprinkle the top crust with

½ teaspoon granulated sugar

Bake at 350°F for 1 hour, or until the filling is bubbly and the crust is lightly browned. Cool on a wire rack. Serve slightly warm or at room temperature.

Makes 6 to 8 servings.

Josephine's Grape Juice Pie

This recipe first appeared in the Second Hoopeston Cookbook, *published in 1950. Although I have made changes, I still consider the idea to be Josephine Petry's.*

Prebake one Foolproof Pie Shell (page 101) and allow time to cool. In a mixing bowl beat

3 large egg yolks

Add, in this order, blending well after each addition

⅞ cup (¾ cup plus 2 tablespoons) sugar
3 tablespoons fresh lemon juice
½ cup bottled grape juice
6 tablespoons cornstarch

In a heavy saucepan, bring to a boil over high heat

2 cups bottled grape juice

Remove the hot grape juice from the heat and add to the yolk mixture in a thin stream, stirring all the while. Pour the mixture into the saucepan and cook over medium heat, stirring constantly, until thick enough to drop in sheets and clumps from a spoon. Remove from the heat. Stir in, 1 tablespoon at a time

2 tablespoons soft unsalted butter

If the filling appears lumpy rather than smooth, press it through a sieve. Let cool at room temperature until just warm, stirring occasionally to prevent a film from forming on top. Spoon and scrape the cooled filling into the baked pie shell. Chill until firm. Serve plain or topped with Sweetened Whipped Cream (page 270). Refrigerate leftovers.

Makes 6 to 8 servings.

Vinegar Pie

A cure for the winter blahs for a cook from early days who didn't have the luxury of lemons. Oldtimers can't get enough of this one.

Line a 9-inch pie pan with dough for Foolproof Pie Shell (page 101). Chill while preparing the filling. Preheat the oven to 450°F. In a heavy nonreactive saucepan stir together, pressing out any lumps with the back of a spoon

1 cup granulated sugar
⅓ cup brown sugar
⅓ cup unbleached all-purpose flour
⅛ teaspoon salt
½ teaspoon ground cinnamon
¼ teaspoon ground nutmeg

Stir into the sugar mixture, in this order

½ cup cider vinegar
2 cups boiling water
½ cup raisins

Cook over high heat, stirring calmly, until the mixture boils. Reduce the heat to medium and cook, stirring briskly, for 1 full minute. Remove from the heat. Continue to stir until the bubbling stops. In a side bowl beat with a fork

3 large eggs

Gradually stir about 1 cup of the hot mixture into the eggs and then slowly stir the warmed eggs into the pot. If you do not do this slowly, while stirring constantly, the mixture may curdle. Stir in until melted

2 tablespoons unsalted butter

Spoon and scrape the filling into the pie shell, taking care not to dump all the raisins in one spot. Bake at 450°F for 10 minutes. Reduce the heat to 350°F and bake 30 minutes longer, or until the filling is beginning to set around the edges. Carefully remove the pie from the oven and place on a wire rack to cool. The filling will still be somewhat liquid, but will firm up as it cools. Serve at room temperature or chilled. Refrigerate leftovers.

Makes 6 to 8 servings.

Old-Fashioned Oatmeal Pie

A cooperative supper differs from a potluck in that the host and hostess plan the menu, rather than leaving things to chance, and provide recipes where needed. Why not plan a cooperative with your friends and make this pie one of your assignments? Don't be put off by the oatmeal. The pie is really good.

Prepare an unbaked Foolproof Pie Shell (page 101). Chill while preparing the filling. Preheat the oven to 350°F. In a mixing bowl beat

2 large eggs

Stir into the eggs, in this order

1 cup granulated sugar
¼ cup dark corn syrup
¾ cup old-fashioned oatmeal (uncooked)
¾ cup packaged, sweetened flaked coconut
½ cup milk
1 teaspoon pure vanilla extract
⅛ teaspoon salt
2 tablespoons melted unsalted butter

Pour the mixture into the pie shell and bake at 350°F for 40 to 45 minutes, or until set except for the very center of the pie. It will continue to set up after it is out of the oven. Cool on a wire rack. Serve warm or cold. Refrigerate leftovers.

Makes 6 to 8 servings.

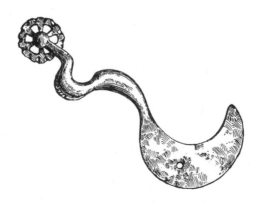

Country Applesauce Pie

Summer apples make good sauce and fall apples slice for pie. In old-time kitchens, when the stored pie apples were gone, summer's sauce came to the rescue. This is best with homemade tart applesauce. If you use sweet store-bought, stir a teaspoon of lemon juice into the two cups used.

Line a 9-inch pie pan with dough for Foolproof Pie Shell (page 101). Chill while preparing the filling. Preheat the oven to 400°F. In a mixing bowl beat

2 large eggs

Mix together and then beat into the eggs

½ cup granulated sugar
⅛ teaspoon salt
½ teaspoon ground cinnamon
¼ teaspoon ground nutmeg

Stir in, in this order

2 cups tart applesauce
½ cup evaporated milk
2 tablespoons melted unsalted butter

Pour into the pie shell and bake at 400°F for 40 to 45 minutes, or until the pie is set in the center. Cool on a wire rack. Serve at room temperature or chilled. Refrigerate leftovers.

Makes 6 to 8 servings.

Mock Apple Pie

*This idea from Civil War days resurfaces from time to time, with more histor-
ical than practical value. The filling does taste surprisingly like real apples,
making it fun to serve to groups interested in American foods. I have adapted
an early version to make a higher, sweeter, and spicier pie for you to try.*

Prepare one recipe Foolproof Pie Dough (page 100). Chill the dough
while preparing the filling. Preheat the oven to 425°F. In a nonreactive
3-quart saucepan, stir together

2 cups granulated sugar
2 teaspoons cream of tartar
2 teaspoons ground cinnamon
¼ teaspoon ground nutmeg
¼ teaspoon ground ginger
¼ teaspoon ground cloves

Stir in

2 cups water

Cook over high heat until the mixture boils, stirring occasionally. Boil
for 2 minutes, stirring constantly. If it threatens to boil over, lift the pan
for a few seconds to let it calm down. Remove from the heat. Stir in

¼ cup fresh lemon juice

Let the mixture cool to lukewarm. Roll out half the chilled pie dough
and line a 9-inch pie pan. Roll out and have ready the second half of
the dough for the top crust. Into the pastry-lined pan coarsely break

49 square saltine crackers (no more, no less)

Pour the cooled syrup over the crackers. Dot with slivers of

2 tablespoons unsalted butter

Cover the filling with the top crust. Fold the top edge over the bottom
edge of the crust, and seal and flute the edge. Cut several slashes in the
top for escape of steam. Bake at 425°F for 30 to 35 minutes, or until the
crust is golden brown and the filling is bubbling. Cool on a wire rack.
Serve at room temperature or slightly warm, topped with a scoop of
vanilla ice cream. This pie, like real apple pie, intensifies in flavor in the
refrigerator overnight.

Makes 6 to 8 servings.

Schnitz Apple Pie

Schnitz (dried apple slices) make an anytime apple pie with a flavor all its own. It's one of my favorites. The word schnitz, sometimes spelled snitz, means "slice" in German.

Prepare one recipe Easy Egg Pastry (page 102). Chill the dough while preparing the filling. In a heavy saucepan combine

8 ounces dried apple slices, cut into ½-inch pieces
2 cups water

Over high heat, bring to a boil. Regulate to a simmer and cook, covered, until the apple slices are tender and much of the water is absorbed, 30 to 45 minutes. In a side bowl, stir together, pressing out any lumps with the back of a spoon

1 cup granulated sugar
⅛ teaspoon salt
2 tablespoons cornstarch
1½ teaspoons ground cinnamon
¼ teaspoon ground mace

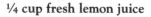

Stir into the sugar mixture

¼ cup fresh lemon juice

Stir the sugar–lemon juice mixture into the stewed apple slices. Cook over medium heat, stirring constantly, until thickened. Remove from the heat and stir in

1 tablespoon unsalted butter

Let cool to lukewarm. Meanwhile preheat the oven to 400°F. Roll out half of the pie pastry and line a 9-inch pie pan. Spoon the filling into the pastry-lined pan. Roll out the second half and cover the filling. Fold the top edge over the bottom edge of the crust, and seal and flute the edge. Cut several slashes in the top for escape of steam. Bake at 400°F for 35 to 40 minutes, or until the crust is nicely browned. Cool on a wire rack. Serve warm or at room temperature.

Makes 6 to 8 servings.

Deep-Dish Pies and Cobblers

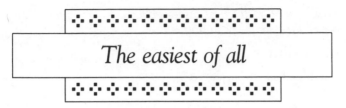

The easiest of all

The computer word "friendly" applies to deep-dish pies and cobblers. They are easy to make, and they're *supposed* to fall apart in serving.

Biscuit Topping for Cobbler

Peach Cobbler

Cherry Cobbler

Strawberry Cobbler

Rich Rhubarb Cobbler

Deep Delicious Apple Pie

Curried Fruit Cobbler

Fresh Blackberry Cobbler with Soft Butter Sauce

Deep-Dish Cherry Pie

Biscuit Topping for Cobbler

This topping is used on the next three cobblers, in which the filling is partially cooked before they are popped into the oven.

Stir or sift together

1½ cups unbleached all-purpose flour
2 teaspoons baking powder
½ teaspoon salt
2 tablespoons granulated sugar

Rub in with your fingers

5 tablespoons shortening

Gently stir in with a fork, just until the dough cleans the bowl

½ cup milk or half-and-half

Toss on a lightly floured surface until no longer sticky, and then pat or roll out to a shape that will fit the top of the casserole to be used. Bake as directed opposite page.

Peach Cobbler

I often use a little jam, jelly, or marmalade in my cobblers to perk up the flavor. Here I've used apricot preserves.

Preheat the oven to 400°F. Butter a 3-quart casserole. Stir together in a large nonreactive saucepan

½ cup granulated sugar
½ cup light brown sugar
½ teaspoon ground cinnamon
¼ teaspoon ground nutmeg
2 tablespoons cornstarch

Stir in, in this order

¼ cup water
2 tablespoons fresh lemon juice
¼ cup apricot preserves
6 cups peeled, pitted, and sliced peaches

Cook over medium heat, stirring often, until the mixture thickens. Remove from the heat. Stir in

1 tablespoon soft unsalted butter

Transfer to the prepared casserole. Cover with Biscuit Topping (see page 156). Bake at 400°F for 25 minutes. Serve warm with cream or ice cream.

Makes 8 servings.

Cherry Cobbler

This recipe is for freshly picked cherries, not canned.

Preheat the oven to 400°F. Butter a 3-quart casserole. Stir together in a large nonreactive saucepan

2 cups granulated sugar
3 tablespoons cornstarch

Stir in, in this order

⅓ cup water
6 cups pitted sour pie cherries, such as Montmorency

Cook over medium heat, stirring often, until the mixture thickens. Remove from the heat. Stir in

2 tablespoons soft unsalted butter
½ teaspoon almond extract

Transfer to the prepared casserole. Cover with Biscuit Topping (see page 156). Bake at 400°F for 25 minutes. Serve warm with ice cream.

Makes 8 servings.

Strawberry Cobbler

This is one of our favorites.

Preheat the oven to 400°F. Butter a 3-quart casserole. Stir together in a large nonreactive saucepan

1½ cups granulated sugar
2 tablespoons cornstarch

Stir into the sugar mixture, in this order

2 tablespoons water
1½ tablespoons fresh lemon juice
6 cups washed and hulled strawberries

Cook over medium heat, stirring often, until thickened. Remove from the heat. Stir in

1 tablespoon soft unsalted butter

Transfer to the prepared casserole. Cover with Biscuit Topping (see page 156). Bake at 400°F for 25 minutes. Serve warm with cream.

Makes 8 servings.

Rich Rhubarb Cobbler

Rich with sugar and butter, this is a special once-a-season treat. The batter rises as it bakes to form a sweet-crusted top.

Preheat the oven to 350°F. Stir together in one bowl

2 cups thinly sliced rhubarb
1 cup granulated sugar

In another bowl mix well

¾ cup unbleached all-purpose flour
¾ cup granulated sugar
⅛ teaspoon salt
⅛ teaspoon ground nutmeg
1½ teaspoons baking powder

Slowly stir into the flour-sugar mixture

¾ cup milk

Melt in an 8-inch-square baking pan

6 tablespoons unsalted butter

Tilt the pan to spread melted butter evenly over the bottom of the pan. Pour the batter evenly over the melted butter. Do not stir. Gently spoon the sugared rhubarb evenly over the batter. Bake at 350°F for 50 minutes, or until the top is nicely browned. Do not underbake. Best served warm. Pass a pitcher of cream.

Makes 9 servings.

Deep Delicious Apple Pie

When Golden Delicious apples are more green than yellow, make deep-dish pie. This has uncomplicated, pure apple flavor.

When buying your apples, pick out green ones. Preheat the oven to 425°F. Prepare 1 recipe Foolproof Pie Shell dough (page 101) and chill while preparing the filling. In a 2-quart casserole, toss together to coat the apple slices

6 cups peeled, quartered, and thinly sliced Golden Delicious apples
2 tablespoons fresh lemon juice

Stir together in a side bowl

1 cup granulated sugar
⅛ teaspoon ground nutmeg
⅛ teaspoon ground ginger
3 tablespoons quick-cooking tapioca

Spoon two-thirds of the sugar mixture over the apples. Toss gently to mix. Spoon the remaining mixture over the apples and do not mix. Dot the top with slivers of

2 tablespoons unsalted butter

Roll out the chilled dough to fit the top of the baking dish and cover the apples with the dough. Cut several slits in the top for escape of steam. Do not attempt to seal the dough to the edge of the baking dish or to flute an edge. Just plop it on there. Bake in the 425°F oven for 40 to 45 minutes, or until the pie is bubbling hot and the crust is golden-brown. Cool on a wire rack. Serve warm or cold. It is so good it needs no topping.

Makes 8 servings.

Curried Fruit Cobbler

A touch of curry spices summer peaches and plums, giving this cobbler come-back-for-more flavor.

Preheat the oven to 400°F. Combine in a 2-quart casserole

3 cups pitted, sliced red plums
1 cup peeled and pitted, sliced peaches

Mix together and then stir into the fruit

1 cup granulated sugar
¼ cup unbleached all-purpose flour
⅛ teaspoon salt
¼ teaspoon curry powder
¼ teaspoon ground cinnamon

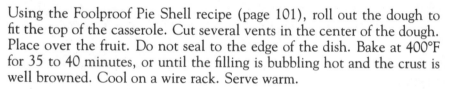

Dot the top of the fruit with slivers of

1 tablespoon unsalted butter

Using the Foolproof Pie Shell recipe (page 101), roll out the dough to fit the top of the casserole. Cut several vents in the center of the dough. Place over the fruit. Do not seal to the edge of the dish. Bake at 400°F for 35 to 40 minutes, or until the filling is bubbling hot and the crust is well browned. Cool on a wire rack. Serve warm.

Makes 8 servings.

Fresh Blackberry Cobbler with Soft Butter Sauce

The best and biggest blackberries always grow on the thorniest bushes in the thickest part of the berry patch. Hot cobbler, dripping with Soft Butter Sauce, makes any scratches you get picking them worthwhile.

Preheat the oven to 425°F. Using Foolproof Pie Dough (page 100), roll out two-thirds of the dough into a 12-inch rectangle to line an 8 x 8 x 2-inch baking pan. Chill the dough in the pan. Wrap the remaining dough and chill separately. Gently wash and then drain until ready to use

5 cups fresh blackberries

Mix together

1 cup granulated sugar
5 tablespoons unbleached all-purpose flour
⅛ teaspoon salt

Remove the chilled dough from the refrigerator. Roll out the remaining third of the dough into a 9-inch rectangle. Cut oval-shaped vents in this dough in a sunburst pattern, cutting 8 vents in all. Spoon 2 tablespoons of the sugar-flour mixture over the pastry-lined pan. Gently toss the remaining sugar-flour mixture with drained blackberries and spoon into the pan. Sprinkle with

1 tablespoon fresh lemon juice

Dot with slivers of

2 tablespoons unsalted butter

Cover with the top crust. Seal and flute the edge. Bake at 425°F for 45 to 50 minutes, or until the crust is well browned and the filling is bubbling hot. If the filling escapes the crust and spreads over part of it, it is O.K. Cool on a wire rack. Serve very warm, in bowls, with a dollop of Soft Butter Sauce (see below) melting on top of each serving.

Makes 9 servings.

SOFT BUTTER SAUCE

Cream together

5½ tablespoons softened unsalted butter
⅔ cup confectioners' sugar

Use at room temperature.

Makes about 1 cup sauce.

Deep-Dish Cherry Pie

Climbing to the top of the cherry tree to pick the first tree-ripened fruit makes me feel like a youngster again. Here is a favorite family recipe for using those first cherries.

Preheat the oven to 425°F. Make the dough for Foolproof Pie Shell (page 101), and chill while preparing the filling. Measure directly into a 2-quart baking dish

6 cups pitted sour cherries

Sprinkle over the cherries

1¾ cups granulated sugar
⅓ cup quick-cooking tapioca
grated rind of 1 lemon

Toss lightly to mix. Roll out the chilled dough to fit the top of the baking dish and cover the cherries with the dough. Cut several slits in the middle of the dough. Do not attempt to seal the dough to the edge of the baking dish. Flute the edge, if you wish. Bake in the 425°F oven for 40 to 45 minutes, or until the pie is bubbling hot and the crust is golden-brown. Cool on a wire rack. Serve warm or cold, topped with a scoop of vanilla ice cream.

Makes 8 servings.

Drop Cookies

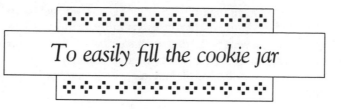

To easily fill the cookie jar

These are the family favorites we make over and over again.

Grandma's Soft Molasses Cookies

Hermits

Chocolate Drops

Old-Fashioned Oatmeal Cookies

Soft Oatmeal Cookies

Absolutely Chocolate Chip Cookies

Coconut Macaroons

Grandma's Soft Molasses Cookies

When Mother made something from her Joy of Cooking, *she measured; when she made one of Grandma's recipes, it was a different story. Cups and tablespoons were always heaping. Anything smaller than a tablespoon was measured in the palm of her hand. I don't know how many times I made these, with level measurements, before they matched my memory. Chewy soft and spicy, and just plain good.*

Preheat the oven to 350°F. Sift or stir together and set aside

1¾ cups unbleached all-purpose flour
¼ teaspoon salt
1 teaspoon baking soda
1 teaspoon ground cinnamon
1 teaspoon ground ginger
¼ teaspoon ground cloves

In a large bowl cream together

½ cup shortening
½ cup granulated sugar

Blend in, in this order, adding the dry ingredients ½ cup at a time

½ teaspoon cider vinegar
1 large egg
½ cup dark New Orleans–style molasses
reserved dry ingredients

Drop by rounded teaspoonful onto lightly greased baking sheets (grease even nonstick), spacing 2 inches apart. Bake at 350°F for 10 minutes. They will still be soft. Let rest about 30 seconds, and then carefully remove to wire racks to cool.

Makes 36 cookies.

Hermits

These childhood favorites were one of my mother's specialties. Great lunchbox treats.

Preheat the oven to 350°F. Stir or sift together and set aside

1¾ cups unbleached all-purpose flour
¼ teaspoon salt
1 teaspoon baking powder
1 teaspoon ground cinnamon
½ teaspoon ground nutmeg
¼ teaspoon ground cloves

In a large bowl cream together

½ cup shortening
1 cup light brown sugar

Add, one at a time, beating well after each

2 large eggs

Add the reserved dry ingredients, ½ cup at a time, blending well after each addition. Stir in

1 cup raisins
1 cup chopped pecans or walnuts

Drop by rounded teaspoonfuls onto lightly greased or nonstick baking sheets, spacing 2 inches apart. Bake at 350°F for 12 to 15 minutes, or until lightly browned. Cool on wire racks.

Makes 48 cookies.

Chocolate Drops

My family loves these simple little chocolate cookies.

Preheat the oven to 375°F. Stir or sift together and set aside

2 cups unbleached all-purpose flour
½ teaspoon salt
½ teaspoon baking soda
½ cup cocoa

In a large bowl cream together

8 tablespoons unsalted butter
1 cup granulated sugar

Add, in this order, beating well after each

1 teaspoon pure vanilla extract
1 large egg

Beginning and ending with the dry ingredients, add them alternately with

¼ cup buttermilk

Drop by rounded teaspoonfuls onto lightly greased or nonstick baking sheets, leaving 2 inches between the drops. Bake at 375°F for 10 minutes, or until just beginning to brown around the edges. Cool on wire racks.

Makes 60 cookies.

Old-Fashioned Oatmeal Cookies

Plan these crisp oatmeal cookies with cold milk for an after-school treat.

Preheat the oven to 350°F. Lightly grease 2 baking sheets, or use non-stick. In a large bowl cream together

1 cup shortening
1 teaspoon pure vanilla extract

Stir together, pressing out any brown-sugar lumps with the back of a spoon, and then gradually cream into the shortening mixture

¾ cup granulated sugar
¾ cup brown sugar
¾ teaspoon salt
¾ teaspoon ground cinnamon

Add, in this order, blending well after each addition

2 large eggs
1 teaspoon baking soda, dissolved in 1 tablespoon water
1½ cups unbleached all-purpose flour

If you are using a mixer, remove the bowl from the stand. Stir in

3 cups old-fashioned oatmeal (uncooked)
1 cup raisins

Drop by rounded tablespoonfuls onto the baking sheets, leaving 2 inches between cookies for spreading. Bake at 350°F for 11 to 13 minutes, or until lightly browned. Cool on wire racks.

Makes 36 large cookies.

Soft Oatmeal Cookies

If you like soft oatmeal cookies, rather than crisp, make these.

Place the oven rack in the top third of the oven and preheat the oven to 350°F. Lightly grease two baking sheets (grease even nonstick). Sift, stir, or whisk together and then set aside

1 cup unbleached all-purpose flour
¼ teaspoon salt
½ teaspoon baking soda
1 teaspoon ground cinnamon

In a large bowl, cream together

6 tablespoons soft butter
⅔ cup granulated sugar

Add, in this order, blending well after each

1 teaspoon pure vanilla extract
1 large egg
1 cup old-fashioned oatmeal (uncooked)
½ reserved dry ingredients
2 tablespoons milk
remaining dry ingredients
⅔ cup chopped raisins
½ cup chopped walnuts

Drop by rounded teaspoonfuls onto the baking sheets, leaving 2 inches between cookies so they can spread. Bake at 350°F for 10 to 12 minutes, or until very lightly browned. Cool on wire racks.

Makes 36 cookies.

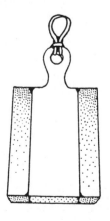

Absolutely Chocolate Chip Cookies

Here is my entry in the never-ending contest for the best chocolate chip cookie in the universe. I like to use enough chips so that none of the cookies is left wanting.

Preheat the oven to 375°F. Lightly grease 2 baking sheets, or use non-stick. In a mixing bowl cream together

1 cup shortening
1 teaspoon pure vanilla extract

Gradually add, creaming well

1 cup granulated sugar

Stir together, pressing out any lumps with the back of a spoon, and then stir into the creamed mixture

½ cup brown sugar
1 teaspoon salt
1 teaspoon baking soda

Add, one at a time, beating well after each

2 large eggs

Stir in, about ½ cup at a time

2 to 2¼ cups unbleached all-purpose flour

After 2 cups flour have been added, check the dough by touching with a finger. If your finger comes away sticky with dough, add additional flour, 1 tablespoon at a time, until the dough is no longer sticky. Stir in

3 cups semisweet chocolate morsels (one 12-ounce package plus one 6-ounce package)

Place the dough on the baking sheets, measuring ⅛ cup (2 level tablespoons) per cookie, spacing cookies at least 2 inches apart on the sheet. Shape into slightly humped rounds. Bake at 375°F for 12 to 15 minutes, or until lightly browned. Cool on wire racks.

Makes about 54 cookies.

Coconut Macaroons

These delicate morsels are what homemade is all about. I use a little extra coconut, making them especially good.

Preheat the oven to 300°F. Lightly grease and flour 2 baking sheets. In a small mixer bowl combine and beat until fluffy

2 large egg whites
¼ teaspoon cream of tartar
¼ teaspoon pure vanilla extract

Add, 1 tablespoonful at a time, beating continuously as you add

1 cup granulated sugar

Continue to beat until stiff but not dry. Fold in

1½ cups packaged, sweetened flaked coconut

Drop teaspoonfuls of batter onto the prepared baking sheets, using a second spoon to help push. Bake at 300°F for about 20 minutes, or until very lightly browned. Remove carefully and cool on wire racks.

Makes 30 macaroons.

Straight-Edged Cookies

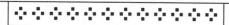

Bars and squares for all occasions

These are great for casual entertaining.

Jeanette's Lemon Bars

Praline Crackers

Peanut Buster Bars

Saucepan Brownies

Blondies

Mabell's Coconut Squares

English Matrimonials

Poundcake Cookies

Jeanette's Lemon Bars

A good lemon bar should melt in your mouth with just-right lemon flavor. These—from my good friend and fellow cook, Jeanette Groves—do.

Preheat the oven to 350°F. In a small bowl stir together

1 cup unbleached all-purpose flour
¼ cup confectioners' sugar

Cut into ¼-inch slices and then cut in with a pastry blender or two knives

8 tablespoons cold unsalted butter

When the butter pieces are the size of small peas, rub in with your fingertips until the mixture resembles coarse cornmeal. Gently press into an even layer in an 8 x 8-inch pan. Bake at 350°F for 20 minutes. Remove from the oven and set aside. In a small bowl beat

2 large eggs

Add in this order, blending well after each addition

1 cup granulated sugar
½ teaspoon baking powder
2 tablespoons unbleached all-purpose flour
grated zest from 1 lemon
3½ tablespoons fresh lemon juice

Pour onto the baked bottom layer (it will still be warm), and bake at 350°F for 20 to 25 minutes, or until the top is just beginning to color. Do not overbake. Cool in the pan elevated on a wire rack. Cut into 1 x 2-inch bars.

Makes 32 bars.

Praline Crackers

These are just as good as they are easy. It's hard to eat just one.

Preheat the oven to 350°F. On a large (about 12 x 16-inch) cookie sheet with sides, place in a single layer with edges touching

⅓ to ½ box graham crackers (about 26 squares)

In a large, heavy saucepan melt over medium heat

2 sticks unsalted butter

Stir into the melted butter

1 cup brown sugar
⅛ teaspoon salt

Stir over medium heat until the sugar dissolves and the mixture begins to bubble. Remove from the heat. Stir in, in this order

1 cup finely chopped pecans
½ teaspoon pure vanilla extract

Pour the sugar mixture over the crackers. Spread to cover. Bake at 350°F for 10 minutes. Cool 10 minutes. Cut individual crackers apart and remove to cool on wire racks.

Makes about 26 crackers.

Peanut Buster Bars

Here's a candy-bar combination: peanut butter and chocolate. The cookies will melt in your mouth.

Preheat the oven to 375°F. Lightly grease a 15½ x 10½ x 1-inch jelly-roll pan. In a large bowl cream together

8 tablespoons unsalted butter
1 cup granulated sugar

Blend in, in this order

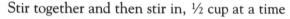

1 cup creamy peanut butter
1 teaspoon pure vanilla extract
1 large egg

Stir together and then stir in, ½ cup at a time

2 cups unbleached all-purpose flour
¼ teaspoon salt
1 teaspoon baking powder

Stir in, or work in with your hands

12 ounces semisweet chocolate morsels

Drop the dough by spoonfuls onto the prepared pan. Use your fingers and palms to spread evenly. Bake at 375°F for 18 minutes, or until lightly browned. Do not overbake. Cool in the pan elevated on a wire rack. Cut into 1½ x 2½-inch bars.

Makes 40 bars.

Saucepan Brownies

I baked pan after pan of brownies, varying the amounts of chocolate, butter, sugar, and flour. After judicious analysis, these were my tasters' choice. The size of the recipe is just right for most families. The method of mixing makes cleanup a breeze.

Preheat the oven to 350°F. Butter an 8 x 8 x 2-inch ovenproof baking dish. In a large heavy saucepan, stir over low heat until melted and smooth

4 squares (1 ounce each) semisweet chocolate, coarsely chopped
8 tablespoons butter cut into pieces

Remove from the heat. Stir in, in this order, adding the eggs one at a time (blend well, but do not overmix)

1 cup granulated sugar
2 large eggs
¼ teaspoon salt
1 teaspoon pure vanilla extract
¾ cup unbleached all-purpose flour
¾ cup chopped walnuts (optional)

Spoon and scrape into the buttered dish, spreading the thick batter into the corners with the back of the spoon. Bake at 350°F for 25 to 30 minutes. The edges should be about dry; the center should still be soft to the touch. Cool in the pan on a wire rack. Good plain or frosted with Brownie Buttercream (see below). Cut into squares to serve.

Makes 16 brownies.

BROWNIE BUTTERCREAM

This makes just the right amount for a thin, creamy layer on the fudgy squares of cake.

Stir together in a small bowl

¾ cup confectioners' sugar
1 tablespoon cocoa
pinch salt

Blend in

1 tablespoon soft unsalted butter
¼ teaspoon pure vanilla extract
1 to 2 tablespoons hot coffee, milk, or water

Add additional liquid, if needed, to make the mixture spreadable. As soon as the mixture is smooth, spread it evenly on the brownies.

Blondies

Blondies, or butterscotch brownies, are chewy and good. At picnics, I serve them with chocolate brownies to give a choice.

Preheat the oven to 350°F. Grease an 8 x 8 x 2-inch pan. In a large saucepan melt over medium-low heat

6 tablespoons unsalted butter

Remove from the heat. Add and stir until smooth

1 cup light brown sugar

Beat in, in this order

1 teaspoon pure vanilla extract
1 large egg

Stir together and then stir into the butter mixture

¾ cup unbleached all-purpose flour
½ teaspoon salt
1 teaspoon baking powder
¾ cup chopped pecans

Spread the batter in the prepared pan. Bake at 350°F for about 30 minutes. Do not overbake. Cool in the pan elevated on a wire rack. Cut into squares while still slightly warm.

Makes 16 blondies.

Mabell's Coconut Squares

These are from my mother-in-law's recipe box. They are rich and oh so tasty.

Preheat the oven to 350°F. Butter an 8 x 8 x 2-inch baking pan. Stir together in a mixing bowl

1 cup unbleached all-purpose flour
1 tablespoon brown sugar
pinch salt (optional)

Cut in with a pastry blender

8 tablespoons unsalted butter

Press the dough into the prepared pan. Bake at 350°F for 20 minutes. Remove from the oven and set aside. In the same bowl you used before, beat

2 large eggs

Beat into the eggs, in this order

1½ cups brown sugar
1 teaspoon pure vanilla extract
½ teaspoon baking powder
½ cup chopped walnuts
1 can (3½ ounces) sweetened flaked coconut

Spoon and gently spread the egg mixture over the partially baked crust and bake at 350°F for exactly 28 minutes. Cool in the pan on a wire rack. Cut into 2-inch squares while still slightly warm.

Makes 16 coconut squares.

English Matrimonials

If you use a food processor, some of the oatmeal gets cut into smaller pieces. It doesn't matter.

Stir together in a mixing bowl, or pulse on and off in a food processor fitted with the metal blade

1½ cups unbleached all-purpose flour
1½ cups uncooked old-fashioned oatmeal
¼ teaspoon salt
1 cup light brown sugar

Cut in with a pastry blender or food processor, just until crumbly

12 tablespoons cold unsalted butter

You should have about 5 cups of the mixture. Pat about half of it into an even layer in a 9 x 12-inch baking dish. Spread over this base

1 jar (12 ounces) red raspberry jam

Sprinkle the remaining mixture over the jam. Gently press to firm. Bake at 325°F for 40 to 45 minutes, or until very lightly browned. Cool in the pan. Cut into 1 x 2-inch bars while still warm.

Makes 54 bars.

Poundcake Cookies

These have poundcake texture with a sugar-coated top. Absolutely divine with a hot cup of tea.

Preheat the oven to 350°F. Grease and lightly flour a 15½ x 10½ x 1-inch jelly-roll pan. In a large bowl cream

2 sticks unsalted butter

Gradually add, creaming well

1 cup granulated sugar

Beat in, in this order, adding the eggs one at a time

1½ teaspoons pure vanilla extract
3 large eggs

Stir or sift together, and then blend into the batter, ½ cup at a time (if using a mixer, use the lowest possible speed)

1¾ cups unbleached all-purpose flour
¼ teaspoon salt
½ teaspoon baking powder
¼ teaspoon ground nutmeg

Drop the batter by spoonfuls onto the prepared pan. Spread evenly with a spatula. Sprinkle evenly over the batter

4 tablespoons granulated sugar

Bake at 350°F for 20 minutes, or until very lightly browned. Cool in the pan elevated on a wire rack. Cut into 1 x 3-inch bars while still slightly warm.

Makes 50 bars.

Rolled and Molded Cookies

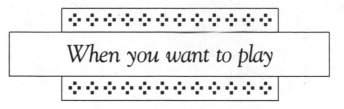

When you want to play

These are fun to make and easy enough for children to help.

Cream and Sugar Cookies

Shortbread Skirts

Snickerdoodles

Nutmeg Butter Cookies

Brown Sugar Cookies

Homemade Gingersnaps

Real Peanut Butter Cookies

Washboard Cookies

Cream and Sugar Cookies

I don't usually like my cookies frosted. These are an exception.

Sift or stir together and set aside

2 cups unbleached all-purpose flour
½ teaspoon salt
1 teaspoon baking powder

Cream until soft and fluffy

8 tablespoons unsalted butter

Gradually add, creaming well

1 cup granulated sugar

Blend in, in this order, adding the dry ingredients ½ cup at a time

2 teaspoons pure vanilla extract
1 large egg
2 tablespoons whipping (heavy) cream
reserved dry ingredients

You should be able to touch the dough lightly with a clean, dry finger without its coming away sticky. If not, add flour, 1 tablespoon at a time, until you can. Use a rubber spatula to scrape the dough into a soft ball. Cover and chill for 2 hours, or long enough to firm the dough. Meanwhile preheat the oven, setting the dial halfway between 350° and 375°F. Using one-third of the dough at a time, roll out to slightly less than ¼-inch thickness. Keep the unused part of the dough chilled. Cut out with a 3-inch cookie cutter. Place on lightly greased or nonstick baking sheets, spacing ¾ inch apart. Bake for about 10 minutes, or until just beginning to color around the edges. Do not overbake. Cool on wire racks. Frost the cooled cookies with Cream and Sugar Frosting (see page 181).

Makes 24 cookies, including rerolling of scraps.

CREAM AND SUGAR FROSTING

Press through a sieve into a medium-size bowl

2 cups confectioners' sugar

Stir together and then stir into the sugar

6 tablespoons whipping (heavy) cream
1 teaspoon pure vanilla extract

Add additional cream or sugar, if needed, to make the mixture spreadable.

Makes about 1 cup frosting.

Shortbread Skirts

These little skirts of shortbread break apart into fan-shaped melt-in-your-mouth goodness. The best thing known to go with homemade ice cream or sherbet.

Preheat the oven to 325°F. In a large bowl beat until softened

2 sticks unsalted butter

Add and beat until creamy and smooth

⅛ teaspoon salt
¼ cup granulated sugar
¼ cup light brown sugar

Gradually add, working in with a wooden spoon

2 cups plus 3 tablespoons unbleached all-purpose flour

Divide the dough into three parts. Pat or roll each into a 5-inch circle on ungreased baking sheets, spacing at least 1 inch apart. Score each circle with the edge of a dull knife into 8 equal wedges. Pierce the dough with the tines of a fork along the score lines, making sure the fork goes through to the baking sheet. Press a decorative edge onto each circle with the tips of the tines held flat. Press gently so as not to make the edge thinner than the rest of the dough. Bake at 325°F for 25 minutes, or until the shortbread is a pale ivory bisque edged with golden brown. Cool slightly in the pans. As soon as cool enough to handle, cut or break apart along the score lines and cool the individual fans on wire racks.

Makes 3 skirts or 24 fans shortbread.

Snickerdoodles

These are thought to have originated with the Pennsylvania Dutch, but they show up in community cookbooks from every region. Here's the best—soft and buttery, with a cinnamony-sweet coating.

Cream together in a large bowl

8 tablespoons unsalted butter
½ cup shortening
1 teaspoon pure vanilla extract

Gradually add, creaming well

1½ cups granulated sugar

Add, one at a time, beating well after each

2 large eggs

Stir or sift together and then add, ½ cup at a time, blending well after each addition

2¾ cups unbleached all-purpose flour
½ teaspoon salt
2 teaspoons cream of tartar
1 teaspoon baking soda

Cover the dough with plastic and chill about 2 hours. Meanwhile preheat the oven to 400°F. Roll pieces of dough between the palms of your hands to form 1-inch balls. Handle the dough gently. Do not pack. Roll the balls in a mixture of

3 tablespoons granulated sugar
2 teaspoons ground cinnamon

Place on a lightly greased or nonstick baking sheet, spacing at least 2 inches apart. Bake at 400°F for about 10 minutes, or until the cookie edges begin to brown. The centers should still be soft. Let them sit for a few seconds to firm before removing from the baking sheets. Cool on wire racks.

Makes 48 snickerdoodles.

Nutmeg Butter Cookies

These cookies will absolutely melt in your mouth.

Preheat the oven to 375°F. Cream

8 tablespoons unsalted butter

Gradually add, creaming well

½ cup granulated sugar

Add, in this order, beating well after each

1 large egg yolk
½ teaspoon pure vanilla extract
pinch of salt (about ¹⁄₁₆ teaspoon)
⅛ teaspoon ground or freshly grated nutmeg

Add, ¼ cup at a time, blending well after each addition

1 cup unbleached all-purpose flour, or more if needed

If using a mixer, you may have to work in the last of the flour by hand. Test the dough by touching it with a finger. If your finger comes away sticky, add additional flour, 1 tablespoon at a time, until the dough is no longer sticky. Cover and chill the dough for ½ hour. Roll the chilled dough on a lightly floured surface to a 9-inch square. Dough should be about ⅛ inch thick. Score lightly at ½-inch intervals, both up and down and sideways. Cut into 1½-inch squares, using score lines as a guide. The remaining score lines will form a tic-tac-toe pattern on each square. Bake at 375°F on ungreased baking sheets, spacing at least 1 inch apart, for 10 to 12 minutes, or until lightly browned. Cool on wire racks.

Makes 36 cookies.

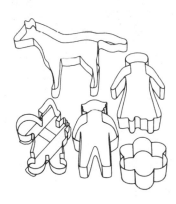

Brown Sugar Cookies

Great lunch-box cookies. Easy to mix and to roll.

Preheat the oven to 350°F. Lightly grease 2 baking sheets, or use non-stick. In a large bowl, mix together thoroughly

4 cups unbleached all-purpose flour
2 cups brown sugar
1 teaspoon salt
1 teaspoon baking powder
1 teaspoon baking soda
¼ teaspoon ground nutmeg

Cut in or work in with your fingertips

1 cup shortening

In a side bowl beat

3 large eggs

Make a well in the dry ingredients and into it pour the beaten eggs. Work the dry mixture in from the sides, and continue to mix, kneading with your hands at the last, until thoroughly blended. The dough should be quite stiff. Working with one-quarter of the dough at a time, roll out on a lightly floured surface to slightly less than ¼-inch thickness. Cut with a 3-inch cookie cutter. Place on baking sheets. Bake at 350°F for 11 to 13 minutes, or until lightly browned. Cool on wire racks.

Makes 36 cookies.

Homemade Gingersnaps

After these, you'll never eat store-bought again. The touch of white pepper is my "secret" ingredient.

Preheat the oven to 350°F. Sift together and set aside

2 cups unbleached all-purpose flour
½ teaspoon salt
2 teaspoons baking soda
1 tablespoon ground ginger
1 teaspoon ground cinnamon
⅛ teaspoon ground white pepper

In a mixing bowl cream together

¾ cup shortening
¼ teaspoon pure lemon extract

Stir together, pressing out any lumps with the back of a spoon, and then gradually cream into the shortening mixture

½ cup granulated sugar
½ cup brown sugar

Add, in this order, beating well after each addition

1 large egg
¼ cup molasses

Gradually stir in, mixing well

sifted dry ingredients

Roll pieces of dough between the palms of your hands to make 1-inch balls. Roll the balls of dough, to coat, in a small dish of

sugar

Place the sugar-coated balls on an ungreased baking sheet, leaving 2 inches in between. Bake at 350°F for 12 to 15 minutes, or until lightly browned. Cool on wire racks.

Makes 48 gingersnaps.

Real Peanut Butter Cookies

For melt-in-your-mouth real peanut butter flavor, these are the best. Enjoy them with a tall, cold glass of milk or buttermilk.

Preheat the oven to 375°F. Lightly grease 2 baking sheets, or use non-stick. In a mixing bowl cream together

8 tablespoons soft unsalted butter
½ teaspoon pure vanilla extract

Stir together, pressing out any lumps with the back of a spoon, and then gradually cream into the butter mixture

½ cup granulated sugar
½ cup brown sugar

Beat in, in this order

½ teaspoon salt
½ teaspoon baking soda
1 large egg
1 cup creamy peanut butter

Stir in

1½ cups unbleached all-purpose flour

Roll the dough into 1-inch balls and place on the baking sheets about 3 inches apart. When one sheet is covered with balls, press each ball flat with a fork that has been dipped in flour. Bake at 375°F for 12 minutes, or until lightly browned on the edges. Cool on wire racks.

Makes about 48 two-inch cookies.

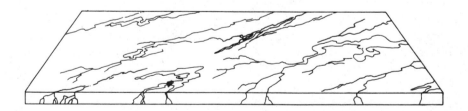

Washboard Cookies

Remember washboards? These delightful cookies are corrugated like that old-fashioned washday helper.

Stir or sift together and set aside

2 cups unbleached all-purpose flour
¼ teaspoon salt
¾ teaspoon baking powder
¼ teaspoon ground cinnamon
¼ teaspoon ground nutmeg

In a large bowl, beat until soft

12 tablespoons unsalted butter

Stir together, pressing out any lumps with the back of a spoon, and then gradually add, creaming well

½ cup granulated sugar
½ cup light brown sugar

Beat in, in this order

1 teaspoon pure vanilla extract
½ teaspoon almond extract
1 large egg

Add the reserved flour mixture, ½ cup at a time, blending well after each addition. Stir in

1⅓ cups packaged, sweetened flaked coconut

Cover and chill the dough for 20 to 30 minutes to firm slightly. Meanwhile, preheat the oven to 375°F. Divide the dough into two parts. On a lightly floured surface, pat or roll each part into an 8 x 10-inch rectangle. Cut each rectangle into four 2 x 10-inch strips. Cut each strip into ten 1 x 2-inch pieces. Place on ungreased baking sheets, spacing 1 inch apart. With a floured fork, gently press ridges into the cookies. Bake at 375°F for 8 to 10 minutes, or until the edges are beginning to brown and the tops are golden. Cool on wire racks.

Makes 80 cookies.

Icebox Cookies

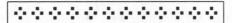

To bake for your break while the coffee perks

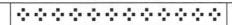

Having a roll of cookie dough in the fridge or freezer is like having money in the bank.

Mumsley's Sour Cream Cookies

Chocolate Wafers

Pinwheel Cookies

Icebox Sugar Cookies

Gingerbread Coins

Peanut Butter Squares

Mumsley's Sour Cream Cookies

This is from a grandmother (me) who never wants to be caught with an empty cookie jar. There's very little sour cream, but I swear it makes a difference.

Beat together until smooth and creamy

8 tablespoons unsalted butter
1 teaspoon pure vanilla extract

Gradually add, creaming well

1 cup granulated sugar

Add, in this order, blending well after each addition

1 large egg
2 tablespoons sour cream

Stir or sift together, and then add, ½ cup at a time, blending well after each addition

2 cups unbleached all-purpose flour
¼ teaspoon salt
¼ teaspoon baking powder
¼ teaspoon baking soda

Cover and chill the dough to firm, 1 to 2 hours. Divide the dough in half. Roll each half on wax paper to form a round log, 1½ by 6 inches. Roll each log separately in wax paper and overwrap in a plastic bag. Refrigerate or freeze. Thaw the frozen logs in the refrigerator overnight, or slice right from the freezer. When ready to bake, preheat the oven to 375°F. Slice the logs into ¼-inch-thick rounds and place on lightly greased or nonstick baking sheets, spacing 1½ inches apart. Bake at 375°F for 8 to 10 minutes, or until just beginning to brown. Cool on wire racks. For variety, roll one of the logs in chopped nuts before slicing, giving the finished cookies an attractive border.

Makes 48 cookies.

Chocolate Wafers

Make the dough for Mumsley's Sour Cream Cookies (see opposite page). Stir into the batter after dry ingredients have been added

2 squares (1 ounce each) unsweetened chocolate, melted and cooled

Proceed as in preceding recipe.

Makes 48 cookies.

Pinwheel Cookies

Make the dough for Mumsley's Sour Cream Cookies (see opposite page). After dry ingredients have been added, divide the dough in half. Stir into one half

1 square (1 ounce) unsweetened chocolate, melted and cooled

Cover and chill the doughs separately. Between two pieces of wax paper, pat or roll each part to a 6 x 12-inch rectangle. Remove the top piece of wax paper from each part. Place the chocolate dough (paper side up) over the plain dough (paper side down). Pull off the top piece of wax paper. Use the remaining piece of wax paper to help roll the two layers together tightly into one 12-inch roll. Cut in half, making two 6-inch rolls. Place the pinwheel rolls in fresh wax paper and overwrap with a plastic bag. Proceed as before.

Makes 48 cookies.

Icebox Sugar Cookies

These are quick to mix and chill. Bake them while heating the water for tea. Scrumptious.

Stir together in a large mixer bowl

2 cups plus 2 tablespoons unbleached all-purpose flour
1 cup granulated sugar
½ teaspoon salt
½ teaspoon baking soda

Add to the dry ingredients

1 cup shortening
1 teaspoon pure vanilla extract
1 teaspoon pure lemon extract
1 large egg
grated zest of 1 lemon

Beat at low speed just until blended. Stop as needed to scrape the bowl and beaters. Divide the dough in half. Roll each half on wax paper into a log, 1½ by 6 inches. Roll in wax paper and overwrap in a plastic bag. Freeze for 1 hour or longer. Thaw the frozen logs in the refrigerator overnight, or slice right from the freezer. When ready to bake, preheat the oven to 375°F. Slice the rolls into ¼-inch-thick rounds and place on lightly greased or nonstick baking sheets. Space the rounds at least 2 inches apart. They spread as they bake. Sprinkle the tops of the cookies lightly with

granulated sugar

Bake at 375°F for 8 to 10 minutes, or until lightly browned.

Makes 48 cookies.

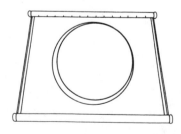

Gingerbread Coins

This dough can also be used for Gingerbread People. After the first chilling period, roll out on a lightly floured surface to ¼-inch thickness. Cut with floured "people" cookie cutters and bake at 375°F for 10 minutes, or until browned just on the edges. You may have to shop a health-food store for the whole-wheat pastry flour. Use all white flour if you prefer.

In a large bowl, beat together until smooth and creamy

½ cup light brown sugar
½ cup shortening

Add in this order, beating well after each addition

½ cup molasses
1 large egg
1 teaspoon cider vinegar

Stir or sift together and then stir in, 1 cup at a time

1½ cups unbleached all-purpose flour, plus more, if needed
1½ cups whole-wheat pastry flour
¼ teaspoon salt
1 teaspoon baking soda
1 teaspoon ground ginger
1 teaspoon ground cinnamon
¼ teaspoon ground allspice

You should be able to touch the dough lightly with a clean, dry finger without its coming away sticky. If not, add flour, 1 tablespoon at a time, until you can. Cover the dough and refrigerate to firm, 1 to 2 hours. Divide the dough in half. Roll each half on wax paper to form a round log, 1½ by 7 inches. Roll each log separately in wax paper and overwrap in plastic bags. Refrigerate or freeze. Thaw the frozen logs in the refrigerator overnight, or slice right from the freezer. When ready to bake, preheat the oven to 375°F. Slice the logs into ¼-inch-thick rounds and place on lightly greased or nonstick baking sheets, spacing 2 inches apart. Bake at 375°F for 8 to 10 minutes, or until just beginning to brown. Cool on wire racks.

Makes 56 cookies.

Peanut Butter Squares

Make the dough for Real Peanut Butter Cookies (page 186). Cover and refrigerate to firm, 1 to 2 hours. Divide the dough in half. Roll each half on wax paper into a square log, 1½ by 8 inches. Roll each log separately in wax paper and overwrap in a plastic bag. Refrigerate or freeze. Thaw the frozen logs in the refrigerator overnight, or slice right from the freezer. When ready to bake, preheat the oven to 375°F. Slice the logs into ¼-inch-thick squares and place on lightly greased or nonstick baking sheets, spacing 1½ inches apart. Bake at 375°F for 8 to 10 minutes, or until lightly browned. Cool on wire racks.

Makes 64 cookies.

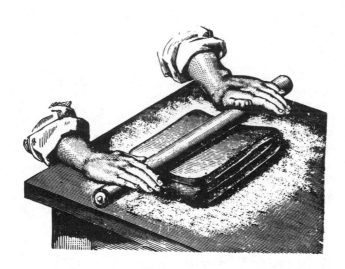

Stovetop Custards

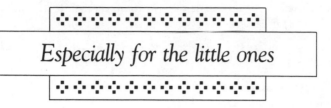

Especially for the little ones

Talk about comfort foods!

Stirred Chocolate Pudding

"Boiled" Custard

Soft Cracker Pudding

Old-Fashioned Blancmange

Almond Blancmange

Orange Blancmange

Creamy Rice Custard

Lemon Cream Custard

Stirred Chocolate Pudding

My mother used to stir this up as she was fixing dinner. It was still warm when we were ready for dessert.

In a heavy saucepan stir together, pressing out any lumps with the back of a spoon

1 cup granulated sugar
⅓ cup unbleached all-purpose flour
¼ teaspoon salt
5 tablespoons cocoa

In a side bowl beat until smooth

2 large egg yolks

Gradually stir into the yolks

2 cups milk

Gradually stir this mixture into the sugar mixture. Place over medium-low heat and cook, stirring constantly, for 10 minutes or until thickened and smooth. Do not allow to boil. Remove from the heat. If lumps have formed, strain through a sieve. Stir in

1 teaspoon pure vanilla extract

Spoon into dessert dishes. Serve warm or chilled. Pass a pitcher of cream.

Makes 5 servings.

"Boiled" Custard

Misnamed, because it should not be allowed to boil or the eggs will curdle. Many recipes call for only egg yolks. I have always used the whole egg.

In a heavy saucepan beat until smooth

2 large eggs

Stir into the beaten eggs, in this order

¼ cup granulated sugar
⅛ teaspoon salt
2 cups milk

Stir constantly over low heat until the mixture begins to thicken and coat a metal spoon. Remove from the heat. Stir occasionally as the mixture cools. When mixture is lukewarm, gently stir in

1 teaspoon pure vanilla extract

Spoon into dessert dishes and chill, or use as sauce for cake or berries.

Makes 4 dessert servings.

Soft Cracker Pudding

One of my tasters introduced me to this. When the threshing crews went through during harvest, her mother made it for a soft pie filling. Crumble the crackers in your hands. If you work them with a rolling pin, the crumbs will be too fine. ·

In a heavy saucepan combine

3 cups milk
⅔ cup granulated sugar
1 cup crumbled saltine crackers (about 15 crackers)
½ cup packaged, sweetened flaked coconut

Cook over medium-high heat, stirring frequently, just until the mixture begins to boil. Remove from the heat. In a side bowl beat until smooth

2 large eggs

Gradually stir 1 cup of the hot mixture into the beaten eggs, and then stir this into the hot mixture. Return to medium heat and cook, stirring constantly, until thickened. Do not allow to boil. It should get just a little thicker than a plain "boiled" custard. Remove from the heat. Stir in

1 teaspoon pure vanilla extract

Spoon into serving dishes. Serve warm or cold.

Makes 6 servings.

Old-Fashioned Blancmange

This is cornstarch custard. It is simple, classic, and easily made. Swirl sweet-ened puréed fruit with any of the flavors for a quick Fruit Fool.

In a heavy saucepan stir together, pressing out any lumps with the back of a spoon

½ cup granulated sugar
¼ cup cornstarch
¼ teaspoon salt

Stir in ¼ cup of milk, to make a smooth paste, and then gradually stir in the remainder of

3 cups milk

Cook over medium-high heat, stirring constantly, until the mixture begins to thicken. Reduce the heat to medium-low and continue to stir and cook until thickened, about 2 minutes. Remove from the heat. Stir gently off heat for about 2 minutes to allow steam to escape. Gently stir in

1½ teaspoons pure vanilla extract

Pour into pudding dishes and chill. Serve with berries or other fresh fruits in season. This can also be used to sauce simple unfrosted cake.

Makes 3 cups or 4 servings.

Almond Blancmange

The combination of vanilla and almond extracts gives this a richer flavor than when almond is used alone.

Reduce the vanilla in the Blancmange recipe to ½ teaspoon and add ½ teaspoon almond extract. Proceed as before.

Makes 3 cups or 4 servings.

Orange Blancmange

Substitute 1 teaspoon pure orange extract for the vanilla in the recipe (see page 198). Proceed as before.

Makes 3 cups or 4 servings.

Creamy Rice Custard

This old-fashioned dessert is easy to make. I like to process all of the rice for a thick, rich custard that tastes like it has cooked for hours.

In a large (about 4-quart) heavy saucepan, cook over high heat until it boils

½ cup regular or parboiled rice
1½ cups water
½ teaspoon salt

Turn the heat to low. Let it settle down, and then cover and cook for 30 to 35 minutes, or until the rice is tender and almost all the water is absorbed. Remove from the heat, but leave covered. In a side bowl, beat until smooth

4 large eggs
¾ cup granulated sugar
¼ teaspoon ground nutmeg
1½ teaspoons pure vanilla extract

Gradually stir in

2 cups half-and-half

Uncover the pot. Stir some of the hot rice into the beaten egg mixture and then stir the combined mixture into the pot. Cook over medium heat, stirring constantly, just until thickened. Once it starts, it thickens quickly. Remove from the heat often and lift the spoon to check. The next step is optional: Pour about half of the custard into a food processor. Process until smooth, or until the rice is a fine texture. Stir the processed custard back into the pot. Process all the custard, if you prefer the smoother texture. Pour into serving dishes. Serve warm or cold. Be sure to refrigerate leftovers.

Makes 6 servings.

Lemon Cream Custard

This creamy custard has a lovely lemon flavor which is repeated in the topping. Outstanding.

Prepare Lemon Syrup to be used in Lemon Whipped Cream (see opposite page), allowing time for the syrup to cool. In a heavy saucepan stir together, pressing out any lumps with the back of a spoon

⅓ **cup unbleached all-purpose flour**
2 **tablespoons cornstarch**
⅞ **cup granulated sugar (¾ cup plus 2 tablespoons)**
¼ **teaspoon salt**

Gradually stir in

½ **cup cold milk**

When the mixture is smooth, stir in

2 **cups scalded milk**

Cook over medium heat, stirring constantly, until the mixture thickens, 5 to 7 minutes. Remove from the heat. In a side bowl, beat until smooth

4 **large egg yolks**

Stir about 1 cup of the hot mixture into the beaten egg yolks, and then stir the warmed yolks into the hot mixture. Return to medium heat and cook, stirring constantly, until thick, 1 to 2 minutes. Remove from the heat. Add in a thin stream, stirring gently all the while

½ **cup strained fresh lemon juice**

Gently fold in until smooth

3 **tablespoons soft unsalted butter**

Let cool 7 to 10 minutes, stirring occasionally to prevent a film from forming on top. Spoon the partially cooled custard into serving dishes. Refrigerate to firm, at least 3 hours. Serve topped with Lemon Whipped Cream (see opposite page). A little home-candied lemon peel (page 263) can be scattered over the cream.

Makes 8 servings.

LEMON SYRUP

In a small saucepan, cook over medium heat, swirling the pan occasionally, until the sugar is dissolved

2 tablespoons strained fresh lemon juice
¼ cup granulated sugar

Boil gently for 3 minutes. Remove from the heat, cool to room temperature, and reserve for the recipe below.

Makes about ¼ cup syrup.

LEMON WHIPPED CREAM

With chilled bowl and beaters, beat until soft peaks form

1 cup whipping (heavy) cream

Fold in

reserved Lemon Syrup (above)

Beat again until soft peaks form.

Makes about 2 cups whipped cream.

Baked Custards and Puddings

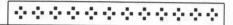

To take you back to Mother's kitchen

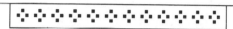

I could live on puddings like this and probably do quite well.

Lemon Cake Pudding

Wild Persimmon Pudding

Devil's Food Float

Raisin Pudding

Cherry Pudding

Indian Pudding

Bread-and-Butter Pudding

Cottage Pudding

Lemon Cake Pudding

This separates into a spongelike cake on top and a tart lemon pudding below. For a child learning to cook, this is always a fun surprise.

Preheat the oven to 325°F. Butter a 1½-quart casserole. Stir together and set aside

1 cup granulated sugar
2 tablespoons unbleached all-purpose flour
⅛ teaspoon salt

Separate, placing the yolks in a large bowl, and the whites in a smaller bowl

3 large eggs

Beat the yolks until smooth. Stir in, in this order

grated zest of 1½ lemons
6 tablespoons fresh lemon juice
stirred dry ingredients
1 tablespoon melted unsalted butter
1 cup milk

Beat the whites until stiff but not dry, and then fold them into the batter. Pour into the buttered casserole. Bake in a preheated 325°F. oven for 45 minutes or until the top portion is firm. Serve warm or cold. Refrigerate leftovers.

Makes 4 to 6 servings.

Wild Persimmon Pudding

An opossum lives at our house. A late-night rustling of leaves signals his arrival to search out supper. Nose to the ground, he moves with surprising speed, looks up once to question the lights, and returns to his repast. Stuffed like a child's toy, he hurries off in a new direction. Knowing that 'possums love persimmons, I gather enough to share, and scatter them in his usual feeding station. I think I saw him smile. Your family will smile like my nocturnal friend when they taste this dark and dense, spicy pudding made with wonderful wild persimmons.

Read about persimmons (page 4). Preheat the oven to 350°F. Butter a 2½-quart casserole. Stir together and set aside

2 cups Wild Persimmon Pulp (see below)
1 tablespoon fresh lemon juice

Stir together, pressing out any lumps with the back of a spoon, and set aside

1½ cups unbleached all-purpose flour
1 cup granulated sugar
¼ cup brown sugar
½ teaspoon salt
1 teaspoon baking powder
1 teaspoon baking soda
2 teaspoons ground cinnamon
¼ teaspoon ground nutmeg

In a large mixing bowl, beat with a wire whisk (use the whisk throughout)

3 large eggs

Add alternately, beginning and ending with dry ingredients

reserved dry ingredients
2 cups milk

Add, in this order, blending well after each addition

reserved persimmon pulp
4 tablespoons melted unsalted butter

Pour and scrape into the prepared casserole. Bake at 350°F for 60 to 70 minutes, or until it appears firm. The pudding will fall as it cools. That is O.K. Serve warm, spooned into dessert dishes. For a choice, pass one pitcher filled with chilled cream and one with warm Tart Lemon Sauce (page 272).

Makes 8 servings.

WILD PERSIMMON PULP

If your persimmons have not been washed by recent rains, they should be rinsed in running water before use. Then simply remove the large calyx from the stem end, and work them through a food mill or a sieve. It will take 1 to 1½ quarts of native persimmons to make 1 cup of pulp. If the pulp is not to be used immediately, it should be treated to prevent darkening. Stir 1 tablespoon lemon juice or 1 teaspoon ascorbic acid into each pint of pulp. Treated persimmon pulp can be stored in the refrigerator for 1 to 2 days and can be frozen for later use.

Devil's Food Float

Try this quick and easy dessert on a day when you crave a little something chocolate. A cakelike layer floats to the top of its own sauce while the pudding bakes.

Preheat the oven to 350°F. Stir together with a fork in an 8 x 8 x 2-inch glass baking dish

1 cup unbleached all-purpose flour
¼ teaspoon salt
2 teaspoons baking powder
2 tablespoons cocoa
¾ cup granulated sugar
¾ cup chopped walnuts

Make a well in the center of the dry ingredients, and pour into that well

½ cup milk
1 teapoon pure vanilla extract
2 tablespoons melted unsalted butter

Stir with the fork just until the dry ingredients are moistened. Spread evenly in the pan. Stir together in a side bowl

½ cup granulated sugar
½ cup brown sugar
5 tablespoons cocoa

Stir in

1 cup boiling water

Gently pour over the batter. Bake at 350°F for 35 minutes. Serve warm. Good plain or with vanilla ice cream. Eat this up. It's not good left over.

Makes 8 servings.

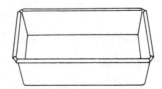

Raisin Pudding

This is an easy and satisfying family dessert.

Preheat the oven to 350°F. In a heavy nonreactive saucepan combine

1 cup light brown sugar
1 cup water
3 tablespoons unsalted butter
1½ tablespoons cider vinegar

Cook over medium-high heat, stirring occasionally, until the mixture boils, the sugar dissolves, and the butter melts. Pour the hot syrup into an 8 x 8 x 2-inch baking dish. In a mixing bowl, stir together

¾ cup unbleached all-purpose flour
⅓ cup light brown sugar
⅛ teaspoon salt
1 teaspoon baking powder
¼ teaspoon ground nutmeg
⅔ cup chopped walnuts
⅔ cup raisins

Add and stir in just until well blended

⅓ cup milk
½ teaspoon pure vanilla extract

Drop the batter by spoonfuls evenly over the syrup in the pan. Bake at 350°F for 25 minutes, or until lightly browned on top. Serve warm. Pass a pitcher of cream.

Makes 6 servings.

Cherry Pudding

*In this family dessert, a cake batter and a cooked cherry sauce bake together
into a tart and tasty pudding.*

In a heavy nonreactive saucepan place

2 cups pitted sour cherries

Stir together and then stir into the cherries

½ cup granulated sugar
1 tablespoon cornstarch

Cook over medium heat, stirring constantly, until thickened and clear.
Remove from the heat and allow to cool while preparing the batter.
Preheat the oven to 350°F. Butter an 8 x 8 x 2-inch baking dish. Sift or
stir together and set aside

1 cup unbleached all-purpose flour
⅛ teaspoon salt
1 teaspoon baking powder

In a mixing bowl beat together, adding in this order

4 tablespoons soft unsalted butter
½ cup granulated sugar
1 large egg
½ reserved dry ingredients
½ cup milk
remaining reserved dry ingredients

Pour and scrape the batter into the prepared pan. Carefully push the
batter to the corners of the pan with the back of a spoon. Spoon the
cooled cherry mixture over the batter. Bake in the 350°F oven for 30 to
35 minutes. Serve plain or with vanilla ice cream.

Makes 9 servings.

Indian Pudding

"Indian," or "Injun," was a colonial name for cornmeal. The earliest Indian puddings were little more than molasses-sweetened mush. This is a far cry from the original.

Preheat the oven to 325°F. Butter a 2-quart casserole. In a heavy saucepan, heat to scalding

4 cups milk
2 tablespoons unsalted butter

The butter may not melt completely. It's O.K. either way. Remove from the heat. Gradually add, in this order, stirring all the while

½ cup yellow cornmeal
¼ cup unsulphured molasses

Over medium-high heat, bring to a boil, stirring constantly. Cook, still stirring, for 1 minute longer, or until thickened. Remove from the heat. Stir together and then stir in

½ cup light brown sugar
½ teaspoon salt
½ teaspoon ground cinnamon
¼ teaspoon ground ginger
¼ teaspoon ground nutmeg

Pour into the buttered casserole. Bake at 325°F for 1½ hours. Remove from the oven after the first 30 minutes and stir well. Return to the oven to bake for the remaining time. Let stand for 45 to 60 minutes before serving. Serve slightly warm with cream or ice cream.

Makes 6 to 8 servings.

Bread-and-Butter Pudding

I have updated a colonial classic to use readily available, albeit high quality, supermarket bread. This is as delicate as it can be. A perfect pudding.

Preheat the oven to 350°F. Butter an 8 x 8 x 2-inch glass baking dish. With a sharp knife, remove the crusts from

8 slices thin-sliced firm white bread

Lay the trimmed bread out on wire racks to dry for 1 hour. Spread on one side of the dried bread, using ½ tablespoon per slice

4 tablespoons unsalted butter

Lay the bread, buttered side up, in the baking dish. You should have two layers, with 4 slices per layer. If necessary, trim the slices to make them fit. In a mixing bowl, beat until smooth

3 large eggs
6 tablespoons granulated sugar
¼ teaspoon salt
¼ teaspoon ground nutmeg
1½ teaspoons pure vanilla extract

Slowly stir into the egg mixture

3 cups milk

Pour the milk mixture through a sieve onto the bread slices. Let stand for 10 minutes. For part of that time, hold down the floating bread to help it soak up the custard. At the end of the soaking time, sprinkle evenly over the surface of the pudding

2 tablespoons granulated sugar

Place the dish of pudding in a larger, shallow baking pan and place in the oven. Pour hot water to a depth of 1 inch into the pan. Bake at 350°F for 45 to 50 minutes, or until a knife inserted halfway between the center and edge comes out clean. Remove the dish from the water bath and set below the broiler just long enough to lightly brown the top. Watch carefully: it won't take long. Cool on a wire rack. Serve warm or cold, with or without Apricot Sauce (see opposite page). Be sure to refrigerate leftovers.

Makes 6 servings.

APRICOT SAUCE

In a small nonreactive saucepan, stir together over medium heat until warm and blended

**⅔ cup apricot preserves
1 tablespoon fresh lemon juice
1 tablespoon unsalted butter**

Makes about ¾ cup sauce.

Cottage Pudding

This is melted-butter cake. It is the saucing that makes it pudding.

Preheat the oven to 375°F. Butter an 8 x 8 x 2-inch baking dish. Whisk together in a large bowl

**2¼ cups unbleached all-purpose flour
½ teaspoon salt
1 tablespoon baking powder
¾ cup granulated sugar**

Melt in a 1-quart utensil on stovetop or in microwave

8 tablespoons unsalted butter

Whisk into the melted butter

**1 cup milk
1 large egg**

Whisk the milk mixture into the dry ingredients. Pour and scrape into the prepared dish. Spread evenly with a spatula. Bake at 375°F for about 30 minutes, or until a wooden pick inserted in the center comes out clean. Serve warm with one or two sauces: Lemon Sauce (page 272), Vanilla Sauce (page 273), "Boiled" Custard (page 196), Blancmange (page 198), Pineapple Sauce (page 272), Blueberry Sauce (page 223), Montmorency Cherry Sauce (page 275). My favorite is Almond Blancmange (page 198) with one of the fruit sauces.

Makes 9 servings.

Steamed Puddings

A heritage of recipes

These carry the cozy warmth of prairie farm kitchens. Recreate one for your family.

Aunt Jakie's Graham Pudding

Mabell's Carrot Pudding

Steamed Date Pudding

Fudge Cake Pudding

Aunt Jakie's Graham Pudding

When I found this, I didn't think it looked complicated enough to be good, but I knew of Jakie Williams's reputation as a fine cook, so I tried it. The long steaming transforms the short and simple list of ingredients into a moist, delicious pudding.

Read about Steaming Puddings (page 11). Grease and flour a 1½-quart pudding mold. Stir together, in this order

2 cups graham flour or sifted whole wheat flour
½ teaspoon salt
1 teaspoon baking soda
2 cups raisins

Stir together and then stir into the flour mixture

1 cup buttermilk
¾ cup molasses

Spoon and scrape into the prepared mold. Cover tightly and steam for 2½ hours. Remove from the pot. Uncover and let cool 5 minutes before unmolding. Serve warm with Tart Lemon Sauce (page 272), Vanilla Sauce (page 273), or Amber Sauce (page 271).

Makes 8 to 10 servings.

Mabell's Carrot Pudding

This is a a typical old-time prairie Christmas pudding and one that has been in our family for generations. I prefer steaming mine in individual molds.

Read about Steaming Puddings (page 11). Grease and flour one 1½-quart pudding mold, or 12 individual ½-cup molds. In a large bowl, beat until light and fluffy

12 tablespoons unsalted butter

Gradually add, creaming well

1 cup granulated sugar

Add, one at a time, beating well after each

3 large egg yolks

Stir or sift together and then stir into the butter mixture

1 cup unbleached all-purpose flour
½ teaspoon salt
1 teaspoon baking soda
1 teaspoon ground cinnamon
1 teaspoon ground cloves
1 teaspoon ground allspice
¼ teaspoon ground nutmeg

Stir in, in this order

1 cup grated carrots
1 cup grated Irish potatoes
1 cup raisins
1 cup currants

The batter will be stiff. You may need to get your hands into it. Beat until stiff, but not dry, and then fold into the batter

3 large egg whites

Spoon into the large mold or individual molds. Cover tightly and steam. The large one should steam for 3 hours. The small ones take only 30 minutes. Remove from the pot. Uncover and let cool for 5 minutes before unmolding. Serve hot with Hard Sauce (page 275) or Tart Lemon Sauce (page 272).

Makes 12 servings.

Steamed Date Pudding

This is moist with the wonderful flavor of dates. A great dessert when winter's snows are piled high against the windows.

Read about Steaming Puddings (page 11). Grease and flour a 1½-quart pudding mold. Stir or sift together and set aside

1 cup unbleached all-purpose flour
¼ teaspoon salt
1 teaspoon baking soda
1 teaspoon ground cinnamon
¼ teaspoon ground nutmeg

In a large bowl, cream until light and fluffy

8 tablespoons unsalted butter

Gradually add, creaming well

1 cup brown sugar

Beat in

1 large egg

Stir in, in this order

reserved dry ingredients
1 cup buttermilk
1 package (8 ounces) chopped dates
1 cup chopped walnuts
1 cup fine dry bread crumbs

Spoon and scrape into the prepared mold. Cover tightly and steam for 3 hours. Remove from the pot. Uncover and let cool 5 minutes before unmolding. Serve warm with Tart Lemon Sauce (page 272) or Vinegar Sauce (page 276).

Makes 10 to 12 servings.

Fudge Cake Pudding

You think of steaming desserts in wintertime, but I have made this in summer to avoid turning on the oven. It's a great chocolate cake.

Read about Steaming Puddings (page 11). Grease and flour a 1½-quart pudding mold. Sift or stir together and set aside

1½ cups unbleached all-purpose flour
¾ teaspoon salt
1 teaspoon baking soda

In a large bowl, cream until light and fluffy

8 tablespoons unsalted butter

Gradually add, creaming well

1½ cups granulated sugar

Add one at a time, beating well after each

3 large egg yolks

Stir in

1 teaspoon pure vanilla extract

Add alternately (three parts dry, two parts buttermilk)

reserved dry ingredients
1 cup buttermilk

Stir in, in this order

3 squares (1 ounce each) unsweetened chocolate, melted and cooled
1 cup chopped walnuts

Beat until stiff but not dry

3 large egg whites

Stir one-quarter of the whites into the batter, and then fold in the remainder until no white streaks remain. Spoon and scrape into the prepared mold. Cover tightly and steam for 1½ hours, or until a wooden pick inserted in the center comes out clean. Remove from the pot. Uncover and let rest 5 minutes before unmolding. Serve warm with Fast Fudge Sauce (page 270), Vanilla Sauce (page 273), or Chocolate Whipped Cream (page 270).

Makes 8 to 10 servings.

Fruit Desserts

With down-home goodness

If I had to pick a favorite, it would have to be one of these.

Individual Strawberry Shortcakes

Southern Ambrosia

Blueberry Buckle with Blueberry Sauce

Alice's Apple Dumplings

Applesauce Charlotte

Simple Summer Pudding

Apple Impromptu

Rhubarb Crisp

Gooseberry Fool

Individual Strawberry Shortcakes

We don't like to oversweeten our strawberries. In this recipe, I use a little sugar in the cake, the butter, and the cream, allowing less sweetener than is ordinarily used for the berries themselves. With gentle handling, the shortcakes will be tender enough to break apart easily in your bowl.

Preheat the oven to 450°F. Mix together and set aside

4 tablespoons soft unsalted butter
½ cup confectioners' sugar

Place in a flat glass container

4 cups washed, hulled, sliced strawberries (about 6 cups whole berries)

Sprinkle over the berries

¼ cup granulated sugar

Cover the berries and chill while making the shortcakes. Sift or stir together

2 cups unbleached all-purpose flour
½ teaspoon salt
1 tablespoon baking powder
1 tablespoon granulated sugar

Cut into the flour mixture

½ cup shortening

Stir in with a fork, just until the dough comes together in a ball

⅔ cup milk

Divide the dough into 6 parts. With lightly floured hands pat each part gently into a circle about ½ inch thick and place on an ungreased baking sheet. Bake at 450°F for 12 to 15 minutes, or until golden-brown. Cool slightly on a wire rack. While still warm, assemble the shortcakes, using one cake per serving. Split the cakes and spread the cut surfaces with

reserved sugar-butter mixture

Place in individual bowls, cut sides up. Spoon over the cakes, using about ⅔ cup per serving

chilled, sugared berries

Top with

Sweetened Whipped Cream (page 270)

Pass any extra cream.

Makes 6 servings shortcake.

Southern Ambrosia

My mother adapted easily to cultural change. Soon after we moved South, she added ambrosia to her menus.

Use the prettiest clear glass bowl you have. Peel, slice, and lay flat in that bowl

4 large, sweet navel oranges

Layer over the oranges slices

1 thinly sliced ripe banana, optional

Spoon over the banana

1 can (8 ounces) crushed pineapple, packed in pinepapple juice

Sprinkle over all

½ cup packaged, sweetened flaked coconut

Cover with plastic wrap and chill until serving time.

Makes 6 to 8 servings.

Blueberry Buckle with Blueberry Sauce

This crunchy-topped cake, bursting with berries and surrounded by its own sauce, is divine. It works equally well at breakfast or supper.

Preheat the oven to 350°F. Butter a 9 x 9 x 2-inch baking pan. Sift together and set aside

2 cups unbleached all-purpose flour
2 teaspoons baking powder
½ teaspoon salt

Wash and then drain on toweling

2 cups fresh blueberries

Cream together

4 tablespoons unsalted butter
1 teaspoon fresh lemon juice

Gradually add, creaming well

¾ cup granulated sugar

Beat in

1 large egg

Add the reserved dry ingredients alternately with

½ cup milk

The batter will be thick. That is O.K. Fold in the blueberries. Spread the batter in the buttered pan. Sprinkle with

Crumb Topping (see opposite page)

Bake at 350°F for 40 to 45 minutes, or until a wooden pick inserted in the center comes out clean. Cool in the pan elevated on a wire rack. Place squares of buckle in small bowls in which you have spooned some of the Blueberry Sauce (see opposite page).

Makes 9 servings.

CRUMB TOPPING

In a small bowl stir together

½ cup granulated sugar
⅓ cup unbleached all-purpose flour
½ teaspoon ground cinnamon

Cut in with a pastry blender

4 tablespoons unsalted butter

BLUEBERRY SAUCE

This is also good on ice cream.

In a saucepan combine

6 tablespoons granulated sugar
1 tablespoon cornstarch
⅛ teaspoon ground cinnamon

Stir in, in this order

1 tablespoon cold water
1½ teaspoons fresh lemon juice
2 cups fresh blueberries

Cook over medium-high heat, stirring frequently, until the mixture begins to boil. Reduce the heat to medium-low and continue to cook, stirring constantly, just until the juice thickens and loses its cloudy appearance. Remove from the heat. Stir in

1 teaspoon soft unsalted butter

Serve warm or chilled.

Makes about 2 cups.

Alice's Apple Dumplings

Generations ago a young girl was expected to produce a cookbook to take to her new home as a bride. This is from a bound volume, hand-written by Alice Wendell.

Preheat the oven to 350°F. Before peeling the apples, cut across the tops and bottoms to flatten them, making it easier to re-form them when assembling the dumplings. Peel, core, and quarter

6 small tart apples (about 2½ inches in diameter)

Roll out into a 10 x 15-inch rectangle

Dumpling Dough (see opposite page)

Cut the dough into six 5-inch squares. Stand 4 apple quarters in the center of each square, re-forming the original apple shape. Mix together and then sprinkle over the apples, dividing evenly between the 6 squares

1 tablespoon granulated sugar
½ teaspoon ground cinnamon
⅛ teaspoon ground nutmeg

Pull the corners of the dough up over the apples. Pick a dumpling up, using a spatula to help if needed, and place it in the palm of one hand. Work the dough to cover the apples completely and use both hands to gently compact the dumpling, much as though you were making a meatball. Place the formed dumpling in a 9 x 12-inch ovenproof baking dish (a metal pan is not suitable). Repeat with the remaining dumplings. Pour over and around the dumplings

Cinnamon Syrup (see opposite page)

Bake at 350°F for 45 minutes, or until the tops are well browned and the syrup has thickened. Cool in the pan elevated on a wire rack. Transfer the warm dumplings into bowls. Spoon the syrup around the dumplings. Pass the pitcher of cream.

Makes 6 servings.

DUMPLING DOUGH

Stir or sift together in a small mixing bowl

2 cups unbleached all-purpose flour
½ teaspoon salt
4 teaspoons baking powder
1 teaspoon granulated sugar

Cut into the dry ingredients

½ cup shortening

Mix in with a fork, just until the dough holds together

⅔ cup milk

The dough will be soft. Toss on a floured surface until no longer sticky.
Roll out as directed.

CINNAMON SYRUP

Combine in a heavy nonreactive saucepan

1 cup granulated sugar
1 cup brown sugar
1 teaspoon ground cinnamon
3 cups water
¼ cup cider vinegar
4 tablespoons unsalted butter

Cook over medium heat, stirring occasionally, until the sugar is dissolved
and the butter melts.

Applesauce Charlotte

This is a buttered bread casing baked with a filling of applesauce marmalade. It is simply delicious.

Prepare Unseasoned Applesauce (see below), or use 1 quart high-quality store-bought. Preheat the oven to 375°F. Place the applesauce in a nonreactive stockpot. Stir together and then stir in

1½ cups granulated sugar
1½ teaspoons ground cinnamon
¼ teaspoon ground mace
1 teaspoon pure vanilla extract

Cook over medium-low heat, stirring often, until the mixture becomes a very thick marmalade. Be careful. A mixture as thick as this can pop like a volcano, burning you with hot apple purée. Stirring helps control the problem. Meanwhile, cut the crusts from

10 slices thin-sliced white bread

Melt

8 tablespoons unsalted butter

Brush both sides of the bread with the butter. Sauté in a skillet over medium heat, turning once, until golden brown on both sides. Line a 1½-quart charlotte mold or soufflé dish with the bread, cutting the pieces where needed to make a tight fit. Fill the lined mold with the thickened apple marmalade. Cover the top of the marmalade with additional bread. Prepare more bread and butter, if needed. Bake at 375°F for about 35 minutes, or until the bread on top is nicely browned. Let cool at least 30 minutes. Turn out on a serving plate or spoon from the dish like cobbler. Serve warm or at room temperature with Tart Lemon Sauce (page 272).

Makes 8 to 10 servings.

UNSEASONED APPLESAUCE

Peel, quarter, and core

3 pounds small, tart cooking apples (about 18)

Cook over medium heat in a covered nonreactive stockpot with

1 cup water

Cook just until tender. Stir occasionally and add water, if needed, to prevent sticking. Some apples will collapse into sauce as they cook. If yours do not, press them through a sieve, or purée in a food processor.

Makes about 1 quart sauce.

Simple Summer Pudding

You can mix several kinds of berries for summer pudding. You can even butter the bread. But simplicity is best.

Trim the crusts from

6 or more slices thin-sliced white bread

Line the bottom and sides of a 1½-quart pudding mold or glass soufflé dish with the bread, cutting the pieces to fit. In a heavy nonreactive saucepan, combine

4 cups red ripe raspberries
¾ cup granulated sugar

Cook over low heat, stirring gently now and then, just until the juices flow, about 10 minutes. With a slotted spoon, transfer the berries to the bread-lined mold. Spoon about half the juice over the berries and bread. Cover the top with the remaining prepared bread. Snugly fit a plate over the top of the pudding and gently press down—not too hard, just a little. Place a weight on the plate, such as an unopened can of food. Cover the whole thing with plastic wrap and refrigerate for 24 hours. No fudging. Time is needed to transform the bread. Cover and refrigerate the remaining juice separately. When ready to serve, run a thin knife or spatula around the edges of the mold to help release and invert on a serving plate.* If some bread remains unstained, pour some of the reserved juice over it. Pass the remaining juice and a pitcher of cream.

Makes 6 to 8 servings.

---

* If your pudding seems too juicy to unmold, don't worry. Slice it like pie, or dip it out like cobbler. Spoon some of the collected juice over each serving.

Apple Impromptu

This is crumb-topped apple pie without a crust. It's fast and easy, and, oh, so good. McIntosh apples are preferred. Jonathans come in second.

Preheat the oven to 375°F. Butter an 8 x 8 x 2-inch baking dish. Fill the dish with

6 cups peeled, thinly sliced tart apples

Stir together and then sprinkle over the apples

1 tablespoon lemon juice or rum
1 tablespoon water

Mix together in a medium-size bowl

½ cup unbleached all-purpose flour
½ cup light brown sugar
⅛ teaspoon salt
½ teaspoon ground cinnamon
⅛ teaspoon ground nutmeg

Cut in

4 tablespoons unsalted butter

Sprinkle the crumb mixture evenly over the apples. Bake at 375°F for 30 minutes. Serve warm with vanilla ice cream.

Makes 6 servings.

Rhubarb Crisp

As soon as asparagus spears poke through the ground, we check the rhubarb patch. When the stalks have lengthened, but before they get tough, we pull the rhubarb for crisps, pies, and sauce. Our favorite crisp uses both white and brown sugar to sweeten rhubarb's very tart flavor.

Butter a 9 x 12-inch baking dish. Preheat the oven to 350°F. Mix together and spread evenly over the bottom of the dish

5 cups thinly sliced rhubarb
1 cup granulated sugar

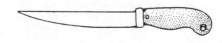

Mix together

1 cup brown sugar
1 cup unbleached all-purpose flour
1 cup old-fashioned oatmeal (uncooked)
¼ teaspoon salt
1 teaspoon ground cinnamon

Cut into the flour mixture with a pastry blender

8 tablespoons unsalted butter

You may need to finish rubbing the butter in with your fingers. Sprinkle the flour-butter mixture evenly over the rhubarb. Combine and sprinkle over all

2 tablespoons water
1 tablespoon fresh lemon juice

Bake in the preheated 350° oven for 30 minutes, or until lightly browned on top. Serve warm or cold, topped with vanilla ice cream.

Makes 12 servings.

Gooseberry Fool

You will need "Boiled" Custard already prepared to make this dessert. Some cooks use only whipping cream, increasing the amount to 1½ cups, and some use 2 cups custard and no cream. I think the combination is best.

Trim the tops and tails from enough gooseberries to make

4 cups trimmed gooseberries

In a heavy saucepan, mix the gooseberries with

1 cup granulated sugar

Cook over medium heat, stirring constantly, until the juices begin to flow. If the pan appears dry, mash some of the berries to get things started. Continue to cook, stirring often, until the berries are soft and most have popped open. Press the cooked berries through a sieve with the back of a wooden spoon to make a purée. Refrigerate the purée until well chilled. About 1 hour before serving, whip until soft peaks form

1 cup whipping (heavy) cream

Gently fold the whipped cream into

1 cup chilled "Boiled" Custard (page 196)

Fold the custard-cream mixture into the chilled gooseberry purée, just until swirled. Do not blend completely. Spoon the swirled mixture into parfait glasses. Chill until ready to serve. Serve with plain sugar cookies.

Makes 6 servings.

Old-fashioned Ice Creams

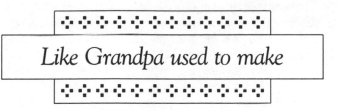

Like Grandpa used to make

Summer isn't really summer without homemade ice cream.

Creamy Custard Ice Cream

Dad's Peach Ice Cream

Pure Vanilla Ice Cream

Easy Chocolate Ice Cream

Fresh Strawberry Ice Cream

Midwestern Cherry Ice Cream

Fresh Banana Ice Cream

Lemon Velvet

Coffee 'n' Cream

Burnt Sugar Ice Cream

Bourbon Ice Cream

Frozen Maple Cream

Peanut Butter Ice Cream

Creamy Custard Ice Cream

I have fond memories of my dad and me making this with a hand-cranked freezer. Always enthusiastic at the start of churning, I readily gave way to his broad shoulders when the cream stiffened and threatened to stop the blades. When the mixture was ready, the dasher was removed and the top replaced. Ice was packed around the can and a burlap sack laid over the top for insulation. This allowed the cream to firm up before serving. As a reward for my labors, I was allowed to lick the fast-melting cream from the pulled dasher blades.

In a heavy saucepan, mix together

1 cup granulated sugar
3 tablespoons unbleached all-purpose flour
¼ teaspoon salt

In a side bowl beat

3 large eggs

Stir into the beaten eggs

3 cups milk

Gradually stir the egg-milk mixture into the contents of the saucepan. Cook over medium heat, stirring constantly, until the mixture thickens slightly, forming a custard base. Do not allow to boil. Remove from the heat. Stir in

1 tablespoon pure vanilla extract

Refrigerate the custard base to chill. Strain the chilled custard base through a sieve and then gradually stir in

2 cups whipping (heavy) cream

Churn-freeze. Remove the churning paddle and cover tightly. Firm in the freezer or by packing in ice for 1 hour before serving. Store leftovers in airtight containers in the freezer.

Makes 2 quarts.

Dad's Peach Ice Cream

Dad used peaches that were home-canned in heavy syrup, but any canned peaches will work.

Drain and finely chop

2 cups canned peaches

Prepare one recipe Creamy Custard Ice Cream (see opposite page). Toward the end of the churning time, add the chopped peaches to the cream. Finish churning.

Makes a little more than 2 quarts.

Pure Vanilla Ice Cream

Pure and simple. It doesn't have to be complicated to be good.

Stir together to dissolve sugar

1 quart half-and-half
1 cup superfine sugar

Stir in

1 cup whipping (heavy) cream
1 tablespoon pure vanilla extract

Churn-freeze. Remove the churning paddle and cover tightly. Firm in the freezer or by packing in ice for 1 hour before serving. Store leftovers in airtight containers in the freezer.

Makes a little more than 1 quart.

Easy Chocolate Ice Cream

Smooth and easy. It'll remind you of the chocolate milk you drank as a kid.

Stir together until blended

2 cups whipping (heavy) cream
2 cups half-and-half
1 can (16 ounces) chocolate syrup
1½ teaspoons pure vanilla extract

Churn-freeze. Remove the churning paddle and cover tightly. Firm in the freezer or by packing in ice for 1 hour before serving. Store leftovers in airtight containers in the freezer.

Makes 1½ quarts.

Fresh Strawberry Ice Cream

This ice cream has fresh-from-the-garden flavor. It takes about 2 cups of whole berries to make 1 cup crushed.

The day before you want to churn your ice cream, stir together in a glass or stainless-steel bowl

1 cup crushed strawberries
1 cup granulated sugar

Cover with plastic and refrigerate. When ready to churn, stir into the berry mixture, in this order

2 cups half-and-half
1 cup whipping (heavy) cream
1 teaspoon pure vanilla extract

Churn-freeze. Remove the churning paddle and cover tightly. Firm in the freezer or by packing in ice for 1 hour before serving. Store leftovers in airtight containers in the freezer.

Makes about 1 quart.

Midwestern Cherry Ice Cream

You need fully ripened pie cherries for this. If you grow your own, watch your crop closely, lest the robins beat you to harvest. It will take about 2 cups pitted cherries to make 1 cup chopped. Use a food processor with a light touch. You don't want a purée.

Using the recipe for Fresh Strawberry Ice Cream (see above) substitute 1 cup finely chopped Montmorency or other "sour" pie cherries for the strawberries. Proceed as before.

Makes about 1 quart.

Fresh Banana Ice Cream

The fresh-banana flavor of this ice cream remains even after it is stored.

In a mixing bowl mash until smooth

3 ripe bananas

Stir in, in this order

1 tablespoon fresh lemon juice
½ cup granulated sugar
¼ cup light corn syrup
1 can (12 ounces) evaporated milk
1 cup milk
1 cup whipping (heavy) cream

Churn-freeze. Remove the churning paddle and cover tightly. Firm in the freezer or by packing in ice for 1 hour before serving. Store leftovers in airtight containers in the freezer.

Makes about 1½ quarts.

Lemon Velvet

This is incredibly smooth for a still-frozen ice cream. The sugar buffers the cream so that it doesn't curdle—it thickens—when the lemon is added.

Stir together gently until the sugar dissolves

2 cups whipping (heavy) cream
2 cups superfine sugar

Gently and gradually stir in, in this order

½ cup strained fresh lemon juice
2 cups half-and-half

Pour into two metal trays and place in the coldest part of your freezer. This will be smooth-frozen without stirring in 3 to 4 hours.

Makes 1½ quarts.

Coffee 'n' Cream

Make subtle variations in the flavor of this ice cream by using "gourmet" beans to make your coffee.

Stir together until the sugar and instant coffee dissolve

1 cup strong, freshly brewed hot coffee
1 teaspoon instant coffee crystals
¾ cup superfine sugar

Chill the coffee mixture. Stir in

3 cups whipping (heavy) cream

Churn-freeze. Remove the churning paddle and cover tightly. Firm in the freezer or by packing in ice for 1 hour before serving. Store leftovers in airtight containers in the freezer.

Makes a little more than 1 quart.

Burnt Sugar Ice Cream

If you're from Kansas, this is an old Kansas recipe. If you're from Missouri, it's an old Missouri favorite—and so forth. I know it sounds like a lot of sugar in the syrup flavoring, but trust me, it will taste just right.

Make one recipe Burnt Sugar Syrup (see page 27). Before you take it off the heat the last time, gradually stir in

2 cups scalded half-and-half

Remove from the heat. In a heavy saucepan beat until smooth

3 large eggs
¼ cup granulated sugar
⅛ teaspoon salt

Gradually stir the hot burnt sugar mixture into the egg mixture. (If you find the skillet heavy to hold in one hand, transfer its contents to a quart measure before you pour.) Cook over medium heat, stirring constantly, until slightly thickened. Be careful not to let it boil, lest it curdle. Remove from the heat. Cool slightly and then refrigerate to chill. Pour through a sieve to be sure it's smooth, and gently stir in

1 cup whipping (heavy) cream

Churn-freeze. Remove the churning paddle and cover tightly. Firm in the freezer or by packing in ice for 1 hour before serving. Store leftovers in airtight containers in the freezer.

Makes about 1½ quarts.

Bourbon Ice Cream

From south of the Mason-Dixon Line, smooooooth ice cream. The bourbon whiskey makes this slow to freeze. Add extra salt to the brine, if you want to speed things up. I keep a small bottle of bourbon in the kitchen, flavored with a floating vanilla bean. If you do the same, you can use it in this ice cream.

In a heavy saucepan, stir together over medium heat just until the sugar dissolves (it doesn't have to get very warm)

2 cups half-and-half
1 cup brown sugar

Refrigerate to chill. Stir into the chilled mixture, in this order

1 cup whipping (heavy) cream
3 tablespoons plain or vanilla-flavored bourbon whiskey

Churn-freeze. Remove the churning paddle and cover tightly. Firm in the freezer or by packing in ice for 1 hour before serving. Good topped with toasted pecans. Store leftovers in airtight containers in the freezer.

Makes a little more than 1 quart.

Frozen Maple Cream

Acid rains are killing some stands of maple trees, making the syrup more precious every year. Let's find an answer to the problem so we can continue to enjoy this delicious ice cream!

Stir together until well blended

**1 cup pure maple syrup
2 cups whipping (heavy) cream
2 cups half-and-half**

Churn-freeze. Remove the churning paddle and cover tightly. Firm in the freezer or by packing in ice for 1 hour before serving. Store leftovers in airtight containers in the freezer. Serve with cookies or pralines—or crumble pralines for garnish.

Makes a little less than 1½ quarts.

Peanut Butter Ice Cream

I like peanut butter any way I can get it, and I love getting it in this ice cream.

In a large bowl place

1 cup creamy peanut butter

Gradually stir into the peanut butter, in this order

**1 can (14 ounces) sweetened condensed milk
1 quart half-and-half
1½ teaspoons pure vanilla extract**

Churn-freeze. Add toward the end of the freezing time (Some freezers have holes for adding nuts while the machine is running. Others have to be stopped for such additions)

1 cup chopped honey-roasted peanuts

Remove the churning paddle and cover tightly. Firm in the freezer or by packing in ice for 1 hour before serving. Store leftovers in airtight containers in the freezer.

Makes about 2 quarts.

Smooth Sherbets

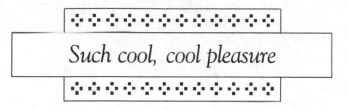

Such cool, cool pleasure

These flavorsome treats will lie on your tongue with light satisfaction. Wonderful any time.

Mabell's Cranberry Ice

Berry Buttermilk Sherbet

Strawberry Sherbet

Fudgy Sherbet

Sour Cream Sherbet

Pineapple Buttermilk Sherbet

Fresh Gooseberry Sherbet

Mabell's Cranberry Ice

Why did I put an ice in the chapter reserved for sherbets? This is sherbetlike, even though our family has always called it an ice. It's my guess that it started out generations ago as a simple ice, and a cook along the way "improved" it with whipping cream. I serve this in individual compotes as a side dish for a holiday turkey dinner, and as a bona fide dessert when the turkey shows up in a casserole.

Simmer in a nonreactive open kettle until all the berries pop

4 cups fresh cranberries
2 cups water

Press the cooked berries through a sieve. Return the sieved berries to the pot. Stir in

2 cups granulated sugar
½ cup light corn syrup

Bring to a gentle boil and cook for 5 minutes, stirring occasionally. Remove from the heat. Stir in

¼ cup fresh lemon juice

Refrigerate to chill. Still-freeze the mixture in metal trays, stirring occasionally with a fork, until it is mushy ice. Whip to soft peaks and then fold into the stirred ice

1 cup whipping (heavy) cream

Freeze until firm. Serve rounded scoops in individual compotes.

Makes 1½ quarts sherbet.

Berry Buttermilk Sherbet

This isn't too sweet, letting the flavor of the berries come through. I prefer blueberries, strawberries, or raspberries. It will take about 4 cups of berries to make 2 cups crushed. I use an old-fashioned potato masher to prepare the fruit. You can use a food processor if you use a light touch and leave some texture.

In a glass or stainless-steel bowl, stir together until the sugar dissolves

2 cups crushed berries
1 cup granulated sugar
1 tablespoon fresh lemon juice

Slowly add, stirring all the while

1 quart buttermilk

Churn-freeze; or still-freeze, stirring often after the ice crystals begin to form. Store leftovers in airtight containers in the freezer.

Makes a little more than 1½ quarts.

Strawberry Sherbet

This is too good to be so easy.

Gently wash and hull

1 quart strawberries

Process them in a blender or food processor just until they form a purée. Rub the purée through a sieve to remove most of the seeds. You should have about 1¾ cups of smooth purée. Stir into the purée

1 tablespoon fresh lemon juice
1 cup granulated sugar

Cover with plastic wrap and refrigerate for 2 hours to chill. Stir the chilled mixture while you slowly pour in

2 cups milk

Churn-freeze. Remove the churning paddle and cover tightly. Firm in the freezer or by packing in ice for 1 hour before serving. Store leftovers in airtight containers in the freezer.

Makes a little more than 1 quart.

Fudgy Sherbet

I think that a fudgy flavor and a sherbet texture make a great combination.

Using a 2-quart container, melt on the stovetop or in a microwave

6 ounces semisweet chocolate morsels

Stir into the melted morsels, in this order, adding the milk 1 cup at a time

1 can (14 ounces) sweetened condensed milk
1 teaspoon pure vanilla extract
4 cups milk

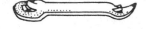

Churn-freeze; or still-freeze, stirring often after ice crystals begin to form. Store leftovers in airtight containers in the freezer.

Makes 2 quarts.

Sour Cream Sherbet

This is slightly tart and very refreshing. A perfect finish for a summer porch supper.

Stir together in a large bowl until smooth

1 cup sour cream
1 cup superfine sugar

Gradually stir in, in this order

3 tablespoons fresh lemon juice
3 cups milk

Churn-freeze. Remove the churning paddle and cover tightly. Firm in the freezer or by packing in ice for 1 hour before serving. Store leftovers in airtight containers in the freezer.

Makes a little more than 1 quart.

Pineapple Buttermilk Sherbet

Although still-frozen and easy to make, this has good old-fashioned flavor from the buttermilk used in the mix. Be sure to read about eggs (page 2) before beginning.

Stir together in a mixing bowl

2 cups buttermilk
⅔ cup granulated sugar
1 can (8 ounces) crushed pineapple, packed in its own juice
2 teaspoons pure vanilla extract

Pour into a 9 x 5-inch loaf-shaped aluminum pan, cover with foil, and freeze until almost firm-frozen, 3 to 5 hours. Stir several times as it freezes. Meanwhile, beat until stiff but not dry

1 large egg white

Remove the mixture from the freezer, transfer to a bowl, and beat until smooth but not thawed. Gently fold in the beaten egg white. Refreeze, covering the pan with foil. If the sherbet is stirred several times during this last freezing, it will have a finer consistency. Store leftovers in airtight containers in the freezer.

Makes a little less than 1 quart.

Fresh Gooseberry Sherbet

I like to make something that cannot be store-bought, and this sherbet fills the bill.

Wash and trim the tops and tails from enough gooseberries to make

8 cups trimmed gooseberries

In a heavy nonreactive saucepan, mix the gooseberries with

2 cups granulated sugar

Cook over medium heat, stirring constantly, until the juices begin to flow. If the pan appears dry, mash some of the berries to get things started. Continue to cook, stirring often, until the berries are soft and most have popped open. Press the cooked berries through a sieve with the back of a wooden spoon to make a purée. Stir into the purée

2 tablespoons fresh lemon juice

Refrigerate the purée to chill thoroughly. After it has chilled, place in a small saucepan

¼ cup cold water

Sprinkle over the cold water to soften the gelatin

1 teaspoon (part of 1 envelope) unflavored gelatin

Heat over low heat, stirring constantly, to dissolve the gelatin. Stir the dissolved gelatin into the chilled gooseberry purée and transfer the gelatinized purée to a metal pan. Cover with foil and freeze until firm, 3 to 5 hours. Stir several times while freezing to break up any large crystals of ice. When frozen, transfer to airtight freezer cartons and store.

Makes about 2 quarts.

Flavored Ices

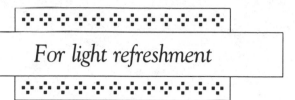

For light refreshment

These combine fruity flavors with icy texture for a refreshing summer treat.

Simple Syrup

Lemon Ice

Orange Ice

Pineapple Ice

Grape Ice

Strawberry Ice

Fresh Peach Ice

Fresh Plum Ice

Fresh Apricot Ice

Watermelon Ice

Cola Slush

Simple Syrup

Make this ahead so it's chilled and ready when you want to make flavored ice.

Stir together in a heavy saucepan over high heat until the sugar dissolves

**4 cups water
2 cups granulated sugar**

Bring to a boil and boil 3 minutes without stirring. Remove from the heat. Cool to room temperature. Refrigerate to chill. If stored in clean glass jars in the refrigerator, it will keep indefinitely.

Makes a little less than 1¼ quarts syrup.

Lemon Ice

This is better than lemonade on a hot summer day.

Stir together until blended

**1 recipe Simple Syrup (see above)
¾ cup fresh lemon juice
½ teaspoon pure lemon extract**

Churn-freeze; or still-freeze, stirring often after the mixture begins to get icy. Freeze until firm. Best eaten before it gets too hard. Store leftovers in airtight containers in the freezer.

Makes about 1½ quarts.

Orange Ice

Here's a trio of ices made from frozen concentrates, giving them the flavor punch they need to stand up to freezing.

Stir together until blended

**1 recipe Simple Syrup (see above)
1 can (12 ounces) frozen orange-juice concentrate, slightly thawed
⅓ cup fresh lemon juice**

Churn-freeze; or still-freeze, stirring often after the mixture begins to get icy. Freeze until firm. Garnish each serving with a sprig of fresh basil.

Makes about 2 quarts.

Pineapple Ice

Substitute 1 can (12 ounces) frozen pineapple-juice concentrate for the orange-juice concentrate in the preceding recipe. Proceed as above.

Makes a little less than 2 quarts.

Grape Ice

Substitute 1 can (12 ounces) frozen grape-juice concentrate for the can of orange-juice concentrate in the Orange Ice recipe above. Increase the lemon juice to ½ cup. Proceed as before.

Makes about 2 quarts.

Strawberry Ice

This captures the very essence of June's strawberry patch. I love it with a summer fruit plate.

Prepare and chill

1 recipe Simple Syrup (see opposite page)

Gently wash and hull

2 quarts strawberries

Process them in a blender or food processor just until they form a purée. Rub the purée through a sieve to remove most of the seeds. You should have about 3½ cups smooth purée. Stir the chilled Simple Syrup into the purée, along with

3 tablespoons fresh lemon juice

Churn-freeze; or still-freeze, stirring often after the mixture begins to get icy. Store leftovers in airtight containers in the freezer.

Makes a little more than 2 quarts.

Fresh Peach Ice

Once, when I was making this, a visitor remarked that anything called an ice could hardly be worth putting his mouth to. I noticed he ate quite a bit before he was through.

Prepare and chill

1 recipe Simple Syrup (see page 246)

Chop and mash, or process in a food processor to form a purée

4 cups peeled, sliced ripe peaches

You should have about 3 cups purée. Stir the chilled Simple Syrup into the purée along with

¼ cup fresh lemon juice

Churn-freeze; or still-freeze, stirring often after the mixture begins to get icy. Store leftovers in airtight containers in the freezer.

Makes a little more than 2 quarts.

Fresh Plum Ice

Substitute peeled, sliced ripe red plums for the peaches in Fresh Peach Ice (above). Proceed as before.

Makes about 2 quarts.

Fresh Apricot Ice

Substitute peeled, sliced ripe apricots for the peaches in Fresh Peach Ice (above). Proceed as before.

Makes about 2 quarts.

Watermelon Ice

This is easier to eat than watermelon, and more refreshing. It will take half of a juicy, ripe 20- to 22-pound melon to make it. Use my primitive method to extract the juice: Hold your hands over a large bowl and squeeze the pulp, a scoopful at a time. Strain the squeezed juice through a sieve to catch any errant seeds and pulp that may drop into the bowl.

In a large bowl, stir together until the sugar is dissolved

6 cups watermelon juice
2 tablespoons fresh lemon juice
1 cup granulated sugar

Churn-freeze; or still-freeze, stirring often after the mixture begins to get icy. Store leftovers in air-tight containers in the freezer.

Makes almost 2 quarts.

Cola Slush

This will freeze solid, but it's best served as slush. Slurpy but good.

Stir together until blended

3 cans (12 ounces each) cola, chilled
3 tablespoons fresh lemon juice
⅓ cup light corn syrup

Churn-freeze until slushy firm, or still-freeze, stirring once every half hour until slushy firm. Serve in tall glasses with long-handled spoons. Leftovers should be frozen as ice cubes and used to chill cola beverages.

Makes about 1½ quarts.

Easy Candies

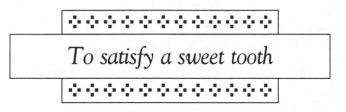

To satisfy a sweet tooth

You can make these in less time than it takes to go shopping. And they're better than what you can buy.

Rocky Road

Cookie Chunk Chocolates

Chocolate Peanut Clusters

Chocolate Raisin Clusters

No Foolin' Fudge

Fast Fudge

Peanut Butter Fudge

Rocky Road

This is the most popular candy I make. You can substitute other nuts, but cashews are best. Some cooks use miniature marshmallows to avoid cutting the larger ones, but cut pieces make the best Rocky Road.

Butter an 8 x 8 x 2-inch glass baking dish. Cut into quarters and have ready

12 large marshmallows

In the top of a double boiler combine

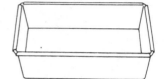

1 pound milk chocolate, broken into chunks
1 teaspoon vegetable oil

Melt over hot, not boiling, water, stirring frequently. Using only one-third to one-half of the melted mixture, pour a thin layer into the prepared pan. Sprinkle evenly with

prepared marshmallows
1½ cups dry-roasted cashews

Gently press the marshmallows and nuts into the bottom layer of chocolate. Pour the remaining chocolate evenly over the top, smoothing the surface with the back of a spoon. Refrigerate until firm. Cut into small squares to serve.

Makes about 1¼ pounds Rocky Road candy.

Cookie Chunk Chocolates

If you hear complaints because your chocolate chip cookies don't have enough chips, turn the tables with this recipe. You can use homemade or purchased cookies, choosing between sugar, butter, and peanut butter. You can choose milk chocolate or semisweet or a combination. For each cup of cookie chunks, melt 6 ounces of chips.

Line 2 large baking sheets with wax paper. Break into small chunks and place in a large bowl

1 package (10 ounces) butter-type peanut butter cookies

Stir together and melt in a double boiler or in a 1-quart glass measure in a microwave

12 ounces semisweet chocolate morsels
11½ ounces milk-chocolate morsels

Pour the melted chocolate over the cookie chunks. Gently stir and fold the mixture to coat the chunks completely with chocolate. Drop by heaping tablespoonfuls onto the prepared baking sheets. Refrigerate for at least 1 hour to firm.

Makes about 30 chocolates.

Chocolate Peanut Clusters

These easy candy clusters are better than store-bought.

Lay a 2-foot-long piece of wax paper on a countertop. In the top of a double boiler over hot, not boiling, water, melt, stirring frequently

6 ounces semisweet chocolate morsels

Shake in a sieve and remove excess salt or crumbs and then stir in

⅞ cup (¾ cup plus 2 tablespoons) dry-roasted peanuts

Drop by rounded teaspoonfuls onto the wax paper. Let stand until firm, at least 1 hour. If the weather is warm, the clusters can be refrigerated to firm.

Makes about 12 clusters.

Chocolate Raisin Clusters

Proceed as for Chocolate Peanut Clusters, substituting ⅞ cup raisins for the peanuts.

Makes about 12 clusters.

No Foolin' Fudge

This easy fudge is as good as Grandma's. No foolin'.

Butter an 8 x 8 x 2-inch glass baking dish. Have all ingredients ready before you start. In a heavy 3-quart saucepan combine

1¾ cup granulated sugar
½ teaspoon salt
1 can (5 ounces) evaporated milk
2 tablespoons unsalted butter

Cook over medium heat, stirring frequently, until the sugar dissolves, the butter melts, and the mixture comes to a boil that can't be stirred down. Boil for 5 minutes, stirring constantly. Remove from the heat and add

12 ounces semisweet chocolate morsels
1½ cups miniature marshmallows
1 teaspoon pure vanilla extract

Stir vigorously until the marshmallows melt. Stir in

1 cup coarsely broken walnuts or pecans

Spoon and scrape into the buttered dish, spreading evenly. Cool in the pan elevated on a wire rack. Cut into squares with a sharp knife.

Makes about 2 pounds fudge.

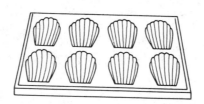

Fast Fudge

This simple recipe makes creamy fudge in a matter of minutes. It's eaten just as fast.

Butter an 8 x 8 x 2-inch glass baking dish. In the top of a double boiler over hot, not boiling, water, melt, stirring frequently

18 ounces semisweet chocolate morsels

When the chocolate is melted, remove from the heat, wiping the bottom of the pan dry. Immediately stir in, in this order

1 can (14 ounces) sweetened condensed milk
1 teaspoon pure vanilla extract
1 cup chopped walnuts

Mix well and spread in the prepared pan. With lightly buttered hands spread and flatten the fudge. Let it stand several hours before cutting.

Makes about 2 pounds fudge.

Peanut Butter Fudge

There's no chocolate here, just peanut butter. Rich and creamy peanut butter.

Butter an 8 x 8 x 2-inch glass baking dish. Combine in a heavy saucepan

2 cups granulated sugar
⅔ cup milk

Cook over medium heat, stirring often, until the sugar is dissolved and the mixture comes to a boil. Continue cooking, without stirring, until the mixture reaches the soft-ball stage (240°F). Remove from the heat and stir in, in this order

1 jar (7 ounces) marshmallow cream
1 jar (18 ounces) crunchy-style peanut butter
1 teaspoon pure vanilla extract

Pour and spread in the prepared pan. Chill for 20 to 30 minutes, or until firm. Cut into squares.

Makes about 1½ pounds fudge.

Confections and Sweetmeats

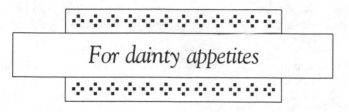

For dainty appetites

These old-fashioned favorites are hard to beat.

Panocha

Pecan Divinity

Creamy Pralines

Brown Sugar Pralines

Vanilla Pralines

Party Mints

Bourbon Balls

Rum Balls

Candied Orange Peel

Candied Grapefruit Peel

Candied Lemon Peel

Panocha

This is brown-sugar candy, sometimes called Penuche. The flavor will remind you of sugary pralines. One taste and my husband is back in his mother's kitchen.

Butter an 8 x 8 x 2-inch glass baking dish. Melt in a heavy saucepan over medium heat

2 tablespoons unsalted butter

Swirl the pan to coat. Place in the butter-coated pan

2 cups light brown sugar
1 cup dark brown sugar
1 cup whipping (heavy) cream
⅛ teaspoon salt

Cook over medium heat, stirring often, until the sugar dissolves and the mixture begins to bubble. Cover and cook for 1 minute to wash down any sugar crystals that may remain on the sides of the pan. Uncover and cook without stirring until it reaches the soft-ball stage (234°F). Remove from the heat and let stand without stirring for 15 minutes. Stir in, in this order

1 teaspoon pure vanilla extract
1 cup chopped pecans

Beat with a wooden spoon until the mixture begins to thicken. Spread in the prepared pan to cool. Cut into squares while still slightly warm.

Makes about 1½ pounds candy.

Pecan Divinity

There are two important things to remember when making this Southern holiday candy: it shouldn't be made on a damp, rainy day; and the syrup has a two-step boiling process. That's about all there is to it. It all goes rather fast, so get everything out before starting.

Butter an 8 x 8 x 2-inch glass baking dish. In a heavy saucepan combine

2¼ cups granulated sugar
⅓ cup water
⅓ cup light corn syrup
⅛ teaspoon salt

Cook and stir over high heat until the sugar dissolves. Reduce the heat to medium. Cover and cook for 1 minute to wash down any sugar crystals from the sides of the pan. Uncover and continue to cook without stirring over medium heat until the syrup reaches the firm-ball stage (249°F). While the syrup cooks, in the large bowl of an electric mixer beat at high speed until soft, almost firm peaks form

2 large egg whites

When the syrup is the right temperature, slowly pour about half of it into the whites, beating all the while at high speed, and taking care not to get syrup on the beaters. Continue beating at low speed while you return the pot of syrup to the heat to cook without stirring until it reaches the hard-ball stage (260°F). It won't take long. Pour the remaining syrup into the beaten whites, beating all the while at high speed. Do not scrape the pan. Continue to beat until the mixture begins to thicken. It may take several minutes. Sprinkle over and fold in

1 teaspooon pure vanilla extract
1 cup chopped pecans

Spread in a prepared dish and allow to cool. Cut into squares while still slightly warm. When completely cool, the pieces should be individually wrapped in plastic wrap, as exposure to air will harden the candy.

Makes about 1 pound fudge.

Creamy Pralines

The secret to making pralines is in knowing how long to beat the cooked mixture before dropping it into patties. If the candy is too thin, it will spread, exposing the nuts. If too thick, it will set up like fudge. Don't worry, you'll get the hang of it.

Cover a countertop, or three baking sheets, with wax paper. Rub a stick of butter over the paper to grease it lightly. In a heavy 3-quart saucepan, combine

1½ cups granulated sugar
1½ cups brown sugar
⅛ teaspoon salt
1 cup evaporated milk

Cook over medium heat, stirring frequently, until the sugar dissolves and the mixture begins to bubble. Cover and cook about 3 minutes to allow steam to wash down any sugar crystals from the sides of the pan. Uncover and stir in

4 tablespoons unsalted butter
1 tablespoon light corn syrup
2 cups pecan halves

Continue to cook over medium heat, stirring constantly, until the mixture reaches the soft-ball stage (about 234°F). Remove from the heat and let stand 5 minutes without stirring, and then stir in

1 teaspoon pure vanilla extract

Beat vigorously with a wooden spoon just until the mixture begins to thicken. Test by dropping one patty. If the mixture spreads too far, exposing all the nuts, you need to beat it a little bit longer. When ready, drop the mixture quickly from a spoon onto the buttered wax paper to form patties, and allow to cool. If the candy becomes too stiff to manage, stir in a few drops of hot water. (If it gets too thick to salvage, press it into a square and call it Praline Fudge.) When it is completely cooled, wrap each patty individually in plastic wrap. *Makes 36 pralines.*

Brown Sugar Pralines

Follow directions for Creamy Pralines (above), using 3 cups brown sugar in place of the two sugars called for. *Makes 36 pralines.*

Vanilla Pralines

Follow directions for Creamy Pralines (above) using 3 cups granulated sugar in place of the sugars called for.

Makes 36 pralines.

Party Mints

Picture these pastel mints together on a silver tray. For the tea table or after-dinner treats.

Cut and have ready 3 pieces wax paper, 12 x 24 inches. In the large bowl of a mixer beat at medium speed until smooth

3 ounces cream cheese
4 tablespoons soft unsalted butter
2 teaspoons peppermint extract

Gradually add, blending well

¼ cup water

Reduce the speed to low and gradually add

2 pounds confectioners' sugar

Scrape the sides of the bowl often with a rubber spatula. If the mixer motor begins to labor, remove the bowl and add the remaining sugar with a wooden spoon. You many need to get your hands into it and knead the last of the sugar in. Divide the mixture into three parts. Leave one part plain. Into one of the other two parts, mix, blending well and using your hands again

2 drops red *or* green food coloring

Blend the other color into the remaining mixture. Keep the parts you are not working with covered with plastic wrap to prevent drying out. Working with one part at a time, shape the mixture into ½-inch balls and place 3 inches apart on one of the pieces of wax paper. Press flat with a flat-bottomed water glass. If the mixture is too sticky to press, let the balls dry for a minute or two before pressing. If it is too sticky to manage, you can sprinkle granulated sugar on the wax paper, and dip the bottom of the glass in sugar before pressing. Lift the edge of the wax paper and gently lift off the mints, transferring them to wire racks to dry. Let dry for at least 1 hour or until the pieces can be moved without distorting their shape. Store in an airtight container, covering the layers with wax paper.

Makes about 2 pounds mints, or 40 of each color.

Bourbon Balls

No baking is required to make these southern sweetmeats for your holiday tables.

Press through a sieve into a large bowl

**1½ cups confectioners' sugar
3 tablespoons cocoa**

Add, in this order, blending well after each addition

**3 cups vanilla-wafer crumbs
1 cup chopped pecans
3 tablespoons light corn syrup
½ cup bourbon whiskey**

Roll pieces of the dough between your hands to form slightly smaller than 1-inch balls. Test the dough's consistency by forming the first ball. Add additional bourbon by the teaspoonful if needed to make the dough come together. Roll the balls in a shallow container filled with

⅓ cup confectioners' sugar

Store in a single layer on wax paper in a tightly closed container. Best if aged a day or two before serving.

Makes 3½ dozen.

Rum Balls

Substitute in the recipe above: 1 teaspoon instant coffee for the 3 tablespoons cocoa, ½ cup dark rum for the ½ cup bourbon whiskey. Proceed as for Bourbon Balls.

Makes 3½ dozen.

Candied Orange Peel

So much better than anything like it you can buy. Adds variety to the tea table or a dessert buffet.

Cut the peel, including the white pith, from

2 oranges

Scrape off any pulp that adheres, and then cut into ¼ x 1½-inch strips. Place the peel in a small (about 1-quart), nonreactive saucepan and cover with cold water. Bring to a full rolling boil, boil 2 minutes, and then pour through a strainer to drain. Repeat 4 or 5 times, or until the peel is tender. In the same saucepan stir together

¼ cup water
½ cup granulated sugar

Cook over medium heat, stirring frequently, until the sugar dissolves. Swirl the pan a couple of times to wash down any sugar on the sides. Add the drained peel. Boil gently until the syrup is absorbed. Stir frequently at first, constantly as the level of the syrup drops, to avoid scorching. Remove from the heat. Line a large baking sheet with wax paper. In a shallow bowl place

¼ cup granulated sugar

When the peel is cool enough to handle, toss, one piece at a time, in the sugar to coat. To avoid sugar buildup on your fingers, use one hand to put the wet peel into the sugar, the other hand to toss and retrieve it. Place the sugared peel on wax paper to dry. This could take as long as 24 hours, depending on the dryness of the air. If covered too soon, the peel will weep. Store in a tightly covered container. Best if used within 3 or 4 days.

Makes about 1½ cups candied peel.

Candied Grapefruit Peel

Substitute 1 grapefruit for the 2 oranges. Proceed as for Candied Orange Peel (opposite).

Makes about 1¼ cups candied peel.

Candied Lemon Peel

Substitute 3 lemons for the 2 oranges. Proceed as for Candied Orange Peel (opposite).

Makes about 1¼ cups candied peel.

Sweet Beverages

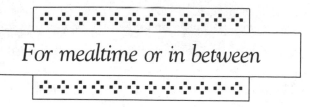

For mealtime or in between

Most of these are summer coolers for lazing in hammock or porch swing, with a couple of cups of warm thrown in to help you out of the cold.

Limeade

Black Cow

'Nilla Milkshake

Hot Cocoa

Iced Coffee

Hot Buttered Rum

Limeade

This was my father-in-law's specialty for cooling off a warm day. He made each glass individually, keeping it up until everyone was satisfied.

In the bottom of a 12-ounce glass, stir together until sugar dissolves

juice of 1 lime
1½ to 3 tablespoons superfine sugar, according to taste

Fill the glass with small ice cubes or crushed ice. Pour to the top

low-sodium sparkling water

Stir well. Float a twist of

zest of lime

Makes 1 glass limeade.

Black Cow

After a hot set of tennis or a round of golf, there's nothing like a black cow.

In a 12-ounce glass, stir together until smooth

1 scoop vanilla ice cream
1 tablespoon chocolate syrup

Continue to stir as you pour to the top

root beer

Float

1 scoop vanilla ice cream

Serve with a long-handled spoon.

Makes 1 black cow.

'Nilla Milkshake

I was never keen about giving my kids chocolate every day. So, when they balked at drinking milk, I made a 'nilla milkshake.

In the bottom of a 12-ounce glass, stir together until smooth

2 scoops vanilla ice cream
1 teaspoon pure vanilla extract

Continue to stir as you pour to the top

ice-cold milk

Makes 1 milkshake.

Hot Cocoa

After you and the kids have built a snow fort, hot cocoa will warm everyone up.

In a heavy saucepan, stir together

⅔ cup cocoa
⅔ cup granulated sugar
pinch salt, optional

Stir in

⅔ cup water

Cook over medium heat, stirring occasionally, until the mixture comes to a boil. Stir in

5½ cups milk

Heat to just under boiling. Remove from the heat. Stir in

½ teaspoon pure vanilla extract

Pour into heavy pottery mugs. Float in each mug

1 large marshmallow

Makes 4 mugs hot cocoa.

Iced Coffee

It's funny—I wouldn't think of putting cream or sugar in my hot coffee.

In the bottom of a 12-ounce heatproof glass stir together until the sugar dissolves

¾ cup strong hot coffee
1 tablespoon granulated sugar, or to taste

Fill the glass with ice cubes. Fill with additional coffee, if needed, leaving just a little room for stirring in cream. Stir in

2 tablespoons whipping (heavy) cream, or to taste

Makes 1 glass iced coffee.

Hot Buttered Rum

If Hot Cocoa is not your style, and you're not the designated driver, perhaps you'd like this Early American nostrum.

Heat an 8-ounce mug by pouring it full of hot water and then pouring out the water. Stir together in the warmed mug

2 teaspoons confectioners' sugar
1 tablespoon unsalted butter
¼ cup rum
¼ cup boiling water

Fill with

boiling water

Stir well, Dust the top with

a dash of nutmeg

Serve with cinnamon swizzle sticks.

Makes 1 serving.

Special Sauces

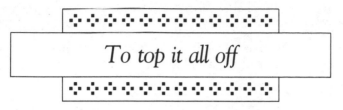

Many of the recipes have a sauce included, because I thought that would be easier for both of us. Anything that didn't fit into that format you will find here.

Sweetened Whipped Cream

Chocolate Whipped Cream

Fast Fudge Sauce

Peanut-Butter Fudge Sauce

Amber Sauce

Pineapple Sauce

Tart Lemon Sauce

Vanilla Sauce

Browned-Butter Rum Sauce

Browned-Butter Bourbon Sauce

Brandied Peaches

Montmorency Cherry Sauce

Hard Sauce

Vinegar Sauce

Sweetened Whipped Cream

Good for a dessert sauce or a soft cake filling. Be sure that bowl, beaters, and cream are chilled before beginning.

If using an electric mixer, use the small bowl. Chill the bowl and beaters for at least 2 hours before beating the cream. Place in the chilled bowl

1 cup whipping (heavy) cream
½ teaspoon pure vanilla extract
2 tablespoons confectioners' sugar, pressed through a sieve

Beat at medium-high speed until the cream begins to thicken. Lower the speed of the mixer and watch carefully. Overbeating will give the cream an undesirable buttery texture. You want the cream to mound into soft peaks. For best control, remove from the mixer early and finish beating with a wire whisk. Refrigerate until ready to use.

Makes about 2 cups whipped cream.

Chocolate Whipped Cream

Using the recipe for Sweetened Whipped Cream (above), omit the vanilla and press through the sieve with the confectioners' sugar

1 tablespoon cocoa

Makes about 2 cups whipped cream.

Fast Fudge Sauce

The quickest sauce is made by simply melting semisweet chocolate, milk chocolate, or a combination, and pouring it warm over ice cream. For something a little more complicated, try this. It will remind you of hot fudge at the local soda fountain.

Place in the top of a double boiler

6 ounces semisweet chocolate morsels
1 cup miniature marshmallows
¼ cup half-and-half

Cook over simmering water, stirring constantly, until smooth. Serve immediately over ice cream. Refrigerate leftovers. May be reheated in the top of a double boiler.

Makes about 1 cup sauce.

Peanut-Butter Fudge Sauce

Try this on your next ice cream sundae.

In a heavy saucepan, stir together over medium heat until smooth

6 ounces semisweet chocolate morsels
½ cup creamy peanut butter
½ cup half-and-half

Serve warm over ice cream. Top with peanuts.

Makes about 1½ cups sauce.

Amber Sauce

This has a butterscotch flavor. Great on steamed graham pudding or squares of unfrosted cake.

In a heavy saucepan melt over low heat

4 tablespoons unsalted butter

Stir in, in this order

1 cup light brown sugar
⅓ cup light corn syrup
⅓ cup half-and-half
⅛ teaspoon ground nutmeg
pinch salt

Cook over medium-high heat, stirring constantly, until the mixture begins to boil. Continue to cook and stir for 1 minute. Remove from the heat. Stir off heat until bubbling stops. Gently stir in

1 teaspoon pure vanilla extract

Serve warm.

Makes about 1 cup sauce.

Pineapple Sauce

This easy sauce is good on ice cream, sponge cake, or cheesecake.

Mix together in a small nonreactive saucepan

4 tablespoons granulated sugar
1 tablespoon cornstarch

Stir in

1 can (8 ounces) crushed pineapple, packed in its own juice

Cook over medium heat, stirring constantly, until the sauce thickens and loses its cloudy appearance. Remove from the heat. Stir in

1 teaspoon fresh lemon juice

Cool to room temperature. Cover and chill to store.

Makes about 1 cup.

Tart Lemon Sauce

This is excellent on gingerbread, cottage pudding, steamed puddings, and bread puddings. One of my favorite sauces.

In a heavy saucepan stir together, pressing out any lumps with the back of a spoon

1 cup granulated sugar
2 tablespoons cornstarch
⅛ teaspoon salt

Gradually add, stirring until smooth

¼ cup cold water

Stir in

1 cup boiling water

Cook over medium heat, stirring constantly, until thickened. Remove from the heat. Gently stir in, in this order

grated zest of 1 lemon
⅓ cup fresh lemon juice
2 tablespoons soft unsalted butter

Serve warm. Store leftovers in the refrigerator. Reheat over low or medium heat, stirring often.

Makes almost 2 cups sauce.

Vanilla Sauce

This has a richer than whipped cream flavor that is delicious.

Combine in a heavy saucepan

4 tablespoons unsalted butter
½ cup granulated sugar
pinch salt
1 cup whipping (heavy) cream

Cook over medium heat, stirring constantly, until the butter melts, the sugar dissolves, and the mixture is smooth. Stir together and then stir into the cream mixture

¼ cup cold water
1 tablespoon cornstarch

Continue to cook and stir until the mixture thickens. Remove from the heat. Gently stir in

1 teaspoon pure vanilla extract

Serve warm or cold.

Makes 2 cups.

Browned-Butter Rum Sauce

Substitute ¼ cup dark rum for the bourbon whiskey in Browned-Butter Bourbon Sauce (page 274). Proceed as before.

Makes 1 cup sauce.

Browned-Butter Bourbon Sauce

Pour this "spiked" sugar sauce over poundcake à la mode.

In a heavy saucepan melt

8 tablespoons unsalted butter

Cook over medium heat, stirring constantly, until the butter is a delicate amber-brown. Remove from the heat. It may continue to color off heat. Stir together and then stir in

1 cup light brown sugar
¼ teaspoon ground cinnamon
¼ teaspoon ground nutmeg

Cook over medium heat, stirring constantly, just until smooth. Do not overcook. Remove from the heat. Avert your face (it may sputter and steam) and add, stirring until smooth

¼ cup bourbon whiskey

Serve warm.

Makes 1 cup sauce.

Brandied Peaches

We love this on vanilla ice cream.

In a glass or stainless-steel bowl, stir together, using a stainless-steel spoon, until all the sugar has turned to juice

4 cups peeled, sliced fully-ripe peaches
¾ cup granulated sugar
¾ cup light brown sugar

Stir in

¾ cup peach or apricot brandy

Transfer to a loosely covered glass jar. An apothecary jar is perfect. Stir once a day. This can be used after 1 day, but improves with aging. After 7 days, refrigerate any remaining peaches.

Makes a little more than 1 quart brandied peaches.

Montmorency Cherry Sauce

The juiciness of fresh pie cherries will vary from year to year. Instead of a precise amount of thickening, I suggest a slurry of cornstarch and water, to be added to suit the liquid in your pot.

Stir together in a heavy saucepan

3 cups pitted Montmorency or other "sour" pie cherries
1 cup granulated sugar

Cook over medium-high heat, stirring constantly. First the mixture will be dry, then the juices will flow. Continue to cook, stirring, until the cherries are cooked through and the juice is boiling. Stir together and then gradually stir in, until the desired thickness is reached (you may not need all of it)

½ cup cold water
3 tablespoons cornstarch

Remove from the heat. Stir in

1 tablespoon soft unsalted butter

Serve warm or cold.

Makes about 2 cups sauce.

Hard Sauce

This is the classic sauce for steamed puddings.

Beat until soft and fluffy

8 tablespoons unsalted butter

Stir through a sieve, then gradually beat into the butter

1½ cups confectioners' sugar

Blend in

1 teaspoon pure vanilla extract or 1 tablespoon brandy

Chill until ready to use.

Makes about 1½ cups sauce.

Vinegar Sauce

This seductive sauce is good on squares of gingerbread or unfrosted spice cake.

In a small saucepan combine

1 cup water
½ cup raisins

Over high heat, bring to a boil, then turn down the heat to low. Cover and cook for 5 minutes to plump the raisins. Remove from the heat and uncover. In a large nonreactive saucepan stir together, pressing out any lumps with the back of a spoon

½ cup granulated sugar
¼ cup brown sugar
1 tablespoon cornstarch
pinch salt (about ¹⁄₁₆ teaspoon)
¼ teaspoon ground cinnamon

Stir in, in this order

¼ cup cider vinegar
cooked raisin mixture

Cook over medium heat, stirring constantly, until thickened and translucent. Remove from the heat. Stir in until melted

2 tablespoons unsalted butter

Serve warm.

Makes 1½ cups sauce.

Epilogue

It's time to get up on my soap box. Anyone who has talked to me since I started on this project knows what's coming.

Although I have hundreds of inherited recipes, there are many that were missed. I wish now that I had asked Aunt Delta for her special lemon pie. I wish I knew how Grandma Nachtigal made her pluma moos. And I wish I had watched my own mother more closely when she was whipping up special things for the family. I know this has happened to others as well. So don't wait until tomorrow to gather together favorite family recipes. Even if you have to visit the cook to watch something made, writing everything down as it is done. Do it now.

If your family has regular reunions, use those occasions to collect. You might produce a reunion cookbook for the benefit of all. And don't neglect your own kitchen. You don't have to cook "old-fashioned" to make things the younger generation loves. Make a small cookbook of their favorites for them to cherish.

And, above all, enjoy!

MARILYN

Bibliography

In addition to the older and community cookbooks that I cherish, I have listed some newer titles that you might enjoy. Out-of-print titles should be located through your local library system.

All About Home Baking. New York: General Foods Corporation, 1933.

Alter, JoAnne, editor. *Family Circle All-Time Baking Favorites.* New York: New York Times Company, 1974.

American Heritage Editors. *The American Heritage Cookbook.* American Heritage Publishing, 1964.

Anderson, Jean, and Hanna, Elaine. *The Doubleday Cookbook, Complete Contemporary Cooking.* Garden City, NY: Doubleday, 1975.

Bailey, Lee. *Lee Bailey's Country Desserts.* New York: Potter, 1988.

Bateman, Mary Michael, editor. *St. Paul's 75th Anniversary Cookbook.* Danville, IL: St. Paul Church, 1988.

Beard, James. *James Beard's American Cookery.* Boston and Toronto: Little, Brown, 1972.

Beery, Lydia Ann. *Mennonite Maid Cookbook.* Harrisonburg, VA: Park View Press, 1971.

Berolzheimer, Ruth, editor. *The American Woman's Cook Book,* revised edition. Garden City, NY: Garden City Publishing, 1955.

Blair, Bevelyn. *Country Cakes.* Columbus, GA: Blair of Columbus, 1984.

Blakely, Lynn, editor. *A Taste of Aloha.* Honolulu: The Junior League of Honolulu, 1983.

Bodger, Lorraine. *Great American Cakes.* New York: Warner Books, 1987.

————, *Great American Cookies.* New York: Warner Books, 1985.

The Boston Symphony Cookbook. Boston: Houghton Mifflin, 1983.

Bowers, Lessie. *Plantation Recipes.* New York: Robert Sepeller & Sons, 1959.

Burpee, Lois. *Lois Burpee's Gardener's Companion and Cookbook.* New York: Harper & Row, 1983.

Campbell's Great American Cookbook. New York: Random House, 1984.

Carson, Jane. *Colonial Virginia Cookery.* Williamsburg: Colonial Williamsburg, Inc., 1968.

Claiborne, Craig. *Craig Claiborne's Southern Cooking.* New York: Times Books, 1957–1987.

————, editor. *New York Times Cook Book.* New York: Harper & Row, 1961.

Cohen, Ben, and Greenfield, Jerry. *Ben & Jerry's Homemade Ice Cream & Dessert Book.* New York: Workman Publishing, 1987.

Cohen, Marlyn. *After All.* New York: Funk & Wagnall's, 1969.

Collection of Favorite Recipes. Rankin, IL: Merry Circle of the Evangelical Lutheran Grace Church, 1944.

Colquitt, Harriet Ross, editor. *The Savannah Cook Book, a Collection of Old Fashioned Receipts from Colonial Kitchens.* New York: Farrar and Rinehart, 1933.

The Cook County Cook Book. Chicago: Associated College Women Workers, 1912.

The Cook's Book. Chicago: Jaques Manufacturing Co., 1935.

Cotton Country Cooking. Decatur, AL: Decatur Junior Service League, 1972.

Crocker, Betty (pseud.). *Betty Crocker's Baking Classics.* New York: Random House, 1979.

Cunningham, Marion. *The Fannie Farmer Baking Book.* New York: Alfred A. Knopf, 1984.

Dalsass, Diana. *Miss Mary's Down-home Cooking.* New York: NAL Books, 1984.

Darden, Norma Jean, and Darden, Carole. *Spoonbread and Strawberry Wine: Recipes and Reminiscences of a Family.* Garden City, NY: Doubleday, 1978.

DeBoth, Jessie M. *The Home Makers' Cooking School Cook Book.* Chicago: Home Makers' Schools of Chicago, Illinois, 1925.

Dickinson, Maude. *When Meals Were Meals.* New York: Thomas Y. Crowell, 1967.

Ellis, Audrey, and Caviani, Mabel. *Farmhouse Kitchen.* Chicago: Henry Regnery Company, 1973.

Family Circle Editors. *Delicious Desserts.* New York: Times Books, 1984.

Farm Journal Food Editors. *Great Home Cooking in America, Heirloom Recipes Treasured for Generations.* Garden City, NY: Doubleday, 1976.

Farmer, Fannie Merritt. *The Boston Cooking-School Cook Book,* revised edition. Boston: Little, Brown, 1923.

The Fifty States Cookbook. Chicago: Culinary Arts Institute, 1977.

Fobel, Jim. *Jim Fobel's Old-Fashioned Baking Book.* New York: Ballantine Books, 1987.

Freehling, Joan, editor. *Noteworthy: A Collection of Recipes from the Ravinia Festival.* Highland Park, IL: Noteworthy Publications, 1986.

Fussell, Betty. *I Hear America Cooking.* New York: Viking, 1986.

Gaspero, Josh. *Hershey's 1934 Cookbook,* revised edition. Hershey, PA: Hershey Foods Corporation, 1971.

Gillum, Mrs. Charles J. and Hadley, Mrs. Robert V., editors. *Sunflower Sampler.* Wichita: Junior League of Witchita, 1983.

Good, Phyllis Pellman, and Pellman, Rachel Thomas, editors. *Cookies.* Lancaster, PA: Good Books, 1982.

———. *Desserts.* Lancaster, PA: Good Books, 1983.

———. *From Amish and Mennonite Kitchens.* Intercourse, PA: Good Books, 1984.

Greene, Bert. *Honest American Fare.* Chicago: Contemporary Books, 1981.

Heatter, Maida. *Maida Heatter's Book of Great American Desserts.* New York: Alfred A Knopf. 1985.

Helton, Ginger, and Van Riper, Susan, editors. *Hermitage Hospitality.* Nashville: Aurora Publishers, 1970.

Hewitt, Jean. *The New York Times Southern Heritage Cookbook.* New York: G. P. Putman's Sons, 1976.

Hirsch, Sylvia Balser. *Miss Grimble Presents Delicious Desserts*. New York: NAL, 1983.

The Hoopeston Cook Book. Hoopeston, IL: The First Presbyterian Church Young Women's Missionary Society, 1930.

Hubbard Trail Country Club: 50th Anniversary Cookbook. Hoopeston/Rossville, IL: Ladies Golf Association, 1975.

Hutchison, Ruth. *The New Pennsylvania Dutch Cook Book*. New York: Harper & Row, 1958.

Johnson, Ronald. *The American Table*. New York: William Morrow, 1984.

Jones, Evan. *American Food, the Gastronomic Story*. New York: E. P. Dutton, 1974, 1975.

Kent, Louise Andrews. *Mrs. Appleyard's Kitchen*. Boston: Houghton Mifflin, 1942.

Kluger, Marilyn. *The Wild Flavor*. Los Angeles: Jeremy P. Tarcher, 1984.

Knox, Gerald, editor. *Better Homes and Gardens All-Time Favorite Recipes*. Des Moines, IA: Meredith Corporation, 1979.

————. *Better Homes and Gardens Classic American Recipes*. Des Moines, IA: Meredith Corporation, 1982.

Kuempel, Sheryl, and Cateora, Nancy, editors. *The Colorado Cook Book*. Boulder: University of Colorado Women's Club and Friends of the Library, 1981.

Lewis, Edna. *The Taste of Country Cooking*. New York: Alfred A Knopf, 1976.

Look What We've Cooked Up! St. Elizabeth Junior Auxiliary Cookbook. Danville, IL: St. Elizabeth Junior Auxiliary, 1980.

Lumbra, Elaine, editor. *The Hoosier Cookbook*. Bloomington, IN: Indiana University Press, 1976.

Lutes, Della T. *The Country Kitchen*. Boston: Little, Brown, 1937.

Manning, Elise W., editor. *Family Favorites from Country Kitchens*. Garden City, NY: Doubleday, 1973.

Masterton, Elsie. *Blueberry Hill Cookbook*. New York: Thomas Y. Crowell, 1959.

McBride, Mary Margaret. *Mary Margaret McBride's Harvest of American Cooking*. New York: Putnam, 1957.

McCullough, Frances, editor. *Holiday Home Cooking: Favorite Recipes from the Members of the Cooking & Crafts Club*. New York: Cooking & Crafts Club, 1986.

McCully, Helen and Noderer, Eleanor. *Just Desserts*. New York: Ivan Obolensky, 1961.

Meade, Martha. *Recipes from the Old South*. New York: Holt, Rinehart and Winston, 1961.

Mickler, Ernest Matthew. *White Trash Cooking*. Berkeley, CA: Ten Speed Press, 1986.

Midwest Old Threshers Cookbook. Mt. Pleasant, IA: Midwest Old Threshers Association, 1987.

Miller, Amy Bess, and Fuller, Persis Wellington, editors. *The Best of Shaker Cooking*. New York: Macmillan, 1970.

Mrs. William Vaughn Moody's Cook-book. New York and London: Scribner's, 1931.

Nichols, Nell B., editor. *Homemade Candy*. Garden City, NY: Doubleday, 1970.

———. *Informal Entertaining Country Style*. Garden City, NY: Doubleday, 1973.

Ojakangas, Beatrice. *Great Old-Fashioned American Desserts*. New York: E. P. Dutton, 1987.

Paddleford, Clementine. *The Best in American Cooking*. New York: Scribner's, 1970.

Page, Linda Garland, and Wigginton, Eliot, editors. *The Foxfire Book of Appalachian Cookery*. New York: E. P. Dutton, 1984.

Park Tudor Treasures. Indianapolis: The Park Tudor Mothers' Association, 1982.

Perl, Lila. *Red-Flannel Hash and Shoo-fly Pie, American Regional Foods and Festivals*. Cleveland and New York: World Publishing, 1965.

Piercy, Caroline B. *The Shaker Cookbook, Not by Bread Alone*. New York: Weathervane Books, 1986.

Pillsbury, Ann (pseud.), editor. *Best of the Bake-Off Collection*. Chicago: Consolidated Book Publishers, 1959.

Pope, Antoinette, and Pope, François. *Antoinette Pope School Cook Book*, revised edition. New York: Macmillan, 1953.

Practical Recipes for the Housewife. Chicago: Chicago Evening American, date unknown.

Presbyterian Cook Book. Jefferson City, MO: Presbyterian Women's Association, 1956.

The Pride of Peoria. Peoria, IL: Junior League of Peoria, 1982.

Purdy, Susan G. *As Easy As Pie*. New York: Atheneum, 1984.

Randle, Bill. *Plain Cooking*. New York: New York Times Book Co., 1974.

Recipe Roundup. La Salle, IL: Radio Station WLPO, 1955.

Recipes from Miss Daisy's. Franklin, Tennessee: Miss Daisy's Tearoom, 1978.

The Ridgefield Cook Book. Ridgefield, Connecticut: The Ridgefield Thrift Shop, 1959.

Roberson, John, and Roberson, Marie. *American Recipes Cookbook*. Englewood Cliffs, New Jersey: Prentice-Hall, 1957.

Rodack, Jaine, editor. *Forgotten Recipes: from the Magazines You Loved and the Days You Remember*. Memphis: Wimmer Brothers Books, 1981.

Rombauer, Irma S. and Becker, Marion Rombauer. *Joy of Cooking*. Indianapolis and New York: Bobbs-Merrill, 1952.

Rowe, Joan, editor. *My Cup Runneth Over*. Omaha: United Methodist Women, 1977.

Schrock, Johnny, editor. *"Wonderful Good Cooking" from Amish Country Kitchens*. Scottsdale, PA: Herald Press, 1974.

The Second Hoopeston Cook Book. Hoopeston, IL: Cross and Circle Guild of the Universalist Church, 1950.

Seranne, Ann, editor. *The General Federation of Women's Clubs Cook Book: America Cooks*. New York: Putnam, 1967.

The Settlement Cook Book. New York: Simon & Schuster, 1976.

Shanks, Laura E., editor. *The Farmer's Guide Cookbook*. Huntington, IN: Guide Publishing, 1927.

Showalter, Mary Emma. *Mennonite Community Cookbook*. New York: Holt, Rinehart and Winston, 1957.

Shuck, Edith G., editor. *The Chicago Daily News Cook Book*. Chicago: Chicago Daily News, 1930.

Silverton, Nancy. *Desserts*. New York: Harper & Row, 1986.

Smith, Jeff. *The Frugal Gourmet Cooks American*. New York: William Morrow, 1987.

Sorosky, Marlene. *The Dessert Lover's Cookbook*. New York: Harper & Row, 1985.

The Southern Heritage Cakes Cookbook. Birmingham, AL: Oxmoor House, 1983.

The Southern Heritage Company's Coming Cookbook. Birmingham, AL: Oxmoor House, 1983.

The Southern Heritage Just Desserts Cookbook. Birmingham, AL: Oxmoor House, 1984.

Southern Sideboards. Jackson, MS: Junior League of Jackson, 1978.

Sturges, Lena, editor. *Country Cooking*. New York: Galahad Books, 1974.

Taber, Gladys. *Gladys Taber's Stillmeadow Cook Book*. Philadelphia and New York: J. B. Lippincott, 1965.

Teeter Tottery Cookery. Milford, IL: Milford Junior Woman's Club, 1978.

The Thirteen Colonies Cookbook. New York: Praeger Publishers, 1975.

Time-Life Editors. *Classic Desserts*. Alexandria, VA: Time-Life Books, 1980.

Tried and True Recipes. Paxton, IL: Women of the United Presbyterian Church, 1913.

Turgeon, Charlotte. *The Saturday Evening Post All-American Cookbook*. Indianapolis: Curtis Publishing Company, 1981.

Truax, Carol, editor. *Ladies' Home Journal Dessert Cookbook*. Garden City, NY: Doubleday, 1964.

Vance, Melinda M., editor. *Connecticut à la Carte*. West Hartford, CT: Connecticut à la Carte, 1982.

Vaughn, Beatrice. *Yankee Hill-Country Cooking*. Brattleboro, VT: Stephen Greene Press, 1963.

Villas, James. *American Taste*. New York: Arbor House, 1982.

Voltz, Jeanne A. *The Flavor of the South*. Garden City, NY: Doubleday, 1977.

Wakefield, Ruth Graves. *Toll House Tried and True Recipes*. New York: Dover, 1977.

Ward, Patricia A. *Farm Journal's Best-Ever Pies*. Philadelphia: Farm Journal, 1981.

Watts, Edith and Watts, John. *Jesse's Book of Creole & Deep South Recipes*. New York: Viking, 1954.

White, Jeanette G., editor. *The Heartland Cookbook: In the Illinois Tradition*. Illinois Home Economics Association. 1975.

Who's Cooking What in Illinois. New York: Who's Cooking What, 1978.

Wilson, Jose. *American Cooking: The Eastern Heartland*. New York: Time-Life Books, 1971.

Winners: Winning Recipes from the Junior League of Indianapolis. Indianapolis: JLI Publications, 1985.

Woman's Day Editors. *Woman's Day Collector's Cook Book*, revised edition. New York: Simon and Schuster, 1973.

Yankee Magazine Editors. *The Yankee Magazine Cookbook*. New York: Harper & Row, 1981.

Yockelson, Lisa. *Country Pies: A Seasonal Sampler.* New York: Harper & Row, 1988.

Zelienka, R.D. and Yoder, E.F., editors. *From Heart to Hearth: A Collection of Amish Recipes & Folklore.* Coloma, WI: Especially for You, 1986.

Zenker, Hazel G. *Cake Bakery: A Book of Recipes.* Philadelphia and New York: M. Evans and Company, 1973.

Index

Alcohols, about, 4–5
Alice's apple dumplings, 224
Almond blancmange, 198
Amber sauce, 271
Ambrosia, southern, 221
Angel food (cake)
  chocolate, 39
  heavenly, 41
  raspberry, 93
Apple(s)
  about, 4
  dumplings, Alice's, 224
  impromptu, 228
  pie
    American, 106
    deep delicious, 159
    mock, 153
    Schnitz, 154
Applesauce
  charlotte, 226
  pie, country, 152
  unseasoned, 226
Apricot
  ice, fresh, 248
  pie, dried, 148
  sauce, 211
Aunt Jackie's graham pudding, 214

Baking powder, about, 3
Balls
  bourbon, 262
  rum, 262
Banana
  cake, layer, 22
  cream pie, my best, 137
  ice cream, fresh, 235
Bars
  lemon, Jeanette's, 172
  peanut buster, 174
Berry buttermilk sherbet, 240
Beverages
  black cow, 266
  hot buttered rum, 268
  hot cocoa, 267
  iced coffee, 268
  limeade, 266
  'nilla milkshake, 267
Biscuit topping for cobbler, 156

Blackberry cobbler with soft butter sauce,
  fresh, 160
Black cow, 266
Black-walnut buttercream cake, 28
Black-walnut buttercream frosting, 29
Blancmange
  almond, 198
  old-fashioned, 198
  orange, 199
Blondies, 176
Blueberry(-ies)
  buckle with blueberry sauce, 222
  pie
    cold, 111
    fresh, 110
Bourbon
  balls, 262
  ice cream, 237
Brandied peaches, 274
Bread and butter pudding, 210
Browned-butter bourbon sauce, 274
Browned-butter rum sauce, 273
Brownie(s)
  buttercream, 175
  saucepan, 174
Brown sugar cookies, 184
Brown sugar pralines, 260
Buckle, blueberry, with blueberry sauce,
  222
Burnt sugar
  buttercream icing, 27
  cake, 26
  ice cream, 236
  syrup, 27
Butter(ed)
  about, 2
  and bread pudding, 210
  browned
    bourbon sauce, 274
    rum sauce, 273
  cakes, to make perfect, 8
  cookies, nutmeg, 183
  pecan
    cake, toasted, 32
    frosting, toasted, 32
  rum, hot, 268
Buttercream
  brownie, 175

Butter(ed) (cont.)
    cake, black-walnut, 28
    frosting, black-walnut, 29
    icing, burnt sugar, 27
Buttermilk
    about, 2
    cake
        lemon, 61
        white, 62
    pie, homestead, 130
    sherbet
        berry, 240
        pineapple, 243
Butterscotch cream pie, 138

Cake(s). See also Cheesecake; Fruitcake
    angel food. See Angel food
    to bake, 9
    butter, to make perfect, 8
    buttermilk
        lemon, 61
        white, 62
    carrot, California, 88
    chiffon, classic, 43
    chocolate. See Chocolate—cake
    to cool, 9–10
    crazy, 89
    crumb, Grandma Martha's, 60
    disappearing, 88
    foam, about, 9
    French-cream, 36
    to frost, 10
    gingerbread, hot-water, 68
    jelly roll, old-fashioned, 76
    layer, 15–33
        banana, 22
        black-walnut buttercream,
            28
        burnt sugar, 26
        caramel, hurry-up, 24
        chocolate, mother's easy, 20
        chocolate angel food, 39
        coconut, fresh, 16
        company dessert cake, 46
        devilish dump, 52
        Illinois jam, 30
        orange, Golden State, 58
        raspberry cream, 44
        rum-flavored spice, 56
        sour cream chocolate, 54
        toasted-butter-pecan, 32
    maple mousse, 94
    mayonnaise
        chocolate, 68
        lemon, 70
    mystery, 71
    persimmon-pecan picnic, 84
    pineapple upside-down, 74

Cakes (cont.)
    poundcake
        sour cream, 64
        traditional, 78
    pudding
        fudge, 217
        lemon, 204
    rotation, 66
    sheet, Prairie State, 82
    spice
        meringue-topped, 83
        pumpkin, 86
    sponge, light milk, 36
    super sundae, 90
    tipsy parson, 96
    toasted-butter-pecan, 32
California carrot cake, 88
Candied grapefruit peel, 263
Candied lemon peel, 263
Candied orange peel, 262
Candies and confections
    about, 12–13
    bourbon balls, 262
    candied grapefruit peel, 263
    candied lemon peel, 263
    candied orange peel, 262
    chocolate peanut clusters, 253
    cookie chunk chocolates, 252
    fast fudge, 255
    mints, party, 261
    no foolin' fudge, 254
    panocha, 258
    peanut butter fudge, 255
    pecan divinity, 259
    pralines
        brown sugar, 260
        creamy, 260
        vanilla, 261
    rocky road, 252
    rum balls, 262
Caramel
    cake, hurry-up, 24
    frosting, hurry-up, 25
Carrot
    cake, California, 88
    pudding, Mabell's, 215
Charlotte, applesauce, 226
Cheesecake
    perfect, 48
    quick refrigerator, 99
Cherry(-ies)
    cobbler, 157
    ice cream, midwestern, 234
    pie
        deep-dish, 162
        sour, 115
    pudding, 208
    sauce, Montmorency, 275

Chess pie, southern, 124
Chiffon cake, classic, 43
Chocolate(s). *See also* Fudge
  angel food, 39
  cake
    icebox, 92
    mayonnaise, 68
    mother's easy, 20
    mousse, 49
    sour cream, 54
  coating, for French cream cake, 38
  cookie chunk, 252
  cookies
    chocolate chip, absolutely, 169
    drops, 166
    wafers, 191
  frosting
    easy, 21
    sour cream, 55
  ice cream, easy, 233
  melting, 7–8
  peanut clusters, 253
  pecan pie, chocolate lover's, 122
  pie
    cream, old-fashioned, 134
    silk, 139
  pudding, stirred, 196
  raisin clusters, 253
  rocky road, 252
  whipped cream, 270
Cinnamon syrup, 225
Cobbler
  biscuit topping for, 156
  blackberry, fresh, with soft butter sauce,
    160
  cherry, 157
  curried fruit, 160
  peach, 156
  rhubarb, rich, 158
  strawberry, 158
Cocoa
  about, 3
  fudge frosting, 63
  hot, 267
  icing, 82
Coconut
  cake, fresh, 16
  filling, 17
  fresh, to prepare, 17
  macaroons, 170
  milk, to prepare, 18
  pie
    cream, classic, 130
    meringue, mother's, 132
    sugared, 126
  squares, Mabell's, 176
  topping for disappearing cake,
    89

Coffee
  'n' cream, 236
  iced, 268
Coins, gingerbread, 193
Cola slush, 249
Company dessert cake, 46
Concord grape pie, 117
Cookies. *See also* Bars; Brownie(s)
  blondies, 176
  brown sugar, 184
  chocolate. *See* Chocolate—cookies
  chunk chocolates, 252
  coconut squares, Mabell's, 176
  cream and sugar, 180
  English matrimonials, 177
  gingerbread coins, 193
  gingersnaps, homemade, 185
  hermits, 165
  molasses, grandma's soft, 164
  nutmeg butter, 183
  oatmeal
    old-fashioned, 167
    soft, 168
  peanut butter
    real, 186
    squares, 194
  pinwheel, 191
  poundcake, 178
  praline crackers, 173
  shortbread skirts, 181
  snickerdoodles, 182
  sour cream, Mumsley's, 190
  sugar, icebox, 192
  washboard, 187
Cottage cheese pie, 142
Cottage pudding, 211
Cracker(s)
  praline, 173
  pudding, soft, 197
Cranberry ice, Mabell's, 240
Crazy cake, 89
Cream
  coffee 'n', 236
  custard, lemon, 200
  pie
    banana, my best, 137
    butterscotch, 138
    chocolate, old-fashioned,
      134
    coconut, classic, 130
  and sugar cookies, 180
  and sugar frosting, 181
  whipped
    chocolate, 270
    lemon, 201
    rum-flavored, 75
    sweetened, 270
  whipping (heavy), about, 3

Cream cheese frosting
  classic, 44
  easy, 72
  ginger, 87
  orange-, 59
  pecan-, 23
  pineapple, 81
  special, 45
  zesty, 85
Crumb cake, Grandma Martha's, 60
Crumb topping, for blueberry buckle with
      blueberry sauce, 223
Curried fruit cobbler, 160
Custard
  about, 10–11
  blancmange. See Blancmange
  "boiled," 196
  filling, for company dessert cake, 47
  ice cream, creamy, 232
  lemon cream, 200
  pie, country, 140
  pouring, 97
  rice, creamy, 199

Dad's peach ice cream, 232
Date pudding, steamed, 216
Devilish dump cake, 52
Devilish frosting, 53
Devil's food float, 206
Disappearing cake, 88
Dixie pecan pie, 121
Drops, chocolate, 166
Dumplings, apple, Alice's, 224

Egg(s)
  about, 2
  whites
    to beat, 8
    to store, 2
English matrimonials, 177
Equipment, 5–7

Flour, about, 1
Foam cakes, about, 9
Fool, gooseberry, 229
French cream cake, 36
Frosting. See also Icing
  about, 10
  buttercream, black-walnut, 29
  caramel, hurry-up, 25
  chocolate
    easy, 21
    sour cream, 55
  cocoa fudge, 63
  cream and sugar, 181
  cream cheese. See Cream cheese frosting
  devilish, 53
  Hungarian, 67

Frosting (cont.)
  lemon, soft, 61
  orange cream cheese, 59
  pecan-cheese, 23
  rum-flavored, 57
  toasted-butter-pecan, 32
Frozen maple cream, 238
Fruit cobbler, curried, 160
Fruitcake, spirited, 72
Fudge
  cake pudding, 217
  fast, 255
  no foolin', 254
  peanut butter, 255
  sauce
    fast, 270
    peanut butter, 271
  sherbet, 242

Gingerbread
  coins, 193
  hot-water, 68
Ginger cream-cheese frosting, 87
Gingersnaps, homemade, 185
Golden State orange cake, 58
Gooseberry
  fool, 229
  pie, green, 116
  sherbet, fresh, 244
Graham pudding, Aunt Jackie's, 214
Grandma Martha's crumb cake, 60
Grandma's soft molasses cookies, 164
Grape
  Concord grape pie, 117
  ice, 247
  juice pie, Josephine's, 149
Grapefruit peel, candied, 263
Green gooseberry pie, 116
Green tomato pie, 147

Half-and-half, about, 3
Hard sauce, 275
Hermits, 165
Homestead buttermilk pie, 130
Hungarian frosting, 67
Hurry-up caramel cake, 24
Hurry-up caramel frosting, 25

Ice. See also Sherbet
  apricot, fresh, 248
  cola slush, 249
  cranberry, Mabell's, 240
  grape, 247
  lemon, 246
  orange, 246
  peach, fresh, 248
  pineapple, 247
  plum, fresh, 248

Ice *(cont.)*
  strawberry, 247
  watermelon, 249
Icebox sugar cookies, 192
Ice cream
  banana, fresh, 235
  bourbon, 237
  burnt sugar, 236
  cherry, midwestern, 234
  chocolate, easy, 233
  to churn, 12
  coffee 'n' cream, 236
  creamy custard, 232
  lemon velvet, 235
  maple, 238
  peach, dad's, 232
  peanut butter, 238
  strawberry, fresh, 234
  vanilla
    black cow, 266
    pure, 233
Icing
  buttercream, burnt sugar, 27
  cocoa, 82
  lemon, quick, 70
  mocha, quick, 69
  seven-minute white, 37
  strawberry, 31
  vanilla, boiled, 18
Illinois jam cake, 30
Indian pudding, 209

Jam cake, Illinois, 30
Jeanette's lemon bars, 172
Jelly roll, old-fashioned, 76
Josephine's grape juice pie,
  149

Lemon
  bars, Jeanette's, 172
  buttermilk cake, 61
  cake
    mayonnaise, 70
    pudding, 204
  cream custard, 200
  frosting, soft, 61
  ice, 246
  icing, quick, 70
  juice, about, 3
  peel, candied, 263
  pie
    meringue, mile-high, 128
    sour cream, 136
  sauce, tart, 272
  syrup, 201
  velvet, 235
  whipped cream, 201
Limeade, 266

Lime meringue pie, 129
Liqueurs, about, 4–5

Mabell's carrot pudding, 215
Mabell's coconut squares, 176
Macaroon(s)
  coconut, 170
  meringue, 135
Maple
  mousse cake, 94
  nut pie, northern, 124
  praline, 95
Marmalade pie, 146
Matrimonials, English, 177
Mayonnaise
  chocolate cake, 68
  lemon cake, 70
Measuring ingredients, 7
Meringue
  macaroon, 135
  pie
    coconut, mother's, 132
    lemon, mile-high, 128
    lime, 129
  spice cake topped with, 83
  topping, 84
  about, 11
Midwestern cherry ice cream, 234
Mile-high lemon meringue pie, 128
Milk, sour, about, 2–3
Milkshake, vanilla, 267
Mints, party, 261
Mocha icing, quick, 69
Montmorency cherry sauce, 275
Mother's coconut meringue pie, 132
Mousse cake
  chocolate, 49
  maple, 94
Mumsley's sour cream cookies, 190
Mystery cake, 71

No foolin' fudge, 254
Northern-maple nut pie, 124
Nut(s). *See also specific types of nuts*
  about, 4
  pie, northern maple, 124
Nutmeg butter cookies, 183

Oatmeal
  cookies
    old-fashioned, 167
    soft, 168
  pie, old-fashioned, 151
Oil, about, 2
Orange
  blancmange, 199
  cake, Golden State, 58
  cream cheese frosting, 59

Orange *(cont.)*
  ice, 246
  peel, candied, 262

Panocha, 258
Party mints, 261
Peach(es)
  brandied, 274
  cobbler, 156
  and cream pie, 108
  ice, fresh, 248
  ice cream, dad's, 232
Peanut
  chocolate clusters, 253
  pie, 125
Peanut butter
  bars, peanut buster, 174
  cookies, real, 186
  fudge, 255
  fudge sauce, 271
  ice cream, 238
  squares, 194
Pecan(s)
  butter
    cake, toasted, 32
    frosting, toasted, 32
  -cheese frosting, 23
  divinity, 259
  hermits, 165
  -persimmon picnic cake, 84
  pie
    chocolate lover's, 122
    Dixie, 121
Persimmon(s)
  about, 4
  -pecan picnic cake, 84
  pudding, wild, 204
  pulp, wild, 205
Pie
  apple
    American, 106
    deep delicious, 159
    mock, 153
    Schnitz, 154
  applesauce, country, 152
  apricot, dried, 148
  banana cream, my best,
    137
  blueberry
    cold, 111
    fresh, 110
  buttermilk, homestead,
    130
  butterscotch cream, 138
  cherry
    deep-dish, 162
    sour, 115
  chess, southern, 124

Pie *(cont.)*
  chocolate
    cream, old-fashioned, 134
    silk, 139
  coconut
    cream, classic, 130
    meringue, mother's, 132
    sugared, 126
  Concord grape, 117
  cottage cheese, 142
  cream. *See* Cream—pie
  custard, country, 140
  dough
    about, 10
    easy egg pastry, 102
    foolproof dough, 100
    foolproof shell, 101
    no-roll crust, 103
    old-fashioned dough, 102
  gooseberry, green, 116
  grape juice, Josephine's, 149
  green tomato, 147
  lemon, sour cream, 136
  marmalade, 146
  meringue. *See* Meringue—pie
  oatmeal, old-fashioned, 151
  peaches and cream, 108
  peanut, 125
  pecan
    chocolate lover's, 122
    Dixie, 121
  pumpkin, old-fashioned, 141
  raisin, 145
  raspberry, red, 114
  rhubarb, 109
  rhubarb-strawberry, 109
  shoofly, wet-bottom, 123
  strawberry
    glazed, 112
    two-crust, 113
  sugar, simple, 120
  sweet potato, southern,
    144
  vanilla, soft, 133
  vinegar, 150
Pineapple
  buttermilk sherbet, 243
  candied, 73
  cream cheese frosting, 81
  ice, 247
  sauce, 272
  upside-down cake, 74
Pinwheel cookies, 191
Plum(s)
  in curried fruit cobbler, 160
  ice, fresh, 248
Poundcake
  cookies, 178

Poundcake (*cont.*)
  sour cream, 64
  traditional, 78
Prairie State sheet cake,
  82
Praline(s)
  brown sugar, 260
  crackers, 173
  creamy, 260
  maple, 95
  vanilla, 261
Pudding
  bread-and-butter, 210
  carrot, Mabell's, 215
  cherry, 208
  chocolate, stirred, 196
  cottage, 211
  date, steamed, 216
  devil's food float, 206
  fudge cake, 217
  graham, Aunt Jackie's,
    214
  Indian, 209
  lemon cake, 204
  persimmon, wild, 204
  raisin, 207
  soft cracker, 197
  steamed, about, 11
  summer, simple, 227
Pumpkin
  pie, old-fashioned, 141
  spice cake, 86

Raisin(s)
  chocolate clusters, 253
  hermits, 165
  pie, 145
  pudding, 207
Raspberry(-ies)
  angel cake, 93
  cream cake, 44
  pie, red, 114
  sauce, 49
Rhubarb
  cobbler, rich, 158
  crisp, 228
  pie, 109
    strawberry-, 109
Rice custard, creamy, 199
Rocky road, 252
Rotation cake, 66
Rum(-flavored)
  balls, 262
  frosting, 57
  hot buttered, 268
  sauce, browned-butter, 273
  spice cake, flavored with, 56
  whipped cream, 75

Sauce
  amber, 271
  apricot, 211
  blueberry, blueberry buckle with,
    222
  brandied peach, 274
  browned butter bourbon, 274
  browned butter rum, 273
  cherry, Montmorency, 275
  fudge
    fast, 270
    peanut butter, 271
  hard, 275
  lemon, tart, 272
  pineapple, 272
  raspberry, 49
  soft butter, fresh blackberry cobbler with,
    160
  vanilla, 273
  vinegar, 276
Saucepan brownies, 174
Scalding liquids, 7
Schnitz apple pie, 154
Seven-minute white icing, 37
Sherbet
  berry buttermilk, 240
  fudgy, 242
  gooseberry, fresh, 244
  pineapple buttermilk, 243
  sour cream, 242
  strawberry, 241
Shoofly pie, wet-bottom, 123
Shortbread skirts, 181
Shortcakes, strawberry, individual,
  220
Shortening, about, 2
Sifting dry ingredients, 7
Slush, cola, 249
Snickerdoodles, 182
Soft cracker pudding, 197
Sour cherry pie, 115
Sour cream
  about, 3
  chocolate cake, 54
  chocolate frosting, 55
  cookies, Mumsley's, 190
  lemon pie, 136
  pound cake, 64
  sherbet, 242
Southern ambrosia, 221
Southern chess pie, 124
Southern sweet potato pie, 144
Spice(s)
  about, 3
  cake
    meringue-topped, 83
    pumpkin, 86
    rum-flavored, 56

Spirited fruitcake, 72
Sponge cake
  light milk, 36
  sunshine, 42
Squares
  coconut, Mabell's, 176
  peanut butter, 194
Strawberry(-ies)
  cobbler, 158
  ice, 247
  ice cream, fresh, 234
  icing, 31
  pie
    glazed, 112
    -rhubarb, 109
    two-crust, 113
  sherbet, 241
  shortcakes, individual,
    220
Sugar(ed)
  about, 1–2
  brown
    cookies, 184
    pralines, 260
  burnt. See Burnt sugar
  cookies
    cream and, 180
    icebox, 192
  and cream frosting, 181
  ice cream, burnt, 236
  pie
    coconut, 126
    simple, 120
Summer pudding, simple, 227
Sundae cake, super, 90
Sunshine sponge cake, 42
Sweet potato pie, southern,
  144

Syrup
  burnt sugar, 27
  cinnamon, 225
  lemon, 201
  simple, 246

Tipsy parson, 96

Vanilla
  about, 3
  ice cream
    black cow, 266
    creamy custard, 232
    pure, 233
  icing, boiled, 18
  milkshake, 267
  pie, soft, 133
  pralines, 261
  sauce, 273
Velvet, lemon, 235
Vinegar
  pie, 150
  sauce, 276

Wafers, chocolate, 191
Walnut(s)
  black
    buttercream cake, 28
    buttercream frosting, 29
  hermits, 165
Washboard cookies, 187
Water, 3
Watermelon ice, 249
Wet-bottom shoofly pie, 123
Whipped cream
  chocolate, 270
  sweetened, 270
White buttermilk cake, 62